RATIONAL CHOICE
AND JUDGMENT

RATIONAL CHOICE AND JUDGMENT
Decision Analysis for the Decider

REX BROWN
George Mason University

With the assistance of
Pascal Paschoud

A JOHN WILEY & SONS, INC., PUBLICATION

Copyright © 2005 by John Wiley & Sons, Inc. All rights reserved.

Published by John Wiley & Sons, Inc., Hoboken, New Jersey.
Published simultaneously in Canada.

No part of this publication may be reproduced, stored in a retrieval system, or transmitted in any form or by any means, electronic, mechanical, photocopying, recording, scanning, or otherwise, except as permitted under Section 107 or 108 of the 1976 United States Copyright Act, without either the prior written permission of the Publisher, or authorization through payment of the appropriate per-copy fee to the Copyright Clearance Center, Inc., 222 Rosewood Drive, Danvers, MA 01923, 978-750-8400, fax 978-646-8600, or on the web at www.copyright.com. Requests to the Publisher for permission should be addressed to the Permissions Department, John Wiley & Sons, Inc., 111 River Street, Hoboken, NJ 07030, (201) 748-6011, fax (201) 748-6008.

Limit of Liability/Disclaimer of Warranty: While the publisher and author have used their best efforts in preparing this book, they make no representations or warranties with respect to the accuracy or completeness of the contents of this book and specifically disclaim any implied warranties of merchantability or fitness for a particular purpose. No warranty may be created or extended by sales representatives or written sales materials. The advice and strategies contained herein may not be suitable for your situation. You should consult with a professional where appropriate. Neither the publisher nor author shall be liable for any loss of profit or any other commercial damages, including but not limited to special, incidental, consequential, or other damages.

For general information on our other products and services please contact our Customer Care Department within the U.S. at 877-762-2974, outside the U.S. at 317-572-3993 or fax 317-572-4002.

Wiley also publishes its books in a variety of electronic formats. Some content that appears in print, however, may not be available in electronic format.

Library of Congress Cataloging-in-Publication Data:

Brown, Rex V.
    Rational choice and judgment : decision analysis for the decider / Rex Brown with assistance of Pascal Paschoud.
       p. cm.
    Includes bibliographical references and index.
    ISBN 0-471-20237-1 (cloth)
    1. Decision making. I. Paschoud, Pascal. II. Title.

BF448.B76 2005
153.8'3—dc22

2004059802

10　9　8　7　6　5　4　3　2　1

In memory of
Marty Tolcott (1922–1996) and
Oleg Larichev (1934–2002)
revered colleagues and precious friends

"The Empire is bearing down on us, Mr. Spock. Should we stand and fight, or make our escape?"   Starship Enterprise Captain Kirk in the TV series *Startrek*

"To be, or not to be—that is the question:—Whether 'tis nobler in the mind to suffer the slings and arrows of outrageous fortune, or to take arms against a sea of troubles and by opposing end them?"   William Shakespeare

Contents

Preface	**xiii**
Who Might Use This Book?	xiii
Background	xiv
Substance of the Book	xvi
Pedagogy	xviii
Demands on Student and Instructor	xx
Other Approaches, Other Materials	xxi
Author Background	xxii
Acknowledgments	xxiii
Prolog: A Baby Delivery Dilemma	**xxv**
1 Basics and Overview	**1**
1.1 Improving Decisions	2
1.2 Decision Modes	5
1.3 Rationality	8
1.4 Quantitative Decision-Aiding Methods	10
1.5 Learning Process	13
2 Uses of Decision Analysis	**21**
2.1 Private Decisions	21
2.2 Corporate Business Decisions	23

		2.3	Government Decisions	25

		2.3	Government Decisions	25
		2.4	Professional Decisions by Individual Practitioners	28
		2.5	Nonstandard Uses of Decision Analysis	28
		2.6	Looking Backward and Forward	30
		Appendix 2A: A Decision Analyst Reflects on His Work		32
3	**Evaluating a Choice Qualitatively**			**37**
		3.1	A Start at Structuring: Pros and Cons	38
		3.2	Goals, Options, and Outcomes: "Going Through the GOO"	38
		3.3	Distinguishing Between GOO Elements	40
		3.4	Assessing Uncertain Possibilities	42
		3.5	Plural Evaluation	44
		3.6	Limitations of Qualitative Analysis	45
4	**Quantitative Aid to Rational Choice**			**51**
		4.1	A Simple Tool: Tallying Pluses and Minuses	52
		4.2	Rationality and Ideal Judgment	54
		4.3	Decision Tools	57
		4.4	Personal Decision Analysis	59
		4.5	Quantitative Substitution of Judgments	60
		4.6	A DA Tool Kit	65
		Appendix 4A: Business Decision Tree Example		68
		Appendix 4B: Personal Example: Study or Play?		74
			4B.1 Need for Decision Aid	74
			4B.2 Initial Model Structure	75
			4B.3 Quantifying Possibility and Preference Graphically	75
5	**Describing Consequences**			**80**
		5.1	Types of Possibility	80
		5.2	Holistic vs. Multicriteria Consequences	82
		5.3	Identifying Criteria	85
		5.4	Metric vs. Rating Scales	86
		5.5	Rating Scale Base	88
		5.6	Rating Scale Units	92
		5.7	Comparison of Scales	95
		5.8	When Describing Outcomes Is Sufficient	96

6	**Taking Value Judgments into Account**	**101**
	6.1 Disaggregating Utility into Multiple Criteria	101
	6.2 Partitioning Criteria	102
	6.3 Decomposing Utility Components into Importance and Criterion Score	105
	6.4 Graphic Representation	109
	6.5 Other Preference Issues	110
7	**Choice Under Uncertainty**	**115**
	7.1 Types of Uncertain Possibility	116
	7.2 Characterizing Uncertainty: Personal Probability	116
	7.3 Average Personal Utility for Option Evaluation	119
	7.4 Simplified Substitutions for Complex Uncertainty	119
	7.5 Balance of Conflicting Criteria and Uncertainty in Modeling	124
	Appendix 7A: Technical Notes	127
	7A.1 Major Elements of DA	127
	7A.2 Decision Theory as a Test of Coherence	127
	7A.3 Schematic Representation of Models	129
8	**Decision-Aiding Strategy**	**132**
	8.1 Requirements of Useful Decision Aid	132
	8.2 Components of an Analytic Strategy	133
	8.3 What Decision to Aid?	134
	8.4 Building on Decider's Thinking	135
	8.5 Specifying Options	136
	8.6 Choice of Model Type	138
	8.7 Modeling Strategy	138
	8.8 Taking Account of Human Factors	141
	8.9 Multiple Approaches: Plural Evaluation	142
	8.10 Integrating Analysis into the Personal Decision Process	145
	8.11 Other Strategy Issues	147
	Appendix 8A: Influence Sketches	151
	8A.1 Diagrammatic Conventions	151
	8A.2 Role of Influence Sketches	153
9	**Aiding the Professional Decider**	**155**
	9.1 Distinctive Features of Professional Decision Aiding	155
	9.2 Factors Affecting Choice of Aiding Tool	157

	9.3	Institution as Interested Party	159
	9.4	Multiple Involved Parties	163
	9.5	Decision-Aiding Organizational Arrangements	165
	9.6	Other Executive Issues	167
		Appendix 9A: Environmental Regulation Case Study	169
		9A.1 Regulatory Problem	169
		9A.2 The Niakuk Permitting Case	170
		9A.3 Aid Description	171
		9A.4 Application to the Niakuk Case	175
10	**Assessing and Inferring Probabilities**		**178**
	10.1	Personal Probability	178
	10.2	Direct Assessment of Discrete Possibilities	181
	10.3	Direct Assessment of Uncertain Quantities	183
	10.4	Indirect Assessment of Discrete Possibilities	184
	10.5	Indirect Assessment of Uncertain Quantities	189
	10.6	General Assessment Issues	190
	10.7	Value of More Information	193
11	**Eliciting Preferences**		**199**
	11.1	Importance of Preference Elicitation	199
	11.2	Meaning of Preference	200
	11.3	Holistic Utility of Prospects	200
	11.4	Disaggregating Utility into Criteria	202
	11.5	Eliciting Additive Criterion Components	204
	11.6	Eliciting ICE Importance Weights	205
12	**Applied Term Project**		**210**
	12.1	Overview	210
	12.2	Stage A: Set the Stage	213
	12.3	Stage B: Evaluate the Choice Informally	214
	12.4	Stage C: Structure Reasoning Qualitatively	215
	12.5	Stage D: Model Reasoning Quantitatively	216
	12.6	Stage E: Integrate Model(s) into the Decision Process	216
	12.7	Stage F: Write the Final Report	217
	12.8	Evaluation of Student Effort	218
		Appendix 12A: Student Project Report	220
		Task Statement	220
		Initial Informal Position	220

Analysis	221
Conclusions	225
Postscript	225
Instructor Comments	226

Epilog 227

References 230

Glossary of Concepts and Terms 235

Index 243

Preface

Decisions permeate all human activity. We all make decisions, all the time, for ourselves or for the organizations we work for. Sometimes we get them wrong and regret the consequences; and sometimes we get them right but can't explain why. This is a textbook for courses to help students with such problems and generally to improve their professional or private decision making, supported by tools of personal decision analysis.

WHO MIGHT USE THIS BOOK?

Decisions can be made in different modes. They can be *professional* (usually for an institution) or *private* (on the decider's own behalf). Private decisions, in turn, can be *personal* (for the decider's own interests) or *civic* (taking a position on a public issue). In fact, decision analysis (DA) is used primarily on professional decisions. Private decisions, on their own, ordinarily do not have high-enough stakes to justify much analysis or much time spent to improve it. However, the rather thorough analysis that students will practice in this mode should hone their *informal* reasoning (in all three modes).

Courses based on this book may be (and have been) offered:

- In public policy, business management, systems engineering, and other professional schools
- In institution-specific professional development programs
- In undergraduate programs of general education
- For self-study by managers and private persons

The technical content and professional–private mix of a course can be customized through the choice of readings (e.g., appendixes, footnotes, and outside materials) and assignments (projects and exercises).

BACKGROUND

Most decisions are made informally, whether intuitively without deliberate thought, or based on careful reflection. However, over the centuries people have recognized the need for better and more defensible decisions and have tried to offer systematic and structured aid. Benjamin Franklin, for example, suggested a way of canceling out equivalent pros and cons of options until the best option became clear.

The theoretical beginnings of decision analysis as a universal logic of making sound decisions were developed some 50 years ago (Savage, 1954; Luce and Raiffa, 1954). Decision analysis consists basically of breaking down a decider's reasoning into separable pieces—about options, uncertainty, and preference—putting numbers to those pieces, and calculating the choice they imply. Many of us in academia and business who were involved early on were confident that DA would revolutionize decision making throughout society—and it still may.

Indeed, by about 1980, DA had penetrated virtually all segments of business, government, and the professions. Examples from my own experience include:

- Should a federal regulator close down a nuclear reactor?
- Should Ford get into the tire business?
- Should Congress conclude that the Clean Air Act is worth its cost?
- Should the Russian government route a pipeline over land or under ice?
- Should a surgeon operate on my arthritic hip?
- Should assisted suicide be legalized?
- Should my daughter split with her boyfriend?

Setbacks

Then the momentum seemed to stall somewhat. DA's adoption and success has not progressed as fast as many of us had hoped and indeed expected (Brown, 1970). A blue ribbon committee of the National Academy of Sciences, headed by Nobel laureate Herb Simon, was puzzled that only a small fraction of decisions that really deserved help were getting it. Some prominent decision analysts who had by then become senior deciders said that they did not often use DA themselves but relied on their unaided judgment. Many DA applications have been reported as successes (Corner and Kirkwood, 1991; Keefer et al., 2004) but with little documentation on what the deciders used and found useful (Grayson, 1973; Simon, 1986; Brown, 2005).

The early exponents of DA developed the essential logical infrastructure of DA, largely in the form of quantitative models adapted to a rich variety of decision tasks. However, it appeared that decision aid needs more than that to be useful. It has to take into account the capabilities and needs of the people who will implement the aid and use it, and be based on a thorough grasp of the specific decision-making setting. Those early decision analysis pioneers, many of them world-class scholars, were largely unfamiliar with the social sciences or with executive decision practice. They focused on developing prescriptive decision models rather than on who would use them, where, why, and how.

As a result, I believe, the craft of decision analysis stayed seriously incomplete. For example, people had trouble providing the inputs that particular models required, much important decider knowledge did not neatly fit the inputs, and the needs of decider and institution were not well understood. This may partly explain why many executives continued to back their own "unaided" judgment.

I was in on the early days of decision analysis at the Harvard Business School in the 1960s before going on to apply it full time and to work on developing better methods. I got to work with a wide variety of deciders (ranging from a class of seventh graders to the head of U.S. nuclear reactor regulation and the president of Ford Motors). Harsh early feedback from the real world of consulting forced me and other decision aiders to try to fill the most serious methodological gaps.

Common Gaps in DA Practice

DA had largely been developed and taught in traditional academic departments with a predominantly quantitative orientation, such as engineering and statistics. I believe that this has often given rise to lopsided methods focused on mathematical "optimization" models rather than on aiding real deciders.[1] In order to outperform an unaided decider, DA needs not only to be logically sound, but also to take full account of the decider's human and institutional requirements and to draw on all of his/her knowledge.

Through persistent and sometimes discouraging trial and error during years of consulting, I have found three common but serious flaws in DA practice:

- Important knowledge that deciders already have, or have available, has been disregarded, because it is not all required by any single model.[2]
- Aiding emphasis has been on modeling logic, to the neglect of other essentials of a useful aid, such as input that real people can provide and output they can use.
- Middlemen, typically technically oriented support staff, have intervened between the aider and the real decider and miscommunicated the decider's needs.

---

[1]This is a controversial position, which I attempt to document in Brown (1992, in press).
[2]*Example.* My nuclear regulator client was deciding whether to close down a reactor as unsafe. An earlier risk analysis, based only on a single-pass "fault tree" model of component failures, had found the reactor to be perfectly safe. However, taking account of a number of recent "near misses" at the reactor and of unfavorable safety inspection reports (which the risk analysis had not addressed), the regulator decided that the reactor was unacceptably *unsafe* and put it on the official "watch" list. Knowledge that did not fit into the single model had been ignored. ♦

Filling the Gaps

Serious though flaws in DA practice may have been, I maintain that they are amenable to remedy, and this book attempts to present some of the remedies that have worked for me. For example, neglected knowledge can be recovered by using *plural evaluation*: that is, by developing multiple approaches (including the decider's instant intuition) that tap into the totality of decider knowledge, and then combining them.

It is only recently that decision analysis methods have evolved to cover the broad range of bases, and for appropriately trained and oriented decision aiders to be available. DA can now, I believe, be generally relied upon to improve unaided decisions, especially those with few options and poorly understood outcomes.

I have engaged in a long personal odyssey to make DA more useful—an odyssey that has by no means run its course. My approach to methodology development has been the classic build–test–build–test. I try to aid live decisions as best I can with the methodology available, to identify critical flaws, to develop corrective methods (often together with colleagues who have complementary expertise), and then to use them in a new round of method development.

Earlier DA practice was basically problem-oriented. It has now become more use- and user-oriented, which when properly implemented, deciders appear to find useful. Decision aiding in general, however, is still very much a work in progress. I believe that its evolution is now moving in an eclectic direction, drawing on a broad array of approaches (not just DA) and focused on narrow fields of application, such as individual industries and even individual organizations. By the time I retired from consulting in the early 1990s, I had some ideas on what had been holding up DA adoption and what to do about it. I taught courses in graduate and professional schools for a few years. This is the textbook that emerged.

SUBSTANCE OF THE BOOK

Decision aids can work in three principal ways; they can:

- *Emulate* the performance of a more qualified decider (e.g., as artificial intelligence and "expert systems") (Henrion et al., 1991)
- *Replace* the decider's current thinking and analyze decisions from scratch (e.g., by relying on data-based models)
- *Enhance* the decider's existing thinking (e.g., by detecting and eliminating logical flaws)

Personal decision analysis,[3] as developed here, does the third of these. It is an enhancement aid. Making and communicating decisions is such a critical part of private,

---

[3] Although "decision analysis" could in theory refer to any way of analyzing a decision (e.g., a description rather than a prescription of the decision process), as used here, "decision analysis" refers specifically to personal decision analysis.

professional, and public life that even "mere" *enhancement* can be of great value. In time, DA-based reasoning may even take its place alongside Reading, 'Riting, and 'Rithmetic (Baron and Brown, 1988) as the fourth R of universal education.

The object of decision aid is not to *prescribe* any particular choice but to improve the process from which a decision may emerge: what questions to ask and what to do with the answers. Students should learn to make good decisions qualitatively right away. However, they are not expected to use the quantitative tools presented here without help, or at least not without substantial practice or apprenticeship. When they become professional deciders, they should be able to make good use of technical specialists, including knowing when to use them, directing their endeavors, and using their results.

Focus on Certain Decision Types

Although the decision-aiding approach is applicable to all types of decisions, I focus here on applying it to the special case of choice among a few options. These are decisions that are the most straightforward to aid and *enhance*.

However, some of the most successful applications of DA involve numerous options, such as allocating a government budget among thousands of items, or designing a complex military system for a fixed cost. The options are so complex that a human decider has very little to contribute, except perhaps some judgmental inputs. An appeal of decision aid in such cases is that it avoids deciders having to handle a task they are ill equipped to deal with or to explain to others. However, this is essentially *replacement*, not enhancement, aid. The tools themselves are technically elaborate (e.g., hierarchical multicriteria models), which would take us beyond the scope of the book.

Similarly, I focus on decisions to be made immediately, although some of the most sought after aid is to preprogram prospective decisions (such as responding to an enemy attack or approving new drugs). Such aid can be immensely difficult to do right, because of the danger of disregarding information that may become known later.[4]

Aiding Approach

This book shares the philosophy and core techniques of the leading "decision analysis" texts (Watson and Buede, 1987; Clemen, 1996; McNamee and Celona, 2001). The tools in our "tool kit" include basic versions of standard DA technique such as decision trees and what have been called *subjective expected utility*, *multiattribute utility analysis*, and *Bayesian updating*.[5] However, the decision-aiding philosophy in

---

[4] I turned down an approach to produce for the Star Wars program an automatic nuclear response to an apparent Russian attack, on the grounds that human judgment was needed to overrule an "aid" in the event of some development that was not foreseen at the time of aid design.
[5] Following the lead of Ron Howard, I have replaced these and other technical terms by others more accessible to a lay decider (Brown, 2004). See the Glossary.

xviii PREFACE

this book features some distinctive perspectives that affect the art of how DA is practiced and what a decider needs to know to use it effectively.

1. There is much more to the decision process of experienced deciders than we can hope (at least yet) to capture in any "single-pass" decision analysis model. It is usually productive to explore why competent unaided deciders take issue with DA results and what the deciders might have to teach aiders.
2. The goal of DA is comprehensive rationality—resolving the myriad of inconsistencies relevant to the choice in the decider's head—rather than just the limited coherence of a single model, although that is certainly a significant move toward comprehensive rationality.
3. The root cause of many aid flaws, such as reliance on single-pass models, is aider orientation: The aider's and decider's interests often conflict (Brown, in press). In virtually all the really successful DAs that I know, the aider has worked directly with the decider, and that is my own practice. Otherwise, I have no confidence that the problem we solve is the one the decider has.
4. Although DA models serve to "divide and conquer," don't divide too finely. Guard against putting too much effort into elaborating the model structure, at the expense of getting the input right.

PEDAGOGY

The text alternates technical exposition with application, interspersed with exercises, consulting experience, and cases. It provides for a term project, where students use the tools to develop their own judgment on a current public policy or personal issue, singly or in groups. Professional, especially public policy, consulting case studies are reviewed.

Developing Skills on Real Judgments

The critical challenge in applying decision analysis successfully is to integrate relatively simple models into how deciders really think about their live choices, in all their complexity and ambiguity. The aim is to lose nothing of value from that thinking, but to add logical rigor. Effective professional as well as private decision making is best developed, I believe, on decisions that are real to deciders and that reproduce, as closely as possible, the state of mind and knowledge-gathering processes that they will face in their profession. How else can they learn how to factor in "gut feel" based on long experience or to dig into their memories to find and extract elusive knowledge? Unless student deciders are currently employed in their chosen professions, they are not likely to have real professional choices to develop starter skills on.

This consideration favors training deciders and aiders on live personal choices or familiar public policy controversies (in which an entire class can participate). Judgments elicited can thus be based on the usual everyday amalgam of personal experience and messy information absorbed over time. They are not hypothetical judgments based on secondhand knowledge [say, from written case studies (e.g., the

Harvard case method) or contrived but convenient experiments]. The question is: "What do you actually think?" rather than "What would you think if you were faced with the situation *described*?" Or again, "What do you predict will actually happen?" rather than "What *would you predict* if this hypothetical situation arose?"[6] Hypothetical analysis has its place where real judgments are not feasible, for example in gathering new information, but it is to be used sparingly.

The skills acquired on personal decisions should be transferable to professional situations on which students cannot yet have judgments worth modeling but which they are preparing to face. Professional decision skills build on personal skills, although professional decisions have distinctive features (such as responding to institutional pressure). These features are addressed passively in this book by examining past professional DA applications (especially consulting case studies) in order to demonstrate the management *potential* of the tools.

Technical Mastery Through Practice

Students master essential model mechanics as soon as possible in a course, so that the main learning effort can be devoted to integrating the mechanics *usefully* into their normal reasoning. This integration is a critical skill.

An important reason for limiting our scope to just a few "simple" tools is so that students can rapidly develop sufficiently fluent mastery of the mechanics that they can focus on problem application. This is similar to getting mastery over a physical skill, such as hitting a tennis ball, to free the mind up for game strategy. A common pitfall in decision aiding is for the modeling to be so ambitious that the aider is preoccupied with technique and stumbles over application. Although the book *can* be used purely as a reader, the material is difficult for students to master without spending most of their learning time doing and discussing assignments rather than learning passively.

Course Planning

The text material can be organized selectively to meet different course needs and to cater to different levels of student aptitude, interest, and experience. It is self-contained but can also be spliced into other courses with a decision-aiding but non-DA orientation (e.g., operations research), or it can prepare the way for technical extensions of DA (e.g., in statistical decision theory). It can also serve as a resource for domain-specific courses such as marketing, capital budgeting, procurement, and public administration.

Different courses can be designed by selecting elements of the text. For example:

- The main text of all 12 chapters except Chapters 2 and 9 could be the sole or principal text for a 30 to 40-hour session of basic introduction to decision analysis for private individuals.

[6]Called for in Bayesian diagnostic updating of uncertainty.

- Chapters 2 and 9 extend the scope to cover professional, especially public policy, applications.
- Plentiful footnotes, literature citations, and appendixes provide enrichment and advanced material for more ambitious or engaged students (or for the instructor), and additional material could double course length.

Assignments and the nature of the term project can also be selected or adapted to the course scope or to topical issues.

Structure of the Book

The first three chapters are nontechnical and address the qualitative essence of DA and review current uses of decision tools. In Chapters 4 to 7 we introduce quantitative tools for analyzing problems dominated by either value judgments or uncertainty, using utility and probability models, respectively. In Chapter 8 we discuss the strategy for using these tools when addressing private or professional decisions. In Chapter 9 we discuss issues of particular relevance for professional decisions. In Chapters 10 and 11 we present approaches for eliciting value judgments and uncertainty inputs for models, respectively.

A course centerpiece is the term project, where students pick a live choice and apply analytic tools as they are introduced, chapter by chapter, and wind up the course with a documented recommendation. The assignments are introduced progressively throughout the course but are gathered together, for convenience, in Chapter 12 (with an illustrative student report in an appendix).

There is a glossary of key terms at the end of the book.

DEMANDS ON STUDENT AND INSTRUCTOR

Student

Although much of the material is intellectually challenging, it uses no mathematics beyond arithmetic and needs no course prerequisites. However, a student who is comfortable with quantitative methods, understands how people think, and has an interdisciplinary orientation is at a definite advantage.

The analytic demands on students are considerable, but they are logical rather than technical. Although the models are simple, integrating them into realistic judgment in real situations is intellectually demanding. Improving on our natural practical thinking skills, which have been virtually untouched over the centuries, is a challenge of the highest order.

The initial qualitative chapters should be quite digestible, but they pave the way for tougher quantitative modeling. I have found that students tend to be either those with an analytic flair who breeze through the course without trouble, or those who struggle throughout the course.

Instructor

The instructor should be well versed in the concepts (but not necessarily the math) of decision analysis as presented in well-known texts (Watson and Buede, 1987; Keeney and Raiffa, 1993; Pratt et al., 1995) and, if possible, have had substantial practice in applying them to real problems. The success of a course will depend largely on instructors' handling of, and their feedback on, assignments.

It certainly helps if the instructor can draw on current events to illustrate (or exercise) ideas. One year I used the sensational ongoing murder trial of sports star O. J. Simpson to illustrate all course material. For example, students were asked to register how surprised they would be (probability) to learn of each of a dozen pieces of evidence *if the defendant were innocent*. Using a simple inference tool, they *all* found that given their own varying assessments, they could have no reasonable (rational) doubt whatsoever about his guilt. (He was found innocent.)

Except for technical exercises, assignments do not have a predetermined "school solution" but allow discretion in how tools are used to solve live practical problems. The instructor must be able to respond to, and give guidance on, free-form student analyses that may not follow a familiar pattern. This may put quite a heavy onus on the instructor.

If instructors do not have much practical decision-aiding experience, the accompanying *teacher's manual* should be a substantial resource. The manual also includes sample schedules, exercise solution notes, classroom handouts, guidance on course strategy, quizzes, and elaboration of technical material (to keep instructors at least one step ahead of students).

OTHER APPROACHES, OTHER MATERIALS

Even if this book does something to advance the art of decision aiding and its teaching, it is far from the balanced primer for the would-be executive, which is still waiting to be written. The instructor may wish to augment it with complementary materials.

Above all, the book focuses attention where my particular background has most to contribute and where I may have some "comparative advantage." As a result, it does not draw on approaches *other than* decision analysis that may also serve the decider well, such as recognition-primed decision making and the analytic hierarchy process. It barely touches the surface of the highly developed modeling methodology that has been the backbone of decision analysis texts (but which I believe should be left until later in the student's DA education).

The book does not use some well-established teaching devices, such as the Harvard case method, where students analyze a past executive decision described in a written document (although that is what I originally cut my teaching teeth on). Instead, my approach has been either to report how a past executive problem was *actually analyzed*, or to have students analyze a nonexecutive problem that is real to them.

This book is also quite parochial in its supporting material. The practical illustrations are tilted toward my own experience: for example, of environmental protection and nuclear risk management in professional examples; of parenting and grandparenting issues in personal examples; and of involvement in Jewish–Israeli affairs in civic examples. In terms of specific methodology, this is, in some ways, a manifesto of what I have found works best for me, and many of the technical references are to my own work.

Here are some suggestions on complementary materials to provide balance:

- Hammond et al. (1996) and Keeney (1999) treat *preformal* analysis more thoroughly and more accessibly than I do, especially in exploring a decider's values and in identifying options to compare.
- Clemen (1996) may be the best of a number of texts covering a traditional, more model-oriented decision analysis, in a business context. It also includes excellent business problem descriptions for student analysis by the Harvard case method.
- Hogarth (1987) reviews the descriptive psychology of decision making, and von Winterfeldt and Edwards (1988) relate it to prescriptive decision analysis.
- Winkler et al. (1990) review the analytic hierarchy process, a popular alternative to decision analysis, and Klein (1989) presents recognition-primed decision making, another alternative.
- Watson and Buede (1987) give a concise but more ambitious treatment of the theoretical underpinnings of decision analysis.
- There is a varied literature on different application areas [such as Weinstein (1996) on medical applications].

AUTHOR BACKGROUND

This text is based on 30 years of decision consulting to executives across government and business, interleaved with methodology research and teaching. I was trained as a social scientist and statistician and taught decision analysis in statistics, psychology, and management programs at Harvard Business School, Cambridge University, and the London School of Economics, as well as to junior high school students.

Where my consulting experience and that of colleagues is referred to, it is usually as part of DSC (Decision Science Consortium, Inc.) or my previous employer, DDI (Decisions and Designs, Inc.). My clients have varied with changing circumstances. When in Michigan, I served the auto industry; in Washington, DC I served the federal government. Under a Democratic administration I worked largely on environmental protection; under a Republican administration, on defense. Clients have ranged in status from an assistant secretary of defense allocating a budget of billions, to a son deciding whether to withhold life support from his dying mother.

ACKNOWLEDGMENTS

I am grateful to a number of colleagues for helpful comments and suggestions, and in particular to Cam Peterson, Susan Tolchin, Jon Baron, Granger Morgan, Stephen Watson, Jim Chinnis, and my patient editor, Andy Sage. I benefited greatly from generations of students, especially at the London School of Economics, the University of Michigan, and George Mason University. Pascal Paschoud, an exceptionally gifted pupil, became my teaching assistant and later helped me extensively with the book, especially on presentation and assignment materials. Theresa Christian has been an outstanding editorial assistant while still in high school (ably aided by her younger sister, Sheila). Many others have given me invaluable feedback and support, including Sean Norton, Bill Tuxworth, Kimberley Gladysz, and my daughters, Karen, Leora, Tamara, and Michele.

Prolog: A Baby Delivery Dilemma

KAREN: Dad, I know you usually work with managers and such, but could you help me make a very personal decision?

REX: Well, I'll try. The principles are much the same.

KAREN: You know I am about to give birth to boy–girl twins. Well, the doctor says there's a problem. Lucy, who will be first, is fine for a natural delivery; but Sam is feet down. Unless he can be "turned" after Lucy is born, I will have to have a caesarian. Should I wait and see what happens with Sam at delivery, or go ahead and have the caesarian for both births?

REX: How do you feel about it now?

K: I'm inclined to deliver Lucy naturally and just hope that I won't need a caesarian for Sam. But I feel uneasy about it. If it turns out that I still need a caesarian, I'll be sorry I didn't do it from the start.

R: How sorry?

K: Either way, having a caesarian is pretty bad. But having a natural birth first is somewhat worse, because, according to the doctor, the delay between the two might harm Sam's health and slow my own recovery. Cost is not an issue, as I am covered by insurance.

R: Is there a good chance that Sam can in fact be turned so that both births could be natural?

K: According to the doctor, it could go either way.

What can you do?	What might happen?	How likely?	How would you feel?
CAESARIAN FIRST	Double caesarian	Certain	Pretty bad (trauma)
NATURAL FIRST	Two naturals OR Natural, then caesarian	Even chance Even chance	Best case Worst case (recovery, Sam's health)

FIGURE P.1 Karen's informal evaluation.

R: Let me sketch out the gist of what you have just said (*draws table; see Figure P.1*). The two rows in this table correspond to your two options. The columns lay out what might happen in each case, how likely, and how you would feel if it did happen. Does organizing them this way help?

K: I suppose so. Just looking at the table does seem to confirm my intuition of having a natural delivery first. But I'm still not quite convinced, and I'd like to be able to review the argument constructively with my husband, Sean.

R: Let's try to put numbers on the pieces of your reasoning. First, your uncertainty about the turning. Can you get your doctor to put a probability on being able to turn Sam?

Later, after consulting with doctor:

K: He still won't be committed. He supposed it was about as likely as not, but he couldn't go further than that.

R: OK. Let's call it 50% for now. Now, about the relative appeal to you of the outcomes—we call that *utility*. On a scale from 0 to 100, where 0 is the worst (natural, then caesarian) and 100 the best (two naturals), how happy would you be with the one in between (double caesarian)?

K: That's a tricky one. A double caesarian is certainly nearer to the worst outcome, (natural, then caesarian) than to the best outcome (two naturals). So a double caesarian would be nearer to 0 than to 100. Let's give it a 20.

R: We can now run the numbers to see what these judgments of uncertainty and utility mean for your choice. The caesarian-first option guarantees that you will have a double caesarian, to which you just gave a 20. If you go natural first, there are two possible outcomes: natural, then caesarian at 0, and two naturals at 100. So you know that the average utility is going to be somewhere between 0 and 100. We get an exact number by multiplying the probability of each outcome (0.5, 0.5) by its utility (0, 100).

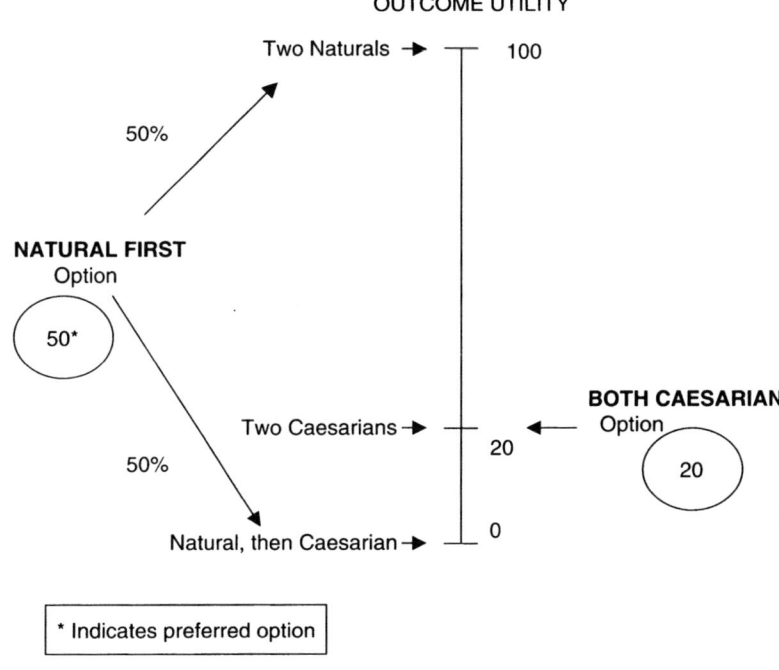

FIGURE P.2 Quantifying delivery options.

The average utility of natural first (as shown in Figure P.2) is therefore

$$(0.5 \times 0) + (0.5 \times 100) = 50$$

This 50 is better than the 20 for caesarian first, so you should apparently go with natural first, and by quite a bit.

K: Why do you say "apparently"?

R: Well, "garbage in, garbage out," they say. Perhaps the numbers you gave me are not very solid. If they change, so might your conclusion. Realistically, could your probability of turning Sam drop below the 50% we used? If it were less than 20%, the average utility of natural first would be lower than 20 (0.2 × 100). So it would then be even worse than we first thought, and therefore certainly ruled out.

K: I don't think my probability could drop that low. In fact, I think the doctor is *more* confident than 50% that he can turn Sam. He might have said "likely as not" just to be on the safe side. Malpractice, you know!

R: So the argument for natural first would be even stronger. How about utility? Could the intermediate utility of having a double caesarian be closer to two naturals (the best) than to natural, then caesarian (the worst)? That is, instead of the

20 you gave originally, could the utility of a double caesarian actually be above 50 on that same scale (i.e., nearer to best than to worst)?

K: Definitely not!

R: Then plausible shifts in your basic judgments wouldn't change your choice. But before you decide, let's look at something else. Perhaps you don't like to take risks. Under one option, you are quite sure of having a double caesarian, which is quite bad. Under the other option, you have a 50:50 chance of *either* natural, then caesarian deliveries, which is even worse, *or* two natural deliveries, which, of course, is best. Do you want to chance it?

K: I think so. Even though I don't like risk much, the gamble looks so much better than the sure thing that I'd take it.

R: So, putting numbers on your judgments like this fits with your original intuition: that you should have a natural delivery first. That choice sounds solid and not likely to change if you dwell on it more, with or without the numbers. You could get another medical opinion, but your obstetrician apparently knows his stuff. The mistake it might conceivably save you from would not be disastrous, surely?

K: I agree, and I feel a whole lot easier in my mind now about what to do. I'll go over what we've discussed with Sean. If he doesn't see anything wrong with it, I'll go ahead and have a natural delivery first.

She did. Both babies were delivered naturally (and did fine, although there was no guarantee that the gamble would pay off).

Chapter 1

Basics and Overview

We make ***decisions***[1] all the time: as private individuals (Should I "pop the question[2]"?); as professionals (Should I take my company public?); and as citizens (Should I support current U.S. foreign policy?). Decisions can have a great impact on the quality of our lives or the success of our organizations. The choices that Napoleon and Bill Gates made surely gave them an edge over rivals (at least for a while).

Sometimes ***choices*** turn out badly. This is not necessarily our fault: We played the cards right, but the trumps were not where they might be expected. However, sometimes we realize (or others do) that we could have used what we knew much better. People blight their lives with ill-considered choices of spouse or career. President Kennedy should probably have known better than to attack Cuba in the ill-fated Bay of Pigs incident in 1961.

The Prolog gave a brief glimpse of what this book is about. It showed my attempt to aid a very personal choice—my daughter's dilemma about what to do about a birth delivery. This case has much in common with situations that seem much different. Suppose that the President of the United States is deciding whether to press the nuclear button that would start World War III. The scale of effort and the analytic resources available, of course, would be very different from my daughter's. But how the President sets about gathering information and makes up his mind, and what it takes to do it right, are much the same. Because all decisions have so much in

---

[1] A *decision* is the broader process within which a *choice* among specific options will be made. Key terms like these appear first in bold italic, are clarified in the Glossary, and put in regular italic type later if a meaning may need refreshing.
[2] Propose marriage.

Rational Choice and Judgment: Decision Analysis for the Decider, by Rex Brown
Copyright © 2005 John Wiley & Sons, Inc.

common, I will initially have you develop decision skills on problems that are real to you (as the Bay of Pigs decision certainly would be to the President) and easier to think about.

1.1 IMPROVING DECISIONS

Much of the time, we feel comfortable about the option we end up choosing in a given decision. However, we sometimes worry that we could have better integrated what we know and what we want and thus given ourselves a better chance of meeting our goals. Even when we know what to do, we may have trouble communicating our reasoning to others, whose perspectives may differ.

1.1.1 The Problem

Muddled thinking—or at least the lack of responsible reflection—is widespread in private and professional circles and may cause serious, but avoidable, harm. For example, thoughtless or passive citizens may be led to support legislation promoted by special interests (Trade restriction? Tax relief?). Regulatory officials may ban— or permit—health practices without trading off risks and costs responsibly. Young people may take the first appealing job that comes along and blight their careers or waste the nation's human resources.

Deciders, D, who are completely **rational** make sound choices, unaided, based on all they know and feel. They reach the same conclusions as they would have by following a rigorous logic. If there were such people, they would not have much use for this book. Fortunately for those of us who make a living trying to get closer-to-ideal decisions, they do not seem to exist.

This book (and any course based on it) is about improving *judgment* and reasoning. However, faulty reasoning is not the only reason that we act unwisely. Thinking smart is no guarantee of acting smart. We can be stubborn, intimidated, or paralyzed as managers or spouses or in other roles. I don't know how to combat such human frailty (as my own failure to diet and exercise testifies), nor do I know who does. Nevertheless, *thinking* smart is still important enough to be worth improving. This is what I focus on—how to make up your mind.

Study of any practice-oriented area, such as medicine or engineering, can address two kinds of question: how the world works (including people) and what can be done about it. Behavioral decision theory is concerned with the first of these: how people *do* decide (Hogarth, 1987). In this book, on the other hand, we are concerned ultimately with the second: how people *should* decide (although this must also take into account how they *do* decide now).

The tools here address various aspects of the decision process to be aided, including:

- Resolving conflicting criteria
- Accounting for uncertainty in outcomes

- Assessing uncertainty directly and indirectly
- Gathering information before a decision and updating uncertainty accordingly
- Combining alternative ways of making a judgment
- Structuring analytic strategy

1.1.2 Role of Decision Aiding

Deciders often get by perfectly well with no more than their intuition, especially for familiar decisions of business and private life. But sometimes the deciders, or those for whom they work, are dissatisfied with their decision making and wish to make certain *target* judgments better or more defensible. This is particularly true in government, where executives are often new to their jobs and are under pressure to defend their actions (e.g., the Bay of Pigs attack).

Decision *aid* can emulate, replace, or enhance judgment.

- **Emulation** imitates or replicates the performance of some more competent decider (e.g., artificial intelligence and "expert systems").
- **Replacement** disregards the decider's current thinking and analyzes decisions from scratch (a common decision-aiding practice).
- **Enhancement** builds on the decider's thinking but improves on it.

Analogy. You wish to compose great music. You can imitate Bach (*emulate*), build a synthesizer (*replace*), or develop your own talent (*enhance*). ♦

Emulation is the least radical contribution, but if D can imitate a more competent decider successfully, he has certainly made progress. *Replacing* D entirely, other than to obtain judgmental inputs, is the most radical and ambitious role, but in most cases, the state of the art is not yet there. *Enhancement*, like emulation, promises to improve D's decisions, but with some innovation. This is the type of aid we develop here.

Decision aid comes in the form of one or more specific analytic *tools*. Some are based on quantitative representations, or *models*, of the personal judgments on which a choice is to be based. They are what we focus on in this book.

1.1.3 The Ivory Tower Trap

A seemingly obvious requirement of a useful decision process, whether aided or not, is that it take into account all relevant available knowledge. This is rarer than one might suppose.

Analogy. Scientists raised in an ivory tower are determining whether heavier-than-air flight is feasible. They report categorically, based on a year of experiments with iron and other objects in their windowless laboratory, that it is quite impossible. The tea-lady, ignoring orders not to meddle in what she doesn't understand, points out the window at a jumbo jet in flight.... ♦

Far-fetched? It is not unknown for a meteorologist to announce a 70% chance of rain just after braving a downpour to get to work. We will be looking at comparable examples in our own field where a major "single-pass" decision analysis is contradicted by a simple reality check (or would have been if anyone had thought to do it).

The point is that rational judgment is *comprehensive.* It must take into account *all* available (or accessible) knowledge, not just that contained in a single study, no matter how internally coherent.

1.1.4 Identifying vs. Evaluating Options

Identifying which options to compare is often the most critical part of D's decision process. A brilliant decider is often recognized by inspired insights into what *might* be done. Phillip of Macedonia is said to have won battles by being the first general in ancient Greece to *consider* arranging his soldiers into a phalanx (then a novel strategy option). However, the distinctive contribution of decision analysis is in *evaluating*[3] specific options, not in *identifying* them. (I address that issue in Chapter 8 after the key concepts and procedures of option evaluation[4] have been driven home.)

1.1.5 Potential Levels of Aid Success

There are three levels of decision-aid success, in increasing order of challenge:

- The lowest level is that D's *informal* decision thinking is enhanced through having worked on *formal* modeling. This enhancement may involve no more than being able to distinguish the role of factual and preference judgments in choice and persuasion.
- Somewhat higher is where explicit simple models are produced and serve as a backdrop to informal thinking. D gains insight from the model but does not necessarily make the choice that its output indicates, because not enough effort and skill have been put into the modeling. This form of success is probably the most that can realistically be achieved on the basis of this book alone.
- The highest success is where D *can* rely on the model to produce a sound decision that D will be confident adopting. The model need not be any more complex

---

[3]In deference to common practice (and with some misgivings), I do not always distinguish the *preference* interpretation of *value, evaluation,* etc. (as in *value judgment*) from their "neutral" interpretation (as in the value of a variable) if the meaning is clear from the context.
[4]There is an excellent nontechnical treatment of identifying options in the "Options" chapter of Hammond et al. (1999).

than those presented here, but its design and input require a great deal of applied experience.

1.2 DECISION MODES

Decision tools can be helpful in any human endeavor where people are making up their own (or other people's) minds. Consider the following decider predicaments:

- A recent graduate is wondering whether to embark on a career in business or academia. He needs help in making up his mind but does not need to persuade anyone else that his choice is sound (see below).
- A nuclear regulator is considering shutting down a reactor that appears to be unsafe. Although the pros and cons are inconclusive, he has to defend his decision before the industry and the public. Moreover, he has bureaucratic considerations in making his choice that he does not care to make public.
- A responsible citizen is debating whether she should protest against an international free trade agreement. She wants to be able to support her position with a rationale that may persuade others, or at least that will withstand criticism. However, her choice will not affect her own interests very directly.

These cases typify three decision *modes* with distinctive decision-aiding needs.

1.2.1 Personal Mode

A *personal* decision is one that D makes on his/her own behalf, for example, about a career. The baby delivery example in the Prolog typifies the personal mode.

Most daily personal decisions are straightforward. Most are small in scope (such as whether to go on a date), but together they determine much of the quality of our lives. Most "only" require Ds to make up their own minds on the basis of their personal interests and what they know, and take no more than a few hours of reflection. However, with some, a misstep (like a bad marriage) may be devastating and the decision will merit greater effort.

Other personal choices include:

- Should D train to be a dancer?
- Should D invest in stocks, bonds, or real estate?
- Should D put her Down's syndrome child in an institution or care for him at home?
- Should D have an arthritic hip replaced now or wait a few years?

Some types of personal decision, although individually small, are relevant to so many people that they justify major public aiding efforts (such as career advisory services).

1.2.2 Professional Mode

A *professional* decision is one that D makes on behalf of others in a work capacity (e.g., in government, business management, or medical practice[5]). The analysis will almost invariably be performed by a specialist decision *aider* (e.g., consultant), who may report through a middleman (e.g., on D's support services staff). The aider may not even meet D.

To some degree, Ds meaningfully influence *action* (if only with a recommendation), say in their capacity as:

- A government inspector closing down an unsafe facility, who acts subject to approval by a higher manager
- A company president buying a factory, or a ship's captain firing on an unidentified plane
- A middle manager: say, a department head hiring a deputy
- A staffer or consultant making marketing recommendations
- A solitary professional: say, an accountant or physician, advising or acting on behalf of a client

A professional choice will generally be made in an organizational context where there are several participating deciders and constituencies with sometimes-conflicting interests. For example, a regulatory official deciding whether to close down a nuclear plant is subject to contradictory pressures from the administration, industry groups, and environmental interveners. He may also take into account his own bureaucratic interests and, of course, whatever laudable concern he may have to serve society.

Professional decisions include the following:

- Should the EPA administrator determine that the Clean Air Act is worth its cost?
- Should a Congress member vote to abolish the death penalty?
- Should a businessperson declare bankruptcy?
- Should a surgeon replace my hip?
- Should a company president move production to Mexico?
- Should a lawyer recommend that her client go to trial, or settle out of court?

Professional decisions will typically involve much larger stakes than private decisions. These decisions thus justify substantially more effort and expertise in decision aiding. (Hundreds of thousands of dollars were spent on decision analysis consultants alone in the nuclear waste case.)

---

[5]See the journal *Medical Decision Making* for examples and Weinstein (1996) for an excellent overview.

As with personal decisions, professional Ds base decisions on judgments that they accept as their own, even if elicited from an informant (see Chapter 10). Although the organization for whom the professional works can be thought of as "making a decision" (e.g., a business filing for bankruptcy), I take the perspective here that the decision is made by an individual professional (who may him/herself, however, treat the organization's interests—whatever that means—as his/her own) (see Chapter 9).

1.2.3 Civic Mode

A *civic* choice is a *private* choice on a public (not personal) issue. D (as voter or citizen) takes a private position on someone else's (e.g., government's) choice, for which s/he has no direct responsibility. For example:

- Should abortion be legalized?
- Should the United States take military action without United Nations authorization?
- Should oil drilling be permitted in the Alaska National Wildlife Refuge?

Civic decisions may *sound* much like *professional* government decisions, but the process is quite different. Civic "deciders" have only a remote influence over action that will be taken and can rarely spend more than an hour or two thinking about it. They are normally under no particular pressure to take great care weighing the pros and cons of a civic choice and would only use the simplest of decision tools, if any. They have the luxury of ill-considered (but perhaps emotionally satisfying) positions, at little personal cost; but possibly, if there are many like-minded voters, with great social impact.

Professional deciders, on the other hand, are directly responsible for comparable choices and may spend several months analyzing them before making a commitment. A congressional staffer (i.e., a professional decider) may spend weeks evaluating legislation and call upon extensive specialized analysis and information.

Example. Broadcasters, catering to civic deciders, devote much more air time to tracking the fortunes of contending positions (e.g., the ups and downs of "gay marriage" legislation) than to evaluating their pros and cons. They recognize that their viewers would prefer to watch a fight or soap opera than listen to a lecture. ♦

Example. I once suggested to a fellow decision analyst who was running for the U.S. Senate: "Present yourself as champion of logical decisions in government." He complained that it wouldn't help, because he needed a sexier sound bite. I concluded from this that the electorate is incompetent to make rational choices in its own interest and that the young need to be educated so that the adults they become are rational voters. This led me to a major research project to develop decision courses for adolescents (Baron and Brown, 1991). ♦

1.3 RATIONALITY

The primary purpose of a decision tool such as decision analysis is to enhance the *rationality* of D's decisions: to improve the prospect that his/her choice will lead to a desirable outcome. I suggest something like the following working definition[6]: *A rational choice is one that advances D's welfare effectively and logically, based on everything D knows, judges, and feels.*

1.3.1 Interpretations

Welfare is an elusive but essential concept, variously referred to as happiness, satisfaction, desirability, and when quantified, **utility**. For our purposes it is whatever caters to D's **preferences** or value judgments.

D would have achieved *ideal* rationality when absolutely everything in his/her mind has been processed with impeccable logic. This is not remotely achievable, given D's finite capacity and the current state of the art of logical analysis. We are all **subrational**.[7] However, ideal rationality serves as a distant beacon toward which we can strive.

A bad outcome does not necessarily mean that the decision was bad (subrational)—or vice versa. It may be rational to wear a seat belt, but against the odds, a seat belt could kill you (say, by trapping you under water). Nevertheless, if the outcomes of my decisions are consistently worse than yours, it is a useful, if inconclusive indication that you are more rational.

A key feature of a rational choice is that it draws on *all* D's knowledge, not just what happens to be used in any particular analysis. A complex and logically coherent analysis may not improve over unaided judgment if the latter draws on more of the available knowledge.

Example. Ford Motor Company UK felt that they had too many car parts depots in the London area. A prestigious university operations research group developed a state-of-the-art math model which indicated that only four of the seven depots were needed. Ford closed three depots, with disastrous results. The four remaining depots proved completely inadequate for the demand. It turned out that depot capacity had been grossly overestimated. Aiders had casually calculated usable depot capacity as height times length times width. They did not take inevitable dead space into account, although they would have if they had taken time to think seriously about it. Thus, the outcomes of the option of closing down depots were grossly distorted. The analysts were high-powered statisticians, with little knowledge of (or, I suspect, interest in) the nitty gritty of inventory management. They presumably did not see the need to take *all* relevant information into account in order to reach a sound decision. ♦

---

[6]My interpretation of rationality is for an individual decision, not for an organization, though it may involve an organization.
[7]*Subrationality* may have elements of rationality, by contrast with *irrationality*.

1.3.2 Elements of a Rational Choice

A sound choice always involves taking into account three considerations, explicitly or implicitly:

- What do I want?—*Goals*
- What can I do?—*Options*
- What might happen?—*Outcomes*

Failure to distinguish among these issues is perhaps the greatest and most common cause of subrational choice (and confusion in debate) on a controversial issue. This book should help D address such distinctions soundly, possibly with the help of quantitative tools. This is not to say that these tools always help or are always worth the trouble. But sometimes they are, especially when the stakes are high and the tools are used skillfully. If rationality is "there" and current subrationality is "here," this book is largely about how to bridge the gap between "here" and "there."

1.3.3 The Value of a Rational Analysis

There are several motivations for explicitly pursuing rationality in a decision.

- The quality of decisions may be enhanced, in the sense that they follow more logically from all available knowledge and expertise. (This is not to say that this object is always achieved. It takes a skilful analysis to outperform a capable intuitive decision maker.)
- It makes the reasoning behind a decision transparent and available to scrutiny. (This may be more valued by skeptical reviewers of the decision than by the deciders themselves.)
- If made public, it discourages the decider from acting on suspect considerations (such as personal advancement or avoiding bureaucratic embarrassment).

Example. The U.S. General Services Administration was deciding whether certain computing services used by government agencies should be provided in-house or contracted out to private firms. A simple decision analysis showed that the in-house option could often be justified only if "administrative morale" (understood by all to mean "empire building") were given a higher importance weight than "service to the public" or "saving taxpayer money." In other words, key actors in the decision process were prepared to give enough weight to "administrative morale" to justify keeping computer service in-house. ♦

1.3.4 Rationality Is No Substitute for Knowledge

A sound decision depends both on how good the knowledge you use is and on how well you reason from that knowledge. Here, we focus mainly on the second, although it is important to recognize that the first can be at least as important. If you are deciding whether to accept an unfamiliar roommate, you may want to take more trouble finding out more about his/her background than pondering what you already know about it.

People often mistakenly assume that my knowing something about rationality puts me instantly in a position to give a superior prescription on what to do, when I have only the sketchiest knowledge of the problem, usually less than they have. "Garbage in–garbage out." Rationality may help to avoid putting garbage in the middle, but it is no substitute for "better garbage."

Business Example. Tom Page, president of Ford's nonautomotive operations, asked me over a social lunch if I thought he should sell off one of his major production facilities. I had to explain lamely that I might be able to help if I were to organize the knowledge that he had or had access to, but that otherwise I had nothing to say that was worth listening to. ◆

Civic Example. I was on a radio talk show and a listener called in to ask me whether I thought the United States should invade Afghanistan. Again, I had to explain that unless I had analyzed and researched the problem carefully, my opinion would be worth no more than the listener's, and possibly less. ◆

1.4 QUANTITATIVE DECISION-AIDING METHODS

This book is not about *prescribing* rational decisions, in the sense of telling people what they should actually do.[8] It is about enhancing the process from which a good decision may emerge. The tools indicate primarily what questions to ask and what to do with the answers. They include both qualitative structure and quantitative models that show the action implications of a decider's goals, judgments, and knowledge. These tools will not necessarily lead to outcomes that deciders should prefer. But the tools may make the deciders more confident that they have given themselves the best chance, through a coherent process for making up their minds.

You should learn here how to use *simple* decision-aiding tools with *sophisticated* art. This book might be likened to a primer on using a hammer and chisel on a block of stone in order to enhance its appearance. Even Michelangelo needed more than that. He also needed substantial apprenticeship and practice before he could turn rough stone into a masterpiece. To pursue the analogy further, Michelangelo's client could enable him to meet her needs better if she acquired some sculpture training. So it is here that some decision analysis training can prepare the decider to use a specialist (but it cannot, on its own, turn the decider into a self-sufficient decision aider).

---

[8]When I first approached the NICHHD (National Institute of Child Health and Human Development) for a grant to develop adolescent decision skills, they assumed that it was to help young people make "correct" choices (e.g., don't do drugs or sex, but do stay in school). However, NICHHD went along, possibly with some regrets, with my proposal to teach people a *process* for achieving their own goals.

1.4.1 Features of Decision Tools

Decision tools that prescribe action have been around at least since the Delphic oracles "helped" ancient Greeks in their sacrificial choices. Since then, various types of decision aid have proliferated. They range from *qualitative* tools, such as "lateral thinking" (de Bono, 1970) and recognition-primed choice, to highly mathematical (*quantitative*) modeling techniques, such as linear programming, operations research, and multiobjective optimization.

Some *prescriptive* tools are *normative*; that is, they specify a logically coherent analysis that would be appropriate for an ideal human being. However, the analysis may or may not be *usable*, that is, adapted to the needs and limitations of real people (and institutions) so that the analysis is actually used and found useful where it matters (Bell et al., 1988). We may be prepared to sacrifice some logical rigor for some greater gain elsewhere (such as practical feasibility).

My modest objective is to present a compact tool kit of *usable* decision-aiding techniques that are versatile enough to address almost any choice among clear-cut options. My philosophical position is *personalist* in the sense that it models some person's judgment. By contrast, an *objectivist* position seeks to be based only on data and to avoid reliance on human judgment.

The benefits sought from quantitative decision aid include:

- Extracting different types of expertise and judgment from different sources. This avoids the technician's having to get into political issues or the high-level manager getting into detail that s/he is not up to providing.
- Pinpointing sources of disagreement, soft spots in an argument, or issues where more study is needed.
- Making the institutional decision process more orderly. (This may or may not be desirable. The British Empire was built, they say, on the art of muddling through!)
- Making it easier to defend a decision to others (e.g., to a court of law or the voting public).

On the other hand, there are potential pitfalls in the use of QDA. Quantification may inspire more confidence than it deserves. It may divert attention from the substance of an argument and to the technique for handling it. It may centralize the power in an organization by making it easier for the boss to micromanage and second-guess junior deciders (which may or may not be a good thing).

1.4.2 Merging Informal and Formal Thinking

The most critical part of rational choice is usually informal: understanding and organizing the important considerations. A mathematician colleague once said to me: "When you're ready to put your argument into numbers, it's time to move on to the next problem." For example, the right choice may well jump out at you, as a result of informal thinking, without any need for quantification. Most day-to-day decisions—and many of greater moment—do not, in fact, justify the time and effort of quantitative analysis.

Nevertheless, this book is aimed particularly at the *exceptions* to this rule, where it *is* worthwhile to quantify. Some problems are important enough to be worth the trouble of quantifying, in order to make decisions that are even slightly sounder. Even with the more routine decisions, mastery of the logical discipline of a sound numerical analysis may help make D's informal reasoning more rational.[9] How useful the effort is depends on the room for improvement, how much of that room can realistically be reduced, and at what cost.

Even when formal models are developed, informal thinking is an integral part of the decision process. I strongly recommend complementing this book with readings on sound informal thinking (see Chapter 3 and Hammond et al., 1999). In this book I try to add to your informal thinking by combining it with formal tools, which often parallel and refine the informal thinking.

1.4.3 Evolution of Decision Analysis

Before the twentieth century, major scientific advances oriented toward decision making had tended to be descriptive more than prescriptive, focusing on how the world works rather than how to make it work better. Decision circumstances changed slowly from year to year, so that decision practice could take its time to improve by trial and error. By the beginning of the twentieth century, however, technology and other fields had begun to change rapidly. The life-and-death perils of poor decisions in World War II spurred the development of the quantitative decision tools of OR (operations research). They were special-purpose tools (e.g., for locating enemy submarines) that may well have been decisive in winning the war.

After the war, OR was adapted to industry, with some success in certain situations. These tended to be where options were complex and consequences were clearly defined and involved processes that could be modeled mathematically (such as in production scheduling and transportation logistics). Progress in applying quantitative methods to choices involving a few clear-cut options with messy outcomes was a good deal slower. Analysis here competed less effectively with unaided humans, and deciders often did better by backing their own judgment.

The mid-twentieth century saw the development of general-purpose statistical decision theory, which can readily adapt to changing circumstances and, *in principle*, analyze any choice whatsoever. It does so by quantifying a decider's judgments about goals, options, and outcomes, however ill defined, and by inferring the preferred choice.[10] Its practical application is personal ***decision analysis,*** or ***DA***.[11]

In the early 1960s, forward-looking research groups at Harvard and Stanford developed and promoted DA as a universal methodology for improving rationality

---

[9]We conducted research to test this hypothesis for adolescents. The results were somewhat encouraging but inconclusive, due to the difficulty of evaluating improvements in informal decision making (Baron and Brown, 1991).

[10]Strictly speaking, decision theory only tests related judgments for consistency. It does not assure that decision judgments will fit with *all* D's other, typically inconsistent judgments, but it makes progress in that direction.

[11]"Personal" is needed as a qualifier only when "decision analysis" on its own is ambiguous, which will not normally be the case in this book.

in a world where poor decisions were damaging lives and communities. Leading corporations (e.g., DuPont, General Electric, and Kodak), and then government departments (e.g., Defense and Energy) began to apply decision analysis to their most challenging (and controversial) decisions (Brown, 1970, 1987). Many impressive successes were reported (Buede and Bresnick, 1992; Clemen and Kwit, 2001), and many of us who had been in decision analysis "on the ground floor" viewed DA with a missionary zeal (Ulvila and Brown, 1982).

Decision analysis has passed through several overlapping phases, characterized by distinctive modes of aiding, each building on the earlier phases (Brown, 1992).

- About 1950 to 1970: The *theory* phase laid the foundations of the parent discipline, statistical decision theory.
- About 1960 to 1980: The *technique* phase focused on specific modeling procedures and sought illustrative applications (Schlaifer, 1978; Keeney and Raiffa, 1993).
- About 1975 to 1990: The *problem* phase selected from among available DA techniques and adapted them to a particular class of problem, such as capital budgeting or environmental protection (Howard et al., 1972).
- About 1980 to present: The *use-and-user* phase addressed all requirements of useful aid in a given context, in which the focus is on usefulness to a particular decider and context (Brown, 1989; Brown and Vari, 1992).

Actual DA practice by no means fits neatly into these categories. Their edges and timings are much more blurred, but they may give some insight into DA's evolution. In some ways, I view this book as a manifesto for a "use-oriented" decision analysis revolution (as contrasted with technique- or problem-oriented DA). It draws equally on logic, people, and practice skills (rather than on logic alone). I believe this development of emphasis can counter the pressures that have slowed down successful DA practice in the past. DA methodology, although useful as it stands, is still very much a work in progress.

1.5 LEARNING PROCESS

1.5.1 Student's "End Product"

From this book you should develop some immediately useful mental skills. In particular, you should be better able to:

- Make rational choices *informally* and appreciate the considerations that go into them, building on how an intelligent person, experienced in making good decisions, already thinks.[12]

---

[12]Nobel laureate Richard Feynman, having performed countless complex mathematical computations over the years, got to the point where he could *intuit* the results of new computations to within a few percentage points of the correct answer. Enough practice with formal decision analyses may do the same for our intuitive decision making (Peterson and Beach, 1967; Fong et al., 1986).

- Build simple, logically sound models. These models need not be particularly ambitious technically compared with what you might find, say, in a typical OR course. They help illuminate your informal thinking but do not supersede it.
- Integrate such models effectively into informal decision processes so that they yield better and more useful choices. (It takes an unusually good student to do this successfully.)
- Effectively specify more authoritative models (to be developed and applied by decision analysis specialists) to use on your own decisions, professional and private.

1.5.2 Teaching Strategy

We alternate discussion of real (often current) decision-aiding cases with expounding the methodological issues involved. In the text we move between technical exposition, homework, case experience, and hands-on projects (group and individual). DA tools are applied to *cases* (real past DA applications), *examples* (unanalyzed real problems), and *exercises* (artificial problems used to demonstrate a method).

I believe applying modeling tools to real problems—rather than to hypothetical worked examples—is critical in mastering quantitative decision analysis. We devote at least equal attention to this art as to model construction, notably through hands-on practice on live problems. We also focus on the interface of tools with live decision making rather than on the technology of specific tools (which you can learn elsewhere) (Clemen, 1996).

If you plan to apply decision analysis yourself, without taking much more course work learning how, it is best to begin by working with these few general-purpose procedures applied to real problems, as we do here. You can then work intensively on a succession of real cases in apprenticeship to a successful practitioner on the way to your quickly becoming a handy amateur decision analyst. Even if your intent is to become a professional decision analyst, I believe this approach is a more effective way to start training than learning technically ambitious *statistical* decision theory removed from practice.

Analogy. If you want to make something that will fly for your daughter's birthday party tomorrow, you should learn how to use hammer and nails to build a simple kite rather than trying to master the carpentry to make a model airplane. Otherwise, you will have the makings of a plane that won't fly. This book can thus be seen as a crash course in using hammer and nails. Using simple tools does not assure that your kite will fly, but you will certainly have a better chance of success than you would with sophisticated tools that you are not yet ready to use. The difficult part is *designing* the kite, not in wielding the tools needed to implement the design. Design should ultimately be the critical focus of your efforts, even though you may have to start by learning how to use the tools (e.g., how to hit the nail and not your thumb). ♦

Although it is as a decider that you are being trained, text and exercises have you also take the role of aider. In the real world the aider is quite likely to be a more experienced analyst, especially in a professional context, but you will work more effectively with him/her by having played that role yourself in the course.

1.5.3 Active Development of Decision Skill

Although the tools are general purpose, the illustrative material is drawn largely from personal or public policy situations that you can relate to readily and make meaningful judgments about. This should enable you to do a useful reality check on the models.

A distinctive feature of this book is its emphasis on modeling *real* judgments. This contrasts with the common teaching practice of having you model only *hypothetical* judgments, as in numerical exercises or traditional Harvard-type case studies, based on reports of other people's knowledge or judgment. Those exercises can be useful for many purposes, such as teaching modeling mechanics, with "school solutions" that can readily be graded. Hypothetical judgment, however, does not exercise the critical skill of assuring that the model corresponds adequately to D's actual—or enhanced—thinking. This, in my opinion, is a major reason that Ds do not use quantitative models more frequently.

Accordingly, many of our examples refer to personal and civic choices that are familiar enough for you to have judgments worth modeling. Many of you will not (yet) have much experience of professional (e.g., management) settings and thus not have professional judgments that can be realistically modeled. I believe, however, that judgment-modeling skills developed on private decisions can usefully be transferred to professional situations.

1.5.4 Assignments

One of my public policy students commented wryly: "Most of my courses are 80% absorption and 20% thinking. This is just the other way around." I expect most of your learning will probably take place during preparation and discussion of assignments (rather than in absorbing text). This requires, I believe, at least two hours of class discussion of assignments for each chapter.

It is extremely important to *master the logical content of each chapter* before moving on to the next, especially Chapters 4 to 7, which are devoted to modeling tools. I have found that if students slip off this escalator at virtually any stage, they will be lost in what follows and may not pass the course without remedial tutoring. An indicator of minimal competence is whether you can complete successfully at least one exercise on each methodological point in a chapter.

Assignments for each chapter are usually split in two sections, marked: *"Prepare for discussion after reading"* and *"Prepare for later discussion or submission."*

1.5.5 Term Decision Project

The capstone of the course is a term project, which exercises and tests the usefulness of what you are learning. Singly or in groups, you work chapter by chapter, topic by topic, throughout the course on a real decision problem of your choosing, applying techniques and concepts as you learn them, and report on your conclusions at the end of the course. The completed project should lead you to make a choice that you really trust and are prepared to act on. Therefore, you need not be limited to course material in your thinking, except to the extent that it helps. Blind faith in what pops out of a model is certainly not what I want to impart. Integrating what you learn here into your everyday decisions *is*.

The project can take various forms, depending on the orientation of a course and your circumstances. If you are learning to make *private* decisions, picking a live, imminent, personal decision that you will commit to by the end of the course usually works well, although working in groups on a civic decision has the appeal of productive interaction with other students. If you are training to become a *professional decision aider*, working on a civic choice in groups (possibly the same civic choice for all groups) may be preferred. If you are already an active decision aider, you can work with a group on a live project with which you are actually involved. A class will usually have either everyone working in groups or all working individually.

The term project is discussed in more detail, along with assignments, in Chapter 12, which you may want to skim now. The assignments will be introduced at strategic points throughout the course, so you will need to look ahead from time to time to parts of Chapter 12. The assignments are grouped into the following "stages":

A. Set up the project and specify the choice to be aided and who is to make the choice. Form teams (group projects only).
B. Evaluate the choice informally.
C. Evaluate the choice formally—but still qualitatively.
D. Evaluate the choice formally—quantitatively.
E. Make the actual choice, integrating model(s) developed in stages C and/or D into the decider's decision process, and ideally commit to action.
F. Submit the final report, including a comparison with the earlier informal choice (stage B), what if any action has or will be taken, and a postmortem on the project.

Each stage has one or more assignments, timed to draw on material covered so far, and identified as:

- WA: written assignment, to be submitted by the next class period, or
- OA: oral assignment, prepared for by the next class period

1.5.6 Professional Illustrations

Although you will learn primarily by working actively on personal or civic decisions, it is useful for you to become *passively* familiar with past cases or experiences similar to those that you might face as a professional. The examples described here draw heavily on consulting and research experience that I can speak most authoritatively about, and hopefully they have enough variety to cover the key issues.

These situations deal with professional choices and you will not ordinarily have the knowledge to second-guess judgments used; therefore, you may not be able to evaluate the realism of the models. However, passive acquaintance with professional cases should help you to adapt skills that you have developed largely on private decisions. This should prepare you to take on the additional challenges of adapting basic skills to problems with higher stakes, greater complexity, multiple players, and other distinctive features that affect decision aiding. In Chapter 2 we preview professional uses of decision analysis, and in Chapter 9 some distinctive issues.

1.5.7 Running Exercise: A Career Choice

To avoid the tedium of having to learn a new factual background for each illustrative case or exercise, the following hypothetical situation illustrates a personal choice on which an individual, Tex, might seek aid. It is used as a running example throughout the book.

Tex has just graduated in social sciences from Cambridge University and is ready to plan his career. In particular, he is weighing the pros and cons of embarking on a career in business or in academia. (This example is, in fact, based quite closely on my own experience of some 50 years ago.) I will return to this career example from time to time, to illustrate analytic tools in use as they are treated in the text.

1.5.8 Technical Footnotes and Appendixes

Mastering DA logic and concepts as you progress through the course is critical. For this reason, I have tried to segregate any material that is not essential to this end into appendixes and footnotes. I recommend ignoring such technical material and references to the literature on a first pass through the material unless you feel in good command of the main text. Footnotes and a knowledge of the material cited should not be needed, for example, to do chapter assignments. They are there, rather, to satisfy any interest you may have in digging deeper into concepts, either through further reading or through more advanced treatment of the same topics. Appendixes have a similar role; I would not generally test mastery of any of this material in quizzes or exams.

1.5.9 Intellectual Challenge of Realistic Modeling

Students have sometimes been misled into anticipating either that a course based on this book would be a "soft option" with a modest intellectual challenge, or that it would be your typical quantitative methods course, heavy on difficult math. It is neither. The book starts off at a fairly slow pace, exploring qualitative issues that motivate and set the stage for what is to follow. This may suggest that the material is going to be straightforward and easy to absorb. However, when we get to the quantitative modeling of informal thinking, the analytic going quickly gets tougher. The principal difficulty is not in the modeling per se, but in assuring that the end result captures (and hopefully improves on) the decider's best judgment.

"Hypothetical" Example. Suppose a star athlete is convicted of murdering his wife and a friend, after a sensational trial that holds the world in thrall. At sentencing, the judge sums up: "I am satisfied that Mr. Athlete committed the murders and here is my rational decision on how to treat him. U.S. environmental regulations specify the value of a life to be about $10 million, giving a total social loss of $20 million for these two deaths. According to a national opinion survey, 100 million TV viewers would pay an average of $10 for the entertainment value of the trial. Thus, the murders produced $1 billion value for society, at the cost of a mere $20 million. I have therefore decided not to punish Athlete, but to commend him for producing a 50:1 benefit–cost ratio for society—an astonishing bargain!"

Do you agree? If not, why not? Think about it before you read on....

The flaw in the judge's reasoning is surely that he takes no account of the immense social cost of condoning *any* murder, which outweighs any entertainment value. (The precedent might spawn a major "murder-for-hire" industry!) ♦

This example shows the dangers of accepting a plausible quantitative argument without robust safeguards (such as a reality check). In the case above, the unrealism is caught easily because it is so powerfully counterintuitive. In less obvious cases, an unsuspecting D may accept and act on flawed models, with harmful results. Modeling a choice so that it improves on unaided judgment requires great skill and training. This fact is often not acknowledged in decision science practice, sometimes with disastrous effects.

An apocryphal story, told among decision scientists themselves, has someone ask a noted decision scientist whether he is using DA on some personal choice. "Of course not," he is said to have replied, "this is an *important* decision." The implication, recognised by the scientists, is that decision analysis *as practiced* does not match up to common sense. I will try to correct that failing here by enhancing, rather than replacing, common sense.

ASSIGNMENTS

Prepare for Discussion or Submission

Decision Mode

1. See the two quotations preceding the table of contents. Which decision mode is each: professional, personal, or civic?

Rationality

2. In the real-life personal problem in the Prolog, the mother had to decide whether to have both her twin babies by caesarian or to have the first, Lucy, naturally and

take a gamble that she also could have the second, Sam, who had complications, naturally. After DA, she opted for the latter option, managed to have both deliveries naturally, and both mother and babies did fine.

  (a) Did that good outcome vindicate the soundness of her choice?

  (b) Later, the mother became persuaded by new medical research that a fetus in the "feet down" position, which Sam was, should always be delivered by caesarian, because of possible injury due to "turning" him. If she had known this at the time, should she have taken the "Caesarian first" option? How do you think this consideration would change the drawing of Figure P.2?

  (c) Does finding out this new information indicate that she made a mistake at the time?

3. One of my students waited to sell his car until the last two days of his stay in the United States. Then he had an accident and collected the entire value of the car in insurance. He was delighted, since he doubted that he could have sold the car in two days. Was it rational of him to have waited? What would that depend on?

Motivation for Course

4. Describe some professional choice you (or someone you have worked with) had to make or recommend, where sounder or better-communicated reasoning would have been useful to D or the organization.

Decision Modes

5. A manager is deciding whether to fire her secretary. What mode is this decision?

6. A bill is being considered by Congress to overturn *Roe v. Wade* (a Supreme Court decision permitting some abortion). List examples of personal, professional, and civic choices *related to* this circumstance. Give two options for each choice.

7. Which of the following are professional, personal, and/or civic decisions?

  (a) Accountant D is making up his mind which candidate to support in the next presidential election.

  (b) Supreme Court Justice D is deciding whether present election laws are constitutional.

  (c) D is deciding whether to accept a job offer in Timbuktu.

Rational Choice

8. In the running Tex exercise, state one goal, one option, and one possible outcome.

9. Describe briefly a real past choice among clear-cut options, made by you, someone you know, or a government agency, of each of the following types:

  (a) The choice was subrational and turned out badly.

  (b) The choice was subrational but turned out well.

(c) The choice was rational but turned out badly.

Why was the choice rational or not in each case?

10. A prime minister dissolves parliament and calls general elections before he would have had to, constitutionally. He loses the election. Was it a subrational choice?

Learning

11. Suppose that your learning objective is to be a more effective surgeon when you qualify in five years. State a relative advantage and disadvantage (one of each) of exercising decision techniques on medical case studies as opposed to exercising them on everyday personal decisions unrelated to medicine.

Chapter 2

Uses of Decision Analysis

At first sight, it might seem that the ends (uses) of decision analysis—if not the means—are straightforward: D has a perplexing choice to make, an aider helps him/her weigh the pros and cons, and s/he makes a sounder decision. In practice, decision analysis is a good deal more complicated. To help you see where we are going, and why, I shall comment briefly on a variety of real applications. By contrast to later parts of the book, this chapter should be a light read, and in fact you can skip or skim it if you are impatient to get to the (tougher) meat of analysis itself.

Your primary explicit use for the tools in this book is likely to be professional. In this chapter we mainly preview professional use of decision analysis in public policy and business, where my own main experience lies. Applied anecdotes will illustrate distinctive features of professional decision making and convey impressionistically the nature of current decision analysis practice, including what it is used for, where, and with what results.

Much of the illustrative case material comes from projects that I conducted as a consultant with DDI (Decisions and Designs, Inc.) and DSC (Decision Science Consortium, Inc.) (see Appendix 2A). That case file is a small fraction of the varied body of DA applications I have accumulated over the past 40 years. They are not necessarily representative of DA practice in general (Keefer et al., 2004).

2.1 PRIVATE DECISIONS

Despite the largely professional motivation of this book, for pedagogical purposes, as discussed in Chapter 1, much of the technical exposition is in the context of familiar

---

Rational Choice and Judgment: Decision Analysis for the Decider, by Rex Brown
Copyright © 2005 John Wiley & Sons, Inc.

private choices—personal and civic. However, compared with professional decisions, the stakes are usually losw and barely justify the trouble of much formal decision analysis. In fact, private decisions will not often be of sufficient moment to warrant quantitative modeling at all, and if they do, only the simplest modeling.

2.1.1 Personal Dilemmas

From time to time I analyze my own decisions with a largely qualitative version of DA. (The problems are rarely large enough to justify more than a few hours of my effort.)

Example. I had to decide whether to have a painfully arthritic hip replaced. The surgeon advised me to wait a few years on the grounds that I was too young (55) and that the pain was still bearable. We agreed, however, to delay the decision two months, during which time I would use it as a running case study in a decision course I was to teach to junior high schoolers. In that course we used a simple plus–minus tally version of DA (see Chapter 4) and at the end of the course I took a vote. Most of the class voted for replacement, a conclusion that I had also come to. I reviewed the analysis with the surgeon; he acknowledged that originally he had overlooked significant factors and agreed that he should operate. He did, and the replacement has worked out fine.[1] ♦

The main benefit of DA to my personal (and civic) decision making is that my formal training in DA over the years hones virtually all my *informal* decision making. As a friendly service, I sometimes try to help other people to make personal choices, including career, marriage, and medical (see the Prolog).

Example. The teenager next door to me had to decide whether to accept a place at a high-powered "magnet" school. A simple decision analysis of what she wanted and what might happen suggested that she should turn it down, based largely on the negatives of a long commute and disruption of her social life. This confirmed her own "gut feeling," but her parents had been urging her to accept. She went over our structured analysis with them; they now understood and appreciated her reluctance and were happy to go along. ♦

2.1.2 Civic Positions

As citizens, we regularly take positions on civic issues. We make up our minds whether we are "pro-choice" or "pro-life" on abortion; whether we favor U.S. military action abroad; whether nuclear power should be abandoned; whether the United States should pressure Israel to leave the West Bank; or whether to protest the activities of the World Trade Organization. As I have noted, decisions like these have their

---

[1]This experience was reported in the Health section of the *Washington Post* (Peters, 1990). See the sequel to this case in Chapter 9.

professional counterparts for public policy makers, but individuals making up their minds on the same issues do not generally have the time or expertise for extensive analysis.

I, and no doubt other decision analysts, try our hands as public citizens from time to time at helping others to marshal their thoughts on topical issues of the day (and occasionally, to press our own points of view) with a qualitative variant of DA. However, the main contribution of DA to the quality of civic choice has probably been—and will continue to be—in giving citizens (or citizens to be) formal DA training that enhances their qualitative reasoning.

Example. House Representative Ed Zschau was running for the Senate and asked me to suggest a platform that he could run on. Since he had earlier taught decision analysis with me and had then become a successful businessman on his way to Congress, I suggested that he put himself forward as "the champion of logical decision making in government."[2] He replied sadly: "In this game, Rex, it doesn't help if they think you make logical decisions. If you can't get the message across in 30 seconds of TV, forget it. Better logic won't cut it." ♦

It then dawned on me that we had an incompetent electorate, unable or uninterested in sound public policy decisions, which are made supposedly on their behalf. They thus leave the field open to whatever vested interest can pay for the most seductive TV spots. This pushed a couple of us to develop courses to teach decision skills to adolescents (Baron and Brown, 1991), in the hope that as adults they would be better equipped to serve their own interests at the polling booth. This mission is now being pursued by the new Decision Education Foundation, based in the Engineering-Economics Department at Stanford University (D'Abbasi et al., 2004).

In the meantime, before that wistful promise can be realized, I and other decision analysts must do what we can to see that public policy discussion is rationally structured. Much of that is a question simply of separating issues of fact from value judgments (which is one of the main tenets of decision analysis—see Chapter 3). When discussing with Israelis whether they should cede the West Bank to the Palestinians unilaterally, I have tried to focus discussion separately on whether it would help or harm Israel's security, and which objective is more important to them, security or controlling land for other reasons.

2.2 CORPORATE BUSINESS DECISIONS

The first operational tools of decision analysis were developed and taught in the early 1960s at Harvard Business School (where I was junior member of the development team). Major corporations such as DuPont, Pillsbury, Ford, Honeywell, Mobil, and

---

[2]His opponent, Alan Cranston, who later became the first U.S. Senator to be censured for unethical behavior, was running on a platform of "integrity in government"!

Firestone began using them on investment and other decisions, to be followed by most Fortune 500 companies by the end of the century (Brown, 1970; Ulvila and Brown, 1982).

2.2.1 The Profit Motive

Business was a good place to introduce decision analysis initially, because it is largely driven by a straightforward measurable objective, profit.

Example. The chief engineer of a Belgian chemical company strongly advocated spending $20 million on a new state-of-the-art boiler, whose technical features had great interest for him. He argued that the old boiler was breaking down all the time. Decision analysis showed that the switch would be profitable only if the old boiler broke down 20 times more frequently than it had been doing. The engineer acknowledged that this was inconceivable, and withdrew his proposal. The old boiler was kept. ♦

2.2.2 Nonprofit Considerations

In the 1960s and 1970s, decision analysis methods (like earlier quantitative decision-aiding methods such as operations research) were limited largely to evaluating choices where utility was measured by money (Schlaifer, 1978). However, even in business, profit is not always the dominant concern.

Example. The president of the European subsidiary of a U.S. tool manufacturer was deciding where to locate his head office. I developed a decision analysis addressing economic considerations, such as access to markets and availability of component suppliers, which pointed clearly to a location in southern Germany. The president studied my report and responded "Thank you. We'll locate in Geneva, Switzerland." It turned out that Geneva had an international school to which he wanted to send his children, and the analysis indicated that locating there would sacrifice profit only modestly. ♦

Sometimes, what initially appears to be a nonfinancial consideration does in fact have financial implications.

Example. Ford Motor Company's vice-president for product planning, Hal Sperlich, was considering dropping convertibles from Ford's line of cars. A decision analysis found that convertibles produced a net profit of under $1 million a year (taking into account business that they took away from other Ford cars). The VP said: "That's not worth taking up precious space in our showrooms" (a consideration that the analysis had not included). The implication was that the loss of showroom space would cost more than the direct profit. He decided to drop convertibles for the time being. (They were later reintroduced.) ♦

2.3 GOVERNMENT DECISIONS

In the 1970s, methods were developed (Keeney and Raiffa, 1993) for dealing with multiple and intangible criteria (not just money). This development opened up public policy as a promising field of application. The government field had several distinctive attractions. By contrast to business, the objectives in government are many, varied, and typically intangible (e.g., aesthetics and quality of life). Decisions are often subject to hostile scrutiny, sometimes all the way up to the Supreme Court. This motivates policy makers to seek a transparent and defensible rationale for their actions. Senior executives, particularly political appointees, are often new to their decision tasks and obliged to rely on the expertise of others. Decision analysis lends itself to breaking one big problem into several smaller problems, each of which taps into a distinctive expertise (i.e., a different expert).

These opportunities and challenges led several of us decision analysts to move over from business to government applications. (My new employers, DDI and later DSC, were based in Washington, DC, the seat of government.)

2.3.1 Regulation

Environmental, health, and safety regulation has proven a particularly fertile ground for decision analysis, due to its controversial and litigious nature.

Example. The Nuclear Regulatory Commission is responsible for assuring the safety of reactors and for shutting them down if it judges them to be unsafe. The administrator for NRC Area III, Tom Murley, considered one reactor particularly risky, yet it was rated one of the nation's safest according to a PRA (probabilistic risk analysis) that had cost $4 million. He asked me to look into it. It turned out that the PRA only took account of risks that could be documented authoritatively, and disregarded others (such as earthquakes and fires). It also ignored informed judgment of the type that led him to doubt the reactor's safety (e.g., based on unfavorable inspection reports). We spent a person-month adapting the PRA to a decision analysis format that included all knowledge that he considered relevant, however tentative. The analysis indicated that the reactor needed a costly "backfit" to come up to regulatory standards. Murley accepted this result and required the backfit (Ulvila and Brown, 1982). ♦

The "cost–benefit analysis" that dominated government decision aid until recently normally quantified only what was readily measurable. This had the effect of emphasizing the *cost* of regulations over their often-intangible benefits, and thus was favored by regulated businesses, since it lowered the value of regulation.

Example. In the early 1990s a Democratic Congress mandated the EPA to determine whether the 1970 Clean Air Act had been worth its cost, with a specific insistence that intangibles be given full weight. A multicontractor research team was put together, where my responsibility was to tie together the contributions from groups of economists, chemists, and other scientific groups (such as the U.S. Geological Survey). I developed a highly aggregated model to estimate the net GDP (gross domestic product) impact of the act, based on inputs we were to receive from the expert contractors.

The specialist contractors themselves declined to produce even tentative findings until these satisfied their stringent scientific standards. In frustration, to show some forward momentum, some colleagues and I put together our own poorly informed input "guesstimates." This produced a highly conjectural net benefit equivalent to $10 to 20 billion a year. Months dragged out into years, without any report to Congress, until Republicans took over and the entire project was shelved, with virtually nothing to show. ♦

2.3.2 Defense

Among government departments, Defense initially took the lead in sponsoring both the development and application of decision analysis, through technical support agencies such as DARPA, ONR, and ARI.

Resource allocation, especially in the budgeting process, has been a particularly popular use, largely because the decisions are standardized and repetitive, which permits investment in methodology and training to be recovered over many applications. In addition, conflicting interests need to be balanced equitably, and decisions are reviewed at several levels of authority.

Weapons procurement, including selection among alternative systems and candidate suppliers, is also a major use (Buede and Bresnick, 1992). Evaluation structures get very complex, with hundreds and sometimes thousands of distinguishable criteria, making decision analysis's "knowledge division of labor" valuable. It also provides a framework for resolving chronic controversy and lends itself to "design-to-cost" procurement practices (i.e., cost is the only given; all else is discretionary). Previously, the cheapest way to meet a preset design requirement was sought, because cost (but not design quality) was thought to be quantifiable. DA's ability to quantify intangibles changed all that.

2.3.3 Foreign Policy

Decision analysis is commonly used on diplomatic strategy.

Example. One of my first projects in Washington was a high-level one. A U.S. diplomatic mission was preparing to visit Saudi Arabia, with a view to a treaty offering economic and other inducements (e.g., a pro-Arab "tilt" in foreign policy) in return for an assured, affordable oil supply. The U.S. NSC (National Security Council) was considering what guidance to give the mission, weighing such issues as public pro-Israeli sentiment as well as oil supply.

The NSC staff asked us to use decision analysis to evaluate alternative levels of concessions to Saudi Arabia. We had access to top foreign policy and other U.S.

experts, to make model inputs as well informed as possible. For example, the consensus of a group of intelligence specialists was a 5% probability of an Arab–Israeli war within four years. Three weeks after we presented our findings but before any action was taken on it, the 1973 war erupted and the entire issue became moot. (We issued a camouflaged version of our classified findings in which we were requested by our intelligence informants to replace the 5% war probability by 50%, supposedly on grounds of national security!) ♦

Example. During a sudden upsurge in hostilities in Lebanon, the United States had to make a rapid decision on whether to evacuate U.S. civilians. The Department of Defense needed to make its urgent recommendation. My DDI colleague, Cam Peterson, met with a group of generals continuously over three days, during which they iterated the following cycle several times before they reached agreement: Interrogate generals on their current thinking; construct a simple decision model based on that thinking; discuss the results with the generals; and revise the model to reflect that discussion. At the end they supported immediate evacuation. ♦

2.3.4 Waste Management

The establishment of a large "Superfund" for toxic waste cleanup in the 1970s, and the controversy that surrounded it, have generated much demand for decision analysis.

Example. A permanent repository for high-level nuclear waste, now in "temporary" surface storage, was needed (and still is, as I write). Funded at over $5 billion, it has been the source of some of the largest decision analysis projects for over 20 years.[3] An award-winning decision analysis by leaders in the DA field ranked candidate sites for a nuclear waste repository based on preliminary evidence and judgments supplied by Department of Energy (DOE) staff. The latter proposed the three top-ranked sites for intensive study—two in salt and one in basalt (U.S. Department of Energy, 1986). The Energy Secretary disagreed and substituted a third rock medium, tuff, in place of one of the salt sites. Political critics accused the administration of disregarding authoritative decision science for improper political purposes.

The DOE staff office chief, Ben Rusche, had me review the exercise. I concluded that the Secretary's decision to include all three rock types in the short list *could* be defended with DA *and* be compatible with the ranking model. If a salt medium appears best *under current knowledge*, it is not surprising that two of the currently top-ranked sites should be in salt. However, if, after subsequent research, salt is rejected, this is informative, and the best choice is now *not* likely to be salt. If it was not now clear which medium was best, it made sense to retain all three to study further. I passed a rough decision analysis to this effect to Rusche. The DOE staff commissioning the

---

[3] I was involved in an advisory and review capacity throughout that period.

earlier study had apparently requested ranking, whereas short listing, which would entail "portfolio diversity,"[4] was what was called for. ◆

2.3.5 Security

Example. Well before the Twin Towers terrorist attack in 2001, an interagency task force on air travel security convened to consider a legislative requirement that all explosive materials be tagged radioactively, to aid inspection of checked luggage for bombs. We made a simple decision model of the choice, calling for about a dozen judgmental inputs, related to such issues as cost, traveler convenience, and the prospect of a terrorist evading the system. It pointed to *not* tagging.

We presented the model to the task force with our own tentative inputs and invited reaction. The issue was highly contentious and there was heated debate, by convinced proponents and opponents of tagging, on what the inputs should be. We focused the discussion by having participants indicate which judgmental inputs they took issue with in order to support their positions. After an hour's discussion, we asked each of the 19 present to enter his/her own input numbers on a standard form that we distributed, and we calculated the implications on a computer we had in an adjoining room. About a third of the participants took part, with results that showed less divergence than the opinions voiced. There was not time at the meeting to review the results together, but we returned the forms with results to their authors, who could use it or work on it in their subsequent deliberations using our computer program (with what results we could not learn). ◆

2.4 PROFESSIONAL DECISIONS BY INDIVIDUAL PRACTITIONERS

Although business and government have so far been the heaviest users of DA, a number of other professions have taken to decision analysis, notably in the context of medical diagnosis and therapy e.g., at the Harvard School of Public Health (Weinstein, 1996).

Example. I was approached by a U.S. Treasury consultant to help him evaluate whether a corporate decision by the Alieska business consortium that avoided "billions" of dollars in federal taxes was "prudent" (i.e., it could reasonably have been made on grounds *other than* tax evasion, which would have been an indictable offense). The approach was not pursued. ◆

2.5 NONSTANDARD USES OF DECISION ANALYSIS

Not all decision aid is designed to help D to select one of his/her current options (although this is the most straightforward use of DA).

---

[4]This was later pointed out by one of the decision analysts involved (Keeney, 1987).

2.5.1 Prospective Decision Rules

Sometimes the object of DA is to aid D to prepare for a future or recurrent decision, although I have rarely found it successful (see Chapter 8).

Example. EPA has many laboratories to test possibly toxic materials. For each testing occasion, a decision has to be made about safety measures: For example, should the testing be done on an open bench or in a special containment space? In collaboration with a company specializing in chemical processes, we developed a computerized tool to match a safety measure to known characteristics of the substance being tested. Lab managers could customize the tool by overriding any part of the model to fit special circumstances, but few of them actually did, so far as I am aware. ♦

2.5.2 "Aiding" Another's Decision

Sometimes an analysis is initiated by one party to aid another's decision. These can be bona fide impartial "think tanks," such as the Congressional Research Service, acting in the public interest to inform government decisions. More often in my experience, however, the research sponsor is really advocating a particular choice, more or less surreptitiously. I have often, in fact, been approached by an interested party to serve as an "expert witness" on some public policy or judicial issue. A litigant's legal counsel will usually only hire expert witnesses after checking that their testimony will be convenient.

Example. The Navy approached us to conduct a decision analysis that would "help" Congress decide whether to spend more on bombers or on aircraft carriers. When I agreed to do it on condition that our findings, whatever they proved to be, would be made public, the matter was dropped. ♦

Sometimes the advocacy aspect of a client's interest is not apparent until a project is well under way.

Example. Industries and environmentalists have long fought over whether the Alaskan National Wildlife Reserve could be drilled for oil. At the urging of the AOGA (Alaska Oil and Gas Association), a federal agency, ARC (Arctic Research Commission) commissioned us to develop a "scientific basis" for land-use regulation decisions of this kind. AOGA may have been expecting the usual industry-friendly cost–benefit approach. As soon as they realized that our decision analysis methods took full account of intangible environmental impacts, AOGA withdrew its support and our contract was "discontinued" for "budgetary" reasons. ♦

Sometimes only the uncertainty portion of the decision process is analyzed formally. Advocacy can again be the motivation.

Example. In the early 1980s there were intelligence indications that Iraq was diverting nuclear material for weapon purposes. I understand that the U.S. State Department hoped to persuade Israel not to take pre-emptive military action, arguing that the United Nations inspections would detect any illegal diversion, with incontrovertible evidence, on the basis of which the international community would put a stop to the Iraqi program in good time.

A study by a national lab had established that over 90% of the strategies that a delinquent state could use to divert nuclear material illegally would be detected. From this they (unrealistically) inferred over a 90% probability of detection. Though encouraged, State had us do a "confirmatory" study, which took into account the informed judgment that an astute adversary will know of and avoid detectable diversion strategies. When our draft findings produced a detection probability of well below 10%, State had our study canceled. A few months later, Israel, apparently sharing our lack of confidence in the effectiveness of international safeguards, bombed and destroyed the Iraqi reactor. ◆

2.6 LOOKING BACKWARD AND FORWARD

2.6.1 Past Record of DA

Half a century ago, in the 1940s, QDA (quantitative decision aid), especially "operations research," was credited with having done much to win World War II. It was then widely believed that QDA could better the welfare of all humankind, and public and private organizations started to use it extensively. Businesses often trusted the analyses enough to overrule the judgment of their own managers. However, the results were often disappointing and the National Academy of Sciences Committee on Risk Analysis and Decision Making found that only a tiny fraction of the potential of QDA was being realized (Simon, 1986).

QDA success stories do abound, however, mainly for problems where humans have particular difficulty unaided (such as optimization over complex options).[5] Nevertheless, many have cautioned against uncritical reliance on QDA and on DA in particular.[6] Early in the 1970s and 1980s, two small impressionistic interview surveys of DA applications (Brown, 1970; Ulvila and Brown, 1982) in business suggested great promise but only modest demonstrable success. Two recent comprehensive literature reviews (Corner and Kirkwood, 1991; Keefer et al., 2004) described hundreds of applications over a wide area of business and government fields, some costing hundreds of thousands of dollars. Although most were *reported* as "successful," they lacked documentation on which decisions were demonstrably changed for the better.

---

[5] Acknowledged by the Edelman Awards of INFORMS, a decision science professional society.
[6] Majone and Quade (1980) and Stephen Watson, coauthor of a major decision analysis text (Watson and Buede, 1987), later cast doubts on its usefulness (Watson, 1992). Jackson Grayson, an early pioneer in decision analysis, cautioned against uncritical use of management science in general after he himself became an influential decider as head of the Federal Price Control Board (Grayson, 1973). Nobel laureate Danny Kahneman also has his doubts (personal communication, 1993). Harvard Business School, the cradle of decision analysis for business, no longer makes the study of decision analysis a requirement in the MBA program.

To check real success would be a massive project and has yet to be done. My own inconclusive experience is that many applications have been neither used nor found useful. Evidence on medical applications, has, however, been encouraging (Weinstein, 1996; Cantor, 2004).

So far, the main benefit of DA, and it is considerable, has been in inducing Ds to practice more rational *informal* reasoning: what DA cofounder Robert Schlaifer called "mental hygiene." Indeed, some of my former MBA students have attributed their success as managers to the "rub-off" influence of DA on their decisions.

I believe that past DA disappointments have largely been due to removable obstacles; for example, decision aiders working through "middleman" staff rather than directly with the decider. The problem that an aider solves may not be the one D has.

2.6.2 Role of Aider Orientation

DA setbacks are also due to aider preoccupation with modeling over the human requirements of a successful aid and due to the models failing to capture all that D knows (Brown, in press). With the burgeoning use of techniques for tapping knowledge in multiple ways, this obstacle to DA success is being chipped away.

Example. A nuclear regulator rejected a favorable evaluation of reactor safety because the probabilistic model used took no account of a series of "near-miss" accidents that he knew of. (It only modeled engineering faults.) DA technology can now incorporate such knowledge into probabilistic risk assessment (Brown, 2002). ♦

Aider motivations can be positive: Examples are pride in useful work and the desire to make D happy. Positive aider motivation to develop useful aids was critical to the above-mentioned Allied success in World War II. The aider then had no conflict of interest with either decider or constituency (the public). Both he and the Ds he served (e.g., military strategists) were at mortal risk and motivated to do whatever it took to defeat the enemy.

However, that overwhelming drive for aiders to produce realistic judgments and sound choices receded after the war. My hypothesis is that aiders' priorities have often been negative and conflicted with D's interests, to the point where their tools fail to meet at least one essential requirement. Aider mismotivations, such as mental comfort and professional standing, can be especially problematic. I believe that greater control by D of the decision-aiding process is having a major influence on aider orientation. As a result, decision analytic tools have greatly improved in scope and technical quality and I think are poised for a great leap forward.

2.6.3 Afterthought

The applications in this chapter illustrate the greater flexibility and sensitivity of decision analysis to users' needs compared with earlier forms of quantitative aid. They illustrate as well how it can better take into account the people, the politics, the time pressures, and all the messy but critical factors that real deciders have to contend with. The nature of decision analysis applications varies by domain, by problem type, and by the role that the analysis plays.

Some cases underline the humbling point that decision analysis is an aid to enhance, not replace, human judgment, and is at risk for dramatic errors (Brown, 2005). Others illustrate how issues beyond—or instead of—improving D's decisions can get entwined with the analysis.

ASSIGNMENTS

Prepare for Discussion After Reading

1. Can you think of any topical government policy issues on which a structured rationale might be useful for the executives involved?

2. What kinds of decisions seem to lend themselves best to DA?

APPENDIX 2A

A DECISION ANALYST REFLECTS ON HIS WORK[7]

Henry Porter (Abridged by Rex Brown)

(The following article, from a popular British magazine, gives some sense of how decision analysis is being used in high-level public policy.)

From the feasibility of weakening the American–Israeli alliance, to helping submarine commanders make decisions about firing torpedoes, a decision analyst can provide "the tools of reason." It works like this: A decision analyst closets himself/herself with decision makers and their assistants and draws out of them all the information relevant to the decision. As they talk, the analyst quantifies their judgments and taps them into a computer terminal. A computer screen makes a diagram that changes as the discussion continues.

So it went when high-level U.S. government officials got together to decide whether to evacuate U.S. citizens from Lebanon. As one decision analyst describes it: "The Joint Chiefs of Staff had to decide whether to evacuate. We closeted ourselves with the key players, trying to understand the nature of the problem for half a day. We then spent half a day constructing a computer program that reflected this. The following morning we played it back to them and told them what the computer model seemed to be saying. We found out where we had gone wrong, modified the program, and then ran it again. They then evaluated the output."

---

[7]Abridged version of "Dr. Logic," *Illustrated London News*, October 1987. Reproduced with permission from *Chance*, Vol. 2, No. 4, 1989.

The phrase "decision analysis" is misleading. It implies that it is a retrospective science that dissects decisions of the past. In fact, almost all analyses are performed on future decisions about to be taken. Naturally enough, the skill of the decision analyst is to interpret the desires and views of the decision makers correctly and to place the right weights on them. The accuracy of the model depends entirely on its input. As one decision analyst puts it: "The computer is like a slide rule and I am just the guy who operates that slide rule."

Slide Rule for Delicate Decisions

This "slide rule" has been applied to some of the most delicate problems that have landed in the laps of the last four U.S. administrations. It has helped the government make foreign alliance and export control decisions and address the issue of underground nuclear waste disposal. So the decision analyst is rather more than the simple technician: The skills required are far more interesting and diverse. Logic and a knowledge of computers are essential, but so, too, is the psychology of individuals and a knowledge of their behavior in large organizations. The decision analyst cannot be an uncommunicative academic wrapped up in his work; he must combine the observations of a novelist with the receptive nonjudgmental air of a family solicitor. Above all, a decision analyst must be very, very discreet, for during the course of his work he will become privy to the mechanics and secrets of the organization that he is helping.

One decision analyst is Rex Brown, the focus of this profile. Being of an analytical and curious bent, he began wondering during his first job with a marketing research company about the advice that he was so glibly handing out. "I found myself advising much grayer and wiser heads than my own, and I began to wonder whether there was such a thing as an absolutely right decision in logical terms." He utilized a year's fellowship at Cambridge University to try and answer his question, and then went to Harvard to work with a well-known mathematical decision theorist.

During the early 1960s, analytical skills emerging from the Harvard Business School were concerned simply with decision making to enable businesses to decide how best to improve profits. Brown was fortunate to be at Harvard at precisely the moment when the science of decision analysis expanded to consider governmental decisions, which are by their nature more difficult to make and in the end infinitely more tricky to evaluate. He later cofounded a company, Decision Science Consortium, Inc., and has been at work in Washington, DC, for the last 17 years.

Brown believes a need exists for his services, particularly in government. "In business there is much less room for improvement. You have people working in the same field and making pretty sound decisions for, say, a period of 20 years. In government it is a different story. It is [often] run by a collection of what one hopes are gifted amateurs who are changed every four years. There is a stronger reason for going through a rational process that can be defended. It is also important [that] the politicians have those vast amounts of data organized for them."

Since the 1970s, the U.S. government has used Brown's services frequently, although the way in which it has been deployed has changed according to the interest and character of the administration. During the Nixon years he was involved closely in major international issues. The analysis, for instance, that Brown completed on the strategic embargoes ended up on Henry Kissinger's desk.

During the Arab–Israeli war, Brown was hired to carry out an analysis on the feasibility of weakening the American–Israeli alliance in favor of the Arab oil states. "The starting point was to decide where we could get a stable and inexpensive supply of oil that we need not worry about. There were experts from CIA and other government agencies attending and we did our analysis in the usual way." The government, of course, decided against such weakening of alliances, but interestingly, Rex Brown would not have known that until he read it in the newspapers.

Brown recalls that when President Carter was replaced by Ronald Reagan: "We were tied up in a number of contracts to do with environmental and welfare programs. They were all canceled and, until Reagan's emphasis on military affairs became apparent, we had very little work." The association with the military had not grown just because of Reagan's predisposition to defense. The pressures of high-speed technology forced the generals to consider at what stage decisions should be taken and if there is time for the human mind to intervene in combat situations. Brown's colleagues have helped to develop computerized decision aids to allow fighter pilots to make tactical decisions without having their control usurped by technology, and have worked with precisely the same aims on top-level war-waging decisions. "We are addressing what the appropriate role of the human is. The temptation in the technical community, which tends to be dominated by engineers, is to design a system that is untouched by the human mind. So when World War III starts, it will trigger a button and we will all sit about for half an hour to see how the war is resolved. Our input is to say that somehow we have to preserve some responsibility for a human judge in the process, even during the throes of a massively complex nuclear battle. There has to be some way that we can impact on this system."

"What was interesting was the different value judgments we got from the generals on when to mobilize. One, for instance, said that the cost of a false alarm was 20 times worse than the U.S. being caught with its pants down. The other said it was 20 times worse to be caught on the hop than to have a false alarm. So you see that there is a very great difference within the military on the values that should drive, say, an automated star wars system."

Perhaps because of this difference, Decision Science Consortium is building artificial intelligence programs that are designed to accumulate military knowledge. "Today a general probably does not know very much more than his counterpart 100 years ago, because each generation has to learn for itself. What we are doing is replicating the experts' knowledge and building on it."

This defense work has led Brown to make some interesting discoveries that have in small ways advanced his own skills. Some years ago he was asked by the U.S. Navy to examine how submarine commanders could make better decisions when it came to firing their torpedoes. "This was interesting because the decision of a submarine commander was always taken in isolated circumstances, which are obviously due to the nature of submarines. They waited too long before giving the order to fire. What we found was that the commanders were capable of making the "right" decisions but were not motivated to do so. They were being evaluated in their exercises on how accurately they could pinpoint the enemy's position, not on the preservation of their own submarines. We told the Navy that they had to sort out the motivation problem and that they did not need us."

When advising companies Brown had quickly learned that his recommendations would never be accepted if they went against the culture of the organization. "You see, you can't get a middle manager to accept an analysis if that act means he is acknowledging that he is not doing his job properly. You have to grasp the institutional setting and assess the territorial instincts... what we call 'turf' in America."

The problems are so magnified in politics that Brown is frequently confounded by powerful turf considerations. He was once asked by the Congressional Office of Technology Assessment to look into the possibility of applying decision analysis throughout the government. Congress considered having the executive branch support all its proposals with systematic logic, which seems a reasonable enough suggestion, especially when the executive advocates something like the costly deployment of MX missiles. "I talked to a member of the cabinet about it. He said: 'I will oppose this to my dying day. Congress meddles enough as it is. If we present them with clear grounds for our recommendations, they will be able to challenge them.' What the cabinet member preferred was creative obfuscation."

"You know, quite a lot of my work revolves around the use of language. On one occasion, we were evaluating new organization arrangements with government officials. I realized that the analysis had to include the empire-building ambitions of the people I was talking to. Obviously we could not call it empire building. But we could call it 'administrative morale.' They were all quite clear about the code and knew exactly what we were talking about. Later I asked them to quantify the importance of various interests. Astonishingly, the government officials were quite prepared to put 10% on serving the public, 10% on saving the taxpayer money, and 80% on administrative morale."

When working with congressional committees, Brown often found himself in the bizarre position of having to compile two sets of books, one that assumes Congress is serving the public and one that assumes that Congress is serving itself. "We had to help a congressional committee decide whether to support an anti-crime bill which would have called for a $100 million investment. We developed two analyses. First we ran one to help the Congressman to decide which side his bread was buttered on. Then we did a separate analysis with the public's point of view and compared them. We learned later that they decided to can the program."

This, of course, leads to certain ethical problems of which Brown is acutely aware. Part of that first analysis included an element that was cosily labeled "electoral security." The congress members then decided in the privacy of their committee rooms what priority to give their own reelection and naturally found many compelling reasons to favor "electoral security" against the wider public interest.

"What my ethics allow me to do is to give them a tool that I place at their disposal. I like to say I am the mindless wielder of the slide rule on these occasions but many of my colleagues ask how I can live with myself when I support these... practices." Brown acknowledges that his science may allow politicians to see more clearly where their interests lie. Before the advent of decision analysis there was a much greater confusion in the politicians' minds between their own interests and the public good, which is not necessarily a bad thing.

What frightens some is that decision analysis may eventually become a tool of authoritarianism. "What has emerged is that everyone wants to rely on a mechanical procedure when it is probably true that a more delicate, subtle application of judgment would be better." Businesses and, to a lesser extent, U.S. government departments become dependent on decision aids in the same way that some patients come to rely on regular visits to a psychoanalyst. Decision making can be agonizing; it can be a relief to offload part of the burden.

Interestingly, Brown finds other similarities with his profession and psychiatry. "It's very odd but people tell me much more than they do their colleagues. It's because I am an outsider and I now think about 20% of my success derives from this fact."

Chapter 3

Evaluating a Choice Qualitatively

In this chapter we discuss some of the principal considerations that reasonable deciders normally take into account when they make a choice and how they can begin structuring and building systematically on these considerations. It is a first step toward creating a quantitative model of D's decision process that can be built into a more powerful tool, but this step on its own may be enough to make more rational and defensible decisions.

In Chapter 1 I quoted a colleague saying: "When you're ready to put your argument into numbers, it's time to move on to the next problem." This is tantamount to saying that the informal stage of thinking about a choice captures most of what needs doing. Quantifying a choice is essentially a refinement of an informal decision analysis that is often substantially complete. I largely agree, but we are interested in the unusually important or perplexing cases that *do* merit numbers.

A key requirement of a successful decision tool is that the resulting choice be at least as sound as the choice D would have made without aid. As the Ancient Greek medical sage Hyppocrates said: "Above all, do no harm." Unfortunately, decision-aiding practice often fails this test (Brown, in press), especially by failing to take into account knowledge that D would ordinarily and sensibly take into account. The most dangerous harm that a tool can do is to lull D into full trust in its output, which he acts on (as happened in the Ford depot case in Section 1.3.1).

D's first step in the decision-aiding process may be to reflect freely and to intuit directly a preferred choice. Tex, for example, might comment, "Business success could make me rich and powerful, and that's more important than the loss of leisure

---

Rational Choice and Judgment: Decision Analysis for the Decider, by Rex Brown
Copyright © 2005 John Wiley & Sons, Inc.

and greater stress I expect from academia." A decision aider might follow up with prompts (to make the knowledge extraction as complete as possible), such as:

- What problem or opportunity triggered the decision issue?
- Is there any option D is currently inclined to take, and why?
- What makes D hesitate?
- What could make D change his/her mind?

3.1 A START AT STRUCTURING: PROS AND CONS

Next, the aider has D list pros and cons for each option (i.e., noting considerations that favor one option or another). Then D considers the relative significance of each pro and con. If there are only two options—as in the Tex business/academia case—a pro for one option is a con for the other, so D need only work with pros.[1] For example, in the Tex case:

- Business pros:
    - Big bucks are possible.
    - Power is possible.
- Academia pros:
    - The risk of poverty is low.
    - The work is professionally fulfilling.

Tex might simply inspect and dwell on this list, and adjust, if necessary, his initial intuition about the preferred option.

A simple variant of this listing of pros and cons, attributed to Benjamin Franklin, is to pair equally important pros and cons, and eliminate each such pair from further consideration. By repeating this cancellation process, eventually D is left with just a couple of pros and cons, whose net effect on the choice may be more apparent than that of the original list.

3.2 GOALS, OPTIONS, AND OUTCOMES: "GOING THROUGH THE GOO"

A step beyond simply listing the pros and cons is for D to reason informally about the three essential decision elements noted in Chapter 1, *goals, options*, and *outcomes* (whence the acronym *GOO*).

---

[1] It may, however, be more convenient to attach pros and cons to the option to which they relate most directly.

3.2.1 Goals

What does D want? What are the objectives D wants to achieve? What are the criteria by which the outcomes of a choice are to be judged (i.e., what D ultimately cares about)? How relatively important are each of these criteria? These are questions of *preferences* among the various criteria. Preferences often involve feelings and emotions, which do not necessarily have any clear rational basis, nor do they need to. ("Degustibus non disputandum": Tastes are not to be disputed.)

3.2.2 Options

These are actions among which D is to choose (i.e., what can D do?). The options can be specified broadly (e.g., emigrate) or narrowly (e.g., join Uncle Ed on his sheep farm in Tasmania), or as a strategy (e.g., emigrate and commit to returning in two years if it doesn't work out). Option specification is discussed further in Section 8.5.

3.2.3 Outcomes

The evaluation of an outcome represents a *factual* judgment. What might happen to the achievement of D's goals as a result of the options? How close to meeting goals will D then be? (The answers will normally be uncertain.)

The *setting* of a decision is not itself an *outcome*, in that it is not affected by the choice, but it can *influence* an outcome. For example, the financial outcome of Tex's business option will be affected by the economic setting; if there should be a protracted economic downturn (which Tex can do nothing about), the prospect of a good financial outcome to the business option will be harmed. A large inheritance is a setting that might make economic criteria less important relative to noneconomic (i.e., the inheritance might affect how important incremental changes in his finances are).

3.2.4 The GOO Table

Even though D may not *explicitly* address all three GOO issues, D will *somehow* need to take them all into account in order to make a wise choice. He may not be the source of judgments involved, but he is the final *judger* of whether they are acceptable.

Figure 3.1 illustrates (using the Tex example) a tabular format for registering thoughts on goals, options, and outcomes. Laskey and Campbell (1991) call this format "going through the GOO" in their junior high school course on decision making. The table displays goals/criteria as rows and options as columns, with option outcomes in the cells. The notations (A+) and (B+) indicate whether a particular criterion appears to favor academia or business, respectively. Impressionistic appraisal of the GOO table may or may not confirm Tex's option *preference* from the earlier pro/con evaluation. If it does not, conflicting results must somehow be merged (see Section 3.5).

Note that although only two criteria are shown, they are *defined* to be exhaustive—criteria are either economic or noneconomic. In general, there can be any number of

                                    OPTIONS

GOALS (Criteria)	BUSINESS	ACADEMIA
Economic (B+)	May make big bucks, but merely respectable income is more likely	Modest and narrow range of income
Noneconomic (A+)	Probably humdrum, with a slight chance at power	At least moderately rewarding, and fulfillment quite likely

Outcomes: in body of table

FIGURE 3.1 Going through the GOO.

criteria (rows) and they should be comprehensive, in order for the GOO exercise to capture the choice in its totality.

Finer-grained evaluation could involve:

- Subdividing the coarse twofold criteria; for example, splitting "economic" into "peak income," "final wealth," and "other economic," and splitting "noneconomic" into "quality of life," "prestige," "work interest," and "other noneconomic."
- Evaluating the outcome descriptions in the boxes by one or more pluses or minuses (see Chapter 4).

Usually, evaluating the choice implications of "going through the GOO" consists of dwelling on each element and letting intuition work, unguided. (This is as far as I go, myself, in aiding most of my own day-to-day decisions.)

3.3 DISTINGUISHING BETWEEN GOO ELEMENTS

It is critical to keep clear the distinction between GOO elements. When you hear a statement about a choice, ask yourself whether it says something about:

- *Goals:* what D prefers or likes ("I don't like broccoli.")
- *Options:* what actions D has to choose among ("broccoli or parsnips, what a dreadful choice!")
- *Outcomes (or settings):* what D thinks is, or will be, the case. ("I expect broccoli will be on the menu today" or "I have an upset tummy, which makes me more finicky.")

Finally, there is what D intends or is considering doing, in the light of the GOO—his choice ("I refuse to eat the broccoli").

The following statements highlight the often subtle differences among goals, options, and outcomes.

- "Disregarding graduation requirements (option) may make you flunk out of school (outcome), which would be sad (goal)."
- "Hedonism (option) does not guarantee a trouble-free life (outcome)."

3.3.1 Goals vs. Outcomes

Keeping goals and outcomes distinct, informally or formally, may be the most important single guideline in rational judgment and they are often confused. A goal judgment has to do with what the decider wants, regardless of what actually happens.

When the distinction is not clear, public controversies are liable to become heated and fruitless. If I advocate gun control and you don't, it might be because I think it will reduce crime more than you do (outcome), and/or it may be because you attach more importance to individual freedom than I do (goal). Clarity on this discrepancy may pinpoint the source(s) of our disagreement and bring about more productive debate.

Example. John Lennon's values were attacked (unfairly, in my opinion) for saying that the Beatles were better known throughout the world than Jesus Christ. If he were *factually* wrong (which I doubt), his knowledge might be at fault, but that says nothing about his values. (Indeed, Christ in His Heavens might make the same factual judgment as Lennon!) For all we know—at least from this statement—Lennon may have had very laudable preferences (goals). He might consider that the Beatles' greater recognition is regrettable and advocate combating it with Bible study. ♦

3.3.2 "Consider the Source": Assessments as Clues to Preference

Paradoxically, factual outcome statements can be *clues* (possibly misleading) to the *preferences* of the author. Ascribing an unfavorable attribute to someone is literally a factual judgment, but it may be a clue to more general disapproval (i.e., preference). It may be unfair to "kill the messenger," but it is reasonable to ask *why* the message was delivered. Could it be that the messenger is citing messages *selectively* in order to favor a preference that s/he would rather not admit to openly, such as racism? If someone says that one race is more intelligent than another, the statement may or may not be true, but perhaps it was said with the *intent* to discredit one race.

Example. Democratic congressional representative Moran was almost forced from office in spring 2003 for having said that "Jewish interests have a major influence on U.S. Middle East policy." Media commentators characterized this statement as "clearly anti-Semitic" (i.e., they were saying that he was admitting to unsavory values). Literally, he was not: He was making a factual judgment (on which he might or might not have been mistaken). Moran *could* be a victim of "killing the messenger" (i.e., he was simply reporting something unpalatable). However, the *fact that he* *made the statement* might be a clue to his preferences. This is especially true if the statement were part of a pattern of Moran selectively citing facts that show Jews in an unfavorable light (ignoring more flattering facts). ♦

Example. Business professor Howard Raiffa was accused in the *Wall Street Journal* of having advocated lying in a course on negotiation. What he had actually said was that a party to a negotiation gains a bargaining advantage by misrepresenting his/her position (because lying may secure an advantageous outcome). He was attacked as amoral for favoring misrepresentation. What he had really done was to make a *factual* judgment about the outcome of misrepresentation. He was simply delivering a message, without approval or disapproval (although I happen to know that he disapproved).[2] ♦

3.4 ASSESSING UNCERTAIN POSSIBILITIES

The outcome element of GOO is normally uncertain. The degree of an ***assessor's*** uncertainty about a ***possibility*** can be described qualitatively with terms such as "unlikely," "possible," "likely," and "certain." These are imprecise terms, but they may correspond to the imprecise state of mind of the assessor. (They can be stated more precisely as probabilities; see Chapter 4.)

An assessor can make an uncertainty assessment, however precise, either directly or by indirect inference. There are two particularly useful lines of indirect assessment, depending on the type of knowledge used: ***conditioned assessment*** and ***assessment updating***. The loose qualitative reasoning below is usually as far as we get in our thinking. (The reasoning is validated and quantified in Chapter 10.)

3.4.1 Conditioned Assessment: "It All Depends"

A common response to a question on assessing (or predicting) a possibility starts with "It all depends on . . . ," which opens the way to *conditioned assessment*. The "unconditional" assessment (i.e., without any hypothetical conditions) of possibility A that depends on condition C is derived indirectly from three other assessments:

- The chances of A being true if condition C is, or is not, true (two assessments)
- The unconditional chance of C

Example. Doctor D notes that patient Sean is feverish and wonders whether he has the flu. D thinks, "it all depends on whether he has had a flu shot." D doesn't yet know whether Sean has had a shot, but judges it "quite likely." If he *has* had a shot, D thinks it "extremely unlikely" that he has flu; if *not*, D thinks that flu is "as likely as not." Based on these three judgments, D may conclude that it is "somewhat unlikely" that Sean has flu. ♦

---

[2]The irony is that if Raiffa himself had been less determined to be intellectually honest and more concerned with his public relations, he might have chosen to misrepresent his factual judgment.

Qualitative *input* judgments are necessarily imprecise, and so, therefore, are the *output* conclusions. Precision requires quantification (see Chapter 10). However, practice with the quantitative procedures should improve an assessor's qualitative performance and avoid the bother of explicit numerical calculations.

3.4.2 Updating Assessments in the Light of New Evidence

We often revise our opinion about matters of fact when we receive new **evidence**. This is *assessment updating*. How much we change our mind depends on:

- *Prior* judgment: assessment of possibility *before* learning evidence
- *Diagnostic* judgment: how surprised we would be (relatively) if the possibility were, or were not, true

Example. Jane is reconsidering her pessimistic forecast that she didn't get an A on a recent exam, given that the professor has just beamed at her as they cross in the corridor. How should that affect her exam forecast? Jane's *prior* judgment is that it is not very likely that she got an A. She notes that the professor *usually scowls* at her. So his beaming today would be most surprising if she had *not* gotten an A, but not at all surprising if she *had* gotten an A. This is quite diagnostic of an A and Jane should become substantially more optimistic.

If, on the contrary, the professor *usually beams* at her, Jane would not be very surprised that he beamed today, whatever her grade. However, she would be a *little bit* more surprised if she had *not* gotten an A than if she had. The "beaming" evidence is only very slightly diagnostic of her getting an A, and her pessimism shouldn't lift much. ♦

In some cases, informal reasoning may be enough to draw a firm conclusion.

Judicial Example. In a murder trial, the defendant had been observed burning his outer clothes immediately after the bloody murder was known to have taken place. A juror thinks this burning behavior would be *extremely* surprising if he were innocent, but not at all surprising if he were guilty. Unless there is other significant evidence pointing toward innocence, the juror might well find the defendant "guilty beyond reasonable doubt." ♦

If, on the other hand, assessor's initial (*prior*) judgment and conflicting diagnostic evidence are *both* very strong, they tend to cancel each other out. A precise conclusion then requires a quantitative analysis (see Chapter 10).

3.4.3 Getting New Evidence Before Deciding

Ds can *seek* new evidence before making a choice. After they receive it, they can use *assessment updating* (see above) to revise their original assessment. A major motivation for doing this is to reduce the *risk* of regret. Ds will have some regret when, with hindsight, an option different from the one chosen turns out to have been best. The risk of regret is related to how likely an error by hindsight is and what the cost to the Ds is if the error does occur. Whether it is worth actually trying to get new information also depends to a large extent on how much that will cost and what the prospects are of its actually reducing uncertainty.

The quantitative logic for determining the value of new but still imperfect information has a well-developed mathematical formulation (Pratt et al., 1995), but it is more difficult to implement successfully than is normally worth the trouble. Informal reasoning along the foregoing lines normally makes more sense than developing a complex model.

3.4.4 Formal Versions of Informal Reasoning

Both lines of reasoning discussed above, *conditioned assessment* and *assessment updating*, can be expressed formally by a rational and quantifiable model. Learning how to analyze formally should help D make sound *informal* arguments if the stakes are not high enough to justify the effort of an explicit model. With good judgment, D may intuitively produce the same conclusion as an explicit numerical model (in which case the model is unnecessary, except to *demonstrate* the soundness of the intuition). Informal argument along these lines is difficult to do effectively, which presents a powerful case for doing it formally (although that is also challenging).

The discussion above has dealt specifically only with binary events (i.e., where there are only two possibilities). The same reasoning can be extended straightforwardly to cases where the uncertainty refers to many possibilities.

3.5 PLURAL EVALUATION

When Ds have an important choice to make, they usually try to think about it in several different ways, even if pressed for time. Don't you? You normally don't want to put all your thinking eggs in one basket, whether the analysis is formal, informal, or purely intuitive. Two half-baked approaches can nearly always be shown to be better than one $\frac{3}{4}$-baked approach (Lindley et al., 1979). Combining several approaches to the same choice or other problem is ***plural evaluation***—by contrast to a ***single-pass evaluation***.[3]

Example. If you are deciding whether to have a child soon, you probably think about it in different ways. Your *single-pass* evaluations might be:

- Having a child just now doesn't feel like a good idea.
- Weighing the pros and cons in a GOO format favors a child.
- Among your recently married friends, those who have had a child seem to have more regrets than the childless friends, which predisposes you against a child.
- An experienced family counselor advises you to have the child.

---

[3]Decision aiders often do not use plural evaluation, which I think is a pity.

Two for, two against. You have generally more confidence in the counselor and the GOO process than straight intuition or canvassing others' opinions. You realize that the contrary implications of the two other lines of thinking could be due to you and your friends over-weighting immediate satisfaction, since you think the greatest rewards of parenthood come later in life. So you decide to have the child. I think this is a sensible way of making up your mind. (I hope it is clear that I am not advocating parenthood, although my own experience tempts me!) ◆

The four arguments in this example illustrate four basic methods of *single-pass* evaluation of a choice (among others):

- *Intuition.* This can be anything from "a feeling in your bones" to more careful reflection.
- *Pros and cons.* This is typified by "going through the GOO," and is built into a numerical model later in the course (see Chapter 6).
- *Analogy.* This involves identifying a similar situation that is easier to analyze (e.g., because it has a known history) and considering how any differences between situations might skew the choice.
- *The opinion of others.* What weight to give to others' opinion depends on their credibility and how persuasive their arguments are. For example, they may alert Ds to important considerations they had not thought of.

I recommend always seeking at least three alternative approaches, qualitative or quantitative, before making a choice.

3.6 LIMITATIONS OF QUALITATIVE ANALYSIS

Even if D's intuitive decision making is known usually to be pretty competent and to follow sound logic (Peterson and Beach, 1967), it is not always easy to identify or communicate the underlying reasoning. An exception is the case, rare in practice, where there is *no* uncertainty in the *inputs* to the argument. (For example, "Sugar is always sweet. This is not sweet. Therefore, this is not sugar."[4])

However, in virtually all interesting choices and inference problems, as in the examples above, uncertainties are great enough that qualitative reasoning may not be up to making a convincing case. Quantitative reasoning, developed in succeeding chapters, can in principle do that, but it can be difficult and burdensome. Chapters 4 to 10 are all concerned with putting numbers to the informal considerations discussed in this chapter (e.g., probabilities to represent uncertainty). Done carefully and skillfully, quantitative analysis should significantly improve on D's informal decisions (though it might not be worth the trouble).

---

[4] As in the syllogisms of classical logic.

ASSIGNMENTS

Prepare for Discussion After Reading

Problem Formulation

1. Imaginary confidential transcript from White House tapes, January 23 1998:

    "Brown, as my private decision consultant, you have only my best interests at heart, right?"
    "Certainly, Mr. President."
    "Should I swear on oath I haven't been having it off with this Lewinsky woman? I have to think about losing my job and my place in history—and doing the right thing, of course."
    "Can I have my class analyze it as a case study, Mr. President?"
    "Well . . . if you're damn sure they won't breathe a word of it."

    Based on a plausible guess of what President Clinton wanted and what might happen (as far as he knew), would you have advised the President to deny on oath any sexual improprieties with Miss Lewinsky?

2. Dolly leaves a reasonable amount of time to get to Gatwick Airport in order not to miss her flight. In midroute, there are inconclusive indications from road signs that she is on the wrong motorway. Should she get off the motorway at the next exit to get directions or keep going and hope for the best? What questions should Dolly ask herself to make a rational choice?

3. In the movie *Ransom*, Mel Gibson's son is kidnapped and a $2 million ransom is demanded. Instead of complying, Gibson goes on TV and refuses the demand. He offers a bounty of $2 million on the kidnapper, dead or alive, which he will withdraw when his son is returned unharmed. If you were the father, what issues would you address in deciding whether to pay the ransom or offer the bounty, if those were the only options you considered?

Civic Choices

4. Should research on human cloning be banned internationally?

5. Should smoking pot be legalized in your country?

6. Identify a controversial current public policy choice and two contending options for it (not necessarily the *only* serious options). List half a dozen significant criteria (grouped if necessary) in order of importance, from your point of view. Indicate which option each criterion favors in this case. Say which option you think is most in the public interest. Submit about half a page explanation in GOO or other format.

7. Study a current newspaper article or editorial (perhaps identified by the instructor) describing a current controversial public issue with a yes–no choice. In about two paragraphs, state your view on what the decider (individual, organization, or society) should do, and why.

Prepare for Later Discussion or Submission
Civic Choices

8. Suppose that there is a bill before Congress to abolish nuclear power: Specifically, no new reactors are to start operations and all the 100+ commercial reactors in the United States are to stop operation by 2020. Off the top of your head, would you support the bill without further clarification of what it would entail? Be prepared to discuss and evaluate more deliberately—but qualitatively—the pros and cons. If your position depends critically on specifics of how the policy is put into effect, take that realistically into account (e.g., do not necessarily assume that the policy is "done right").

9. (Letter submitted to *The Washington Post*). "At the risk of upsetting Muslim friends, I must speak up for what has been called 'profiling'—i.e. focusing airport security screening on certain ethnic and religious groups. To be sure, it selectively inconveniences innocents, which is certainly to be regretted. (Why not compensate them for it? $10 per 'friskee' would surely help calm indignation.) But profiling also promises to make investigative effort more efficient in uncovering the guilty, and that is surely the dominant concern.

    "I don't need to be a racist to want to use all available clues to target scarce screening resources where the guilty are most likely to be found. The clues surely include ethnicity and religion (along with age, physique, behavior, etc.), particularly if I observe that most terrorist attackers have been Moslem. If all I know about a passenger is that he is Moslem, that will raise my probability (however small) that he is a terrorist. Who should you look at more carefully: an elderly nun en route to Lourdes; or a young Arab with a one-way ticket? If I were picking suspects in the theft of a menorah, I would search Jews before gentiles."

    On what grounds might someone disagree with this position?

GOO

10. You are feeling peckish in midafternoon and find a veggie burger and a costly sweet dessert in the fridge.
    (a) Discuss plausibly which you should eat, in a short sentence.
    (b) Restate this argument as a list of pros for each.
    (c) Restate as GOO table.

11. Find and submit a copy of a short (at most one page) newspaper article advocating a particular public action. Recast it concisely in GOO form. Note significant material in the article that does not appear to fit the GOO format and whether it is relevant to the argument. What are the strongest grounds on which a critic might take issue with the article's author?

Distinguishing Factual from Value Judgments

12. "If single mothers expect generous welfare checks, it will encourage them not to worry so much about getting pregnant." Does this demonstrate that the speaker is opposed to welfare?

13. Bill Maher, host of the TV talk show *Politically Incorrect*, after an administration spokesman referred to the 2001 Twin Towers attacks as "cowardly," said of the suicide bombers, "Whatever else they are, they are not cowards." He was taken off the air immediately, on the grounds of his having expressed pro-terrorist sentiments. Did he?

14. For the following statements, indicate whether they: imply judgments of choice (advocacy); only factual assessment (possibly uncertain or wrong); only values (trade-off); or are ambiguous. Use C for choice, P for possibility, V for value judgment, and C or V, etc. for ambiguous. For example, if statement *x* is "ambiguous" and could either be a value judgment or a choice, you would write: "*x*: V or C." Add a brief explanation only if you think it necessary for clarity.

(a) "Al Gore would have become the President of the United States in 2000 if all the ballots in the state of Florida had been recounted."

(b) "Thirty percent of the company's workforce are required to be black."

(c) "Animals in experiments have rights, but saving human lives is more important."

(d) "The rich should have a lower tax rate than the poor as a reward for their superior contribution to society."

(e) "A 'foot and mouth' outbreak cannot be contained by vaccination."

(f) "Sustained economic growth should always take precedence over pollution reduction."

(g) "Letting colored immigrants into England without limit will produce rivers of blood (violent conflict)."[5]

(h) "A woman's place is in the home."

(i) "Eating people is wrong."[6]

The following subtle or arguable cases are only for advanced students, and may confuse others.

(j) "Youth is too good for the young of today. They don't deserve it."

(k) "If the poor don't have bread, let them eat cake."[7]

(l) Radio interviewer: "What do you think of American restaurants?"
Visiting French food critic: "The air conditioning is superb."

---
[5] Enoch Powell, British politician, 1977, whose prospects of becoming prime minister were destroyed by this statement.
[6] Title of song by comedians Flanders and Swan, satirizing critics of anti-Vietnam war protesters.
[7] Marie Antoinette, c. 1770.

(m) Wife to marriage counselor: "My husband never says a word."
Husband: "I don't like to interrupt."
(n) Wealthy suburbanite: "We can't afford children."

"It All Depends"

15. Dolly: "Do you think they're going to fire you from your lectureship at the end of this term?"
Tex: "Well, it all depends. . . ."
Imagine two things that it might depend on, in a typical academic context.

Updating Assessments

16. "What does our daughter's new boyfriend do for a living?"
"When I asked her, she looked embarrassed and mumbled something like 'He's in sales,' or it might have been 'He's in jail.'" On that evidence alone, which statement is more likely, and why?
"Oh, and his parents are Sicilian."
Does this change your opinion, and why?

17. In early 2003, war with Iraq appeared to hinge on proof that Iraqis were hiding WMDs (weapons of mass destruction). Iraqis were not cooperating with UN inspectors. How indicative of guilt was this evidence (regardless of what you may now know by hindsight)?
Suppose that the Iraqis *had* been cooperating and inspectors discovered empty storage with traces of a toxic chemical agent for which Iraqis had an unconvincing explanation. Would that have been stronger evidence of guilt? What would it depend on?
(This exercise can be adapted to fit more current information or a more topical issue.)

18. In DOE procedural guidelines on how to choose a federal site for burying nuclear waste, I came across an instruction to "confer with Indian tribal chiefs." How conclusive is this as evidence that potential sites were expected to be on Indian territory?

Plural Evaluation

19. You are wondering what price to ask for a parcel of land that you own. How many different approaches to making that determination can you think of? Which approach do you have most confidence in? Which might have built-in bias?

20. (Advanced exercise) Barroom customer A: "I'm against going to war for any reason other than a direct threat to us, but at least it helps the economy. Think of all the jobs it creates."
Barroom customer B: "On the contrary, I'm in favor of making the world a better place, even if it takes using military force. But I don't see that it helps

the economy. It's basically throwing the resources that go into arms, etc. down the drain. Battle doesn't contribute to our economic welfare."

A and B disagree on the economic impact of war, using different arguments. Can you think of a third argument for or against the *economic* benefits of war (without addressing *any other* issues, including ethical)?

Advising Others

21. True story. A married couple have disappeared for four months, with two foster daughters aged 3 and 5, after being informed by social service authorities that they cannot adopt the girls and must give them up. They have nearly run out of money and are the subjects of a nationwide hunt. They have been told through official TV announcements that their case will be reviewed if they turn themselves in. Would you advise them to? What would it depend on?

Multiple DA Issues

22. *Two-by-two.* You are on a rescue mission to the island (previously, mountain) of Ararat, ravaged by floods. Dr. Noah and his ark of animals are sinking fast in the raging waters. Nearby, a leaking container with the last remaining pair of fabulous Uzlem birds is bobbing about. As a volunteer rescue worker, you can only try to save either Noah or the birds.
    (a) Which do you try to save? State why informally. Are there any critical questions you would need to address before making up your mind, including any not mentioned above?
    (b) Making any necessary realistic assumptions about Noah's case:
      - List your (rescuer's) options.
      - List your choice criteria of main considerations, in decreasing importance.
      - List key uncertainties, with plausible outcomes and probabilities.
    (c) Then you spot a jutting dry rock that Noah might just be able to get to in time to save himself. State informally what you would do now.
    (d) Which of the answers to part (b) would now change, and in what direction?
    (e) Before you can act, Noah cries out, "For nature's sake, save the birds! My life's work is done." What do you do now? How does part (b) change now?
    (f) You save the birds, and Noah drowns. You discover that both birds are male. Noah's family sues you for negligent manslaughter. You wail, "My God, I made a terrible mistake!" Did you?

Fact vs. Preference

23. It has been urged that social and criminal sanctions on adult–child sex should be reduced on the grounds that it will reduce extortion and child murder. Discuss, distinguishing clearly factual from preference (value) judgments.

Chapter 4

Quantitative Aid to Rational Choice

In Chapter 3 we examined ways of clarifying deciders' thinking about a decision by introducing some structure to their knowledge without departing very much from their familiar ways of thought. This has value in its own right, and Ds will often need to do no more than this to help them make up their minds on what to do. Acting on Chapter 3, Ds will have taken some steps toward making sure that they have reasonably taken into account what is important. Sometimes, especially with professional decisions, Ds will want to refine this thinking with more ambitious analysis. Chapter 4 introduces quantitative decision aid (QDA), which involves structuring choice considerations in the form of a quantitative model. QDA either indicates some action by a person or institution, or takes over some part of the decision process (such as predicting outcomes).

There are a number of QDA tools in common use. One broad class is ***objectivist***, which avoids recourse to human judgment, relying only on authoritative data.[1] Much of the quantitative modeling that goes by the name "operations research" is of this type. The ***personalist*** approach, on the other hand, translates all elements of a choice into quantitative representations of human judgment. ***Personal decision analysis (DA)*** is a prime example of personalist QDA. The approach and tools presented here are a variant of DA.

You will soon notice that the intellectual challenge increases sharply. (No pain—no gain!) However, mastering the principles in this chapter is essential if you, as potential decider D, are to benefit practically from the quantitative tools. Even then,

---

[1] Using, for example, "frequencies" in place of personal judgments.

Rational Choice and Judgment: Decision Analysis for the Decider, by Rex Brown
Copyright © 2005 John Wiley & Sons, Inc.

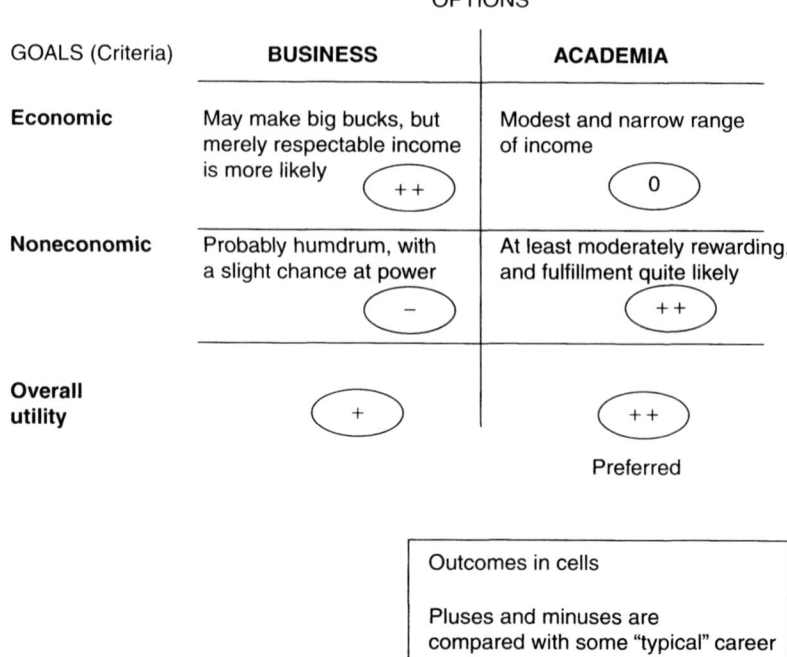

FIGURE 4.1 Tallying plus–minus.

D cannot expect to be able to conduct a successful DA without more training or the assistance of an experienced aider, but you should be able to make better informal decisions and make effective use of an aider.

4.1 A SIMPLE TOOL: TALLYING PLUSES AND MINUSES

A semiquantitative variant of "going through the GOO" (introduced in chapter 3) is ***plus–minus tally,*** which involves judging how much each criterion contributes to the total *utility* of each option, and expressing relative contributions as one or more pluses and minuses (measured from some base situation). The options can be compared by netting out or "tallying" the plusses and minuses for each option, and favoring the one with the most net plusses or the fewest net minuses.[2]

A table with columns for options and rows for criteria is a convenient format. Figure 4.1 tallies +/− for the Tex case (superimposed on Figure 3.1). The figure shows academia better than business by one +, so academia would be preferred on that basis.

---

[2]This computation is strictly proper only if there is no interaction between criteria (e.g., no redundancy or synergy). If there is interaction, the conclusion can be adjusted informally (e.g., adding pluses for synergy, subtracting for redundancy).

Personal Example. My daughter Karen recently called to see if I could come over for a few days to help her husband Sean look after her twins (see the Prolog) while she was out of town. The visit was not really critical, but they'd enjoy it and so would I. "Sure," I reacted immediately, and bolstered my response with the following preliminary plus–minus tally (restricting myself for now to a single plus or minus for each criterion).

Criterion	Visit Option (compared with not visit)
Provide practical help	+
My enjoyment	+
Their enjoyment	+
Karen's good opinion of me	0
Slow progress on this book	−
Disrupt other plans	−
Embarrassment at changing mind	+
Net	+ +

The pluses outnumber the minuses by two, so it might seem that going would clearly be the thing to do. But this simple netting out pluses and minus took no account of their relative significance. I thought harder about each criterion, quantified the plusses and minuses, as below, and added some rationale to remind me of what I had in mind).

	Visit	
Provide practical help	+ +	Moderate, but they'll manage fine without me
My enjoyment	+	No big deal
Their enjoyment	+	Small effect, but I do care about them
Karen's good opinion of me	0	Unaffected, quite solid now
Slow progress on this book	− − − − −	Critically increased risk of missing deadline
Disrupt other plans	− −	Numerous small disappointments
Embarrassment at change	−	Slight, given K and S's supportive attitude
Net	− − − −	

These $+/-$'s netted out as four minuses and I decided not to go. The analytic effort involved had been modest (half an hour) but that was about as much as the stakes justified. ♦

Although the *form* of plus–minus tally appears trivial, getting it to be equivalent to D's judgment (i.e., getting the pluses and minuses right) is certainly not trivial.

A critical requirement is for D to be absolutely clear on what the plus or minus is being *compared* with (i.e., the meaning of *zero* pluses or minuses).

For example, "Karen's good opinion of me" is put at zero (in both tables), reflecting my judgment that whether I visit or not won't make a *difference* to Karen's opinion. Suppose that I had mistakenly interpreted the "good opinion" entry as Karen's *overall* good opinion of me, including any good will that does *not* depend on my visit, which smugly, I might put at + + + + +. Then the sum for visit would be increased by five pluses, and visit would appear to be the right choice, but it would be completely misleading.

The critical requirement is that the assessment of the +/− is in relation to the visit option. This issue may be obvious here, but the mistake is often made in more complex problems. However, Ds may find they don't need to go further than this simple plus–minus tally if the right choice becomes obvious. But having started asking the right questions can set the stage for developing the analysis in more ambitious directions. The following chapters introduce some of these developments.

4.2 RATIONALITY AND IDEAL JUDGMENT

Chapter 1 loosely defined rationality as follows: *A rational choice is one that advances D's welfare effectively and logically, based on everything D knows, judges, and feels.*

Let us look at this more closely. A rational choice identifies the option that promises the greatest welfare for D, based logically on *all* knowledge and judgments available to D. *Utility* is any numerical measure of D's welfare such that D prefers more of it than less. Utility can be given a more precise meaning, such that the best option is always the one with the highest **probability-weighted average** utility.[3] This is **gamble-defined** utility (see Section 4.4.1 and Chapter 7).

Perfectly rational reasoning produces *ideal* personal[4] judgment: the judgment logically implied by the totality of a person's **psychological field**, including knowledge, preferences, and anything else in one's head that might have a bearing.[5] Deciders' uncertain prospects are worse than they might be to the extent that the utility of their decisions departs from the ideal. Since Ds (with or without help) are fallible and cannot achieve ideal judgment, they should try to get as close as possible to the ideal, using a decision process that is informal or formal, or some combination of the two. Ds have to do the best they can with available time and resources.

---

[3]An average is the sum of all possible values, each multiplied by its probability. I use the term "average" in place of the more familiar "expected value" because you don't really expect exactly 65, etc., since you are uncertain (see Howard, 2004).
[4]Not to be confused with the more controversial concept of *ideal impersonal judgment*, which is not specific to any person and which is not addressed here.
[5]My working hypothesis is that a unique such ideal exists (whether or not we know how to derive it).

4.2.1 Features of Rationality

A completely rational choice can be thought of as some ideal personal evaluation of options, which Ds *would* produce if only they were capable of reasoning impeccably on the evidence (i.e., if they take all the time needed to apply flawless analytic expertise to *all* available evidence). A rational judgment is based on everything Ds know and on nothing that they don't know.[6]

Example. Dolly complains that Tex has made poor investment decisions because they had a stock that he failed to sell as its value dropped to zero over several months. Periodically, she would say "You should have sold last week; of course, it's too late now," but the stock kept dropping. Tex's defense was (and should be) that in the light of what he knew *at the time*, it was not unreasonable to expect that the stock would go back up. Dolly could just as well have rebuked Tex for not backing a winning horse. ♦

A bad outcome does not necessarily imply that a bad (irrational) decision was made. Although the apparent prospects of a favorable outcome, given the evidence, may be good enough to justify D's choice, the unexpected may still happen. If, however, Tex *consistently* sells stocks at a loss (or backs losing horses), that would cast *doubt* about the quality of his decision making, but no more than doubt. Bad outcomes are *indicative*, but not conclusively, of bad decisions—and vice versa.

4.2.2 Apparent Irrationality

Sometimes, what appears irrational may, strictly speaking, not be. If D has unconventional or antisocial interests, it is not irrational for D to pursue them as well as possible, although it may incite disapproval from others. (I believe Stalin to have been highly and successfully rational... but evil.)

Example. Jon Baron and I faced the following dilemma while teaching decision skills to teenagers. A student confided that he was debating whether to become a drug dealer (really!). After questioning him closely on his "goals, options, and outcomes," it dawned on us that drug dealing might well be rational *for him*. He wanted material wealth and local status and did not care if he went to jail or got killed. He was indifferent to the welfare of others in a society that had badly treated him and other blacks like him. Pumping gas was not an attractive career alternative. Implication: What may be a sound decision for a person may not be good for society. Contrary to businessman Charles Wilson's famous dictum, What's good for GM may *not* be good for America. ♦

---

[6]The possibility that rationality takes account of "everything D knows" is an important issue in analytic strategy for quantified decision tools, discussed in Chapter 8.

4.2.3 The Prevalence of Subrationality: Room for Improvement

There is general agreement that decision practice throughout society has plenty of room for improvement (i.e., it falls well short of the ideal) and that this deviation costs us dearly,[7] notwithstanding the apparent complacency of the man in the street. Psychological laboratory experiments have uncovered major *subrationalities* in their subjects.[8] For example, subjects switch choices arbitrarily if the same decision situation is described to them in a different form of words (Tversky, 1996). We can all call to mind examples of people making ill-considered decisions where "they should have known better;" that is they had knowledge that rationally implied a different choice (e.g., the friend who married an obvious scoundrel).

Private *civic* decisions are particularly prone to subrationality. People jump to hastily determined and unshakable positions on such issues as the legality of abortion, free trade, and school vouchers. Hence, they see the issue in black and white and pay little attention to evidence supporting a contrary position. Like the Red Queen in *Alice in Wonderland*, they say "Verdict first, trial second!" This may be because they usually risk little personally from an unsound choice and are thus saved the discomfort of hard thinking or "cognitive dissonance" (Festinger, 1957).

We are all well aware of the prevalence of "organizational foolishness," where public and other institutions behave less rationally than the people within them would individually (March and Shapira, 1982). There are well-documented cases of U.S. foreign policy being made in ways that are clearly not that of a "rational unitary actor." For example, during the 1962 Cuban missile crisis, both the Soviet Union and United States took actions that unwisely brought them to within a hair's breadth of World War III (Allison, 1971).

4.2.4 The Motivation for Rationality

Given that irrational action is widespread, what harm does it do? What benefit can D expect to gain by acting more rationally? Is it worth learning analytic tools that will make him/her more rational? Theoretical procedures have been proposed for addressing the value of analysis (Watson and Brown, 1978), but I know of no empirical research with substantive results. All I can say is anecdotal and impressionistic: I have seen many private and professional cases where I am persuaded that D made

---

[7]The cost of *subrationality* might be expressed along the lines of "ideal rationality would make D 10% happier," where a life of misery is 0 and a life of bliss is 100. On this basis, D could judge whether increased rationality is worth pursuing (e.g., if 5% improvement is all D can hope for realistically, it may not be worth the trouble).

[8]However, people may not be quite as irrational as some research suggests. For example, experimental subjects appear too "conservative" in their thinking; that is, they do not change their minds enough when they get new evidence. I suspect that such results are often due to the subjects' (e.g., college students) being put in unfamiliar hypothetical situations (say, drawing balls from an urn), where their normal sound thinking does not work. People in their normal real lives are much less prone to fall into such traps. They do fine in situations that are common enough that they have learned from experience feedback. For this reason, I favor paying careful attention first to how people think now and building on it, before replacing it with the analyst's models.

a subrational decision and had a bad outcome that I believe (but cannot prove) would have been averted had D made a more rational choice.

However logically compelling the self-interest of acting rationally, I have found it most difficult to persuade people to pursue it seriously. In political campaigns, voters seem more interested in following whoever is winning than in deciding rationally who they *should* want to win. They would sooner watch a fight than listen to a lecture. Possibly they are not persuaded that anything is amiss in their reasoning, or do not care.[9]

4.2.5 Opponents of Rationality

There is little mystery about why advocates of a particular point of view might discourage *others* from rational thinking, as in politics and advertising.

Examples. The rector of Leningrad University (in the old Soviet days) told me that they tried teaching a variant of rational choice, but students kept coming to the wrong conclusions, so it was dropped. I more recently got similar responses from fundamentalist Christian parents reluctant to have us teach decision analysis to their children. A student in the environmental science department at Birmingham University told me in 1990 that faculty discouraged "rational choice," I suppose because they considered environmental protection to be a sacrosanct cause, not to be balanced against any other considerations (e.g., economic). ♦

Subrational arguments can sometimes be defensible. It may be a kindness to motivate a spineless friend to act on a rationally defensible New Year's resolution (say, to exercise) by using an "irrationally" strong argument on him, that is, by exaggerating the pros (say, by overstating the health benefits of exercise), even though we believe that the real pros still outweigh the "cons." This is just a benign form of advocacy.[10]

4.3 DECISION TOOLS

All sorts of aid can enhance decision rationality, in the sense of producing choices that get closer to the ideal choice. Some aid is purely ***descriptive***, in that it *describes* how Ds actually *do* make decisions. Other aid is ***prescriptive***, in that it *prescribes* what Ds *should* do. We are most directly concerned with *prescriptive* tools, although we need to take carefully into account *descriptive* features of D's thinking.

4.3.1 Quantitative Tools

A major group of *prescriptive* decision tools involves a quantitative procedure. Most of these, such as linear programming and our special interest, decision analysis,

---

[9] In which case I suppose they could be perversely rational.
[10] The real danger here, as with any deliberate distortion for advocacy, is that you lose credibility as a disinterested decision aider.

involve some kind of model. A *model* is an entity substituted for another that it resembles (in some respect), for some useful purpose (such as convenience) (e.g., a model airplane). Our interest is in quantitative models, generally in the form of a mathematical expression (e.g., $t = ax + by + c$ means that $ax + by + c$ is a model of *target* judgment, t). A model has ***input*** judgment (e.g., x and y) and ***output*** judgment (e.g., t).

Quantitative models can be exact. For example, a company's world sales of a product can be expressed exactly as: number of customers × average sales per customer. Models can also be approximate. For example, product sales can be *estimated* as sales in United States divided by the U.S. fraction of world population. This expression is an approximate model of sales (because if per capita sales are not the same in the United States and the rest of the world, the correspondence will not be exact). For any given target judgment, many exact and approximate models can be constructed at different levels of complexity.[11]

4.3.2 Qualitative Tools

Useful decision tools do not have to be quantitative. Some qualitative tools include recognition-primed decisions (Klein, 1989) and lateral thinking (de Bono, 1970). Verbal decision analysis (Larichev et al., 1995) only asks questions familiar to the decider or expert informant. These questions may, for example, be: "Do you like this more than that?" "Is this more likely than that?" A qualitative approach may miss important information (e.g., the *degree* of preference) that a quantitative approach can capture. On the other hand, quantitative models may specify more than is necessary for sound choice and may not represent it accurately.

4.3.3 Contribution of Tools to Improved Rationality

What part of the room for improvement in D's decision quality can D actually realize from using decision tools? No real D is capable, of course, of ideal rationality, with or without aid, but we can evaluate his actual decisions (and his decision process) by *judging* subjectively how close they come to the ideal (see Chapter 1) (i.e., how much room for improvement is left). In fact, this is a good criterion of choice among contending decision tools: The one you prefer is the one you judge will best approximate the ideally rational decision.

There is no inherent superiority of formal over informal, or quantitative over qualitative, decision aid. Formal analysis imposes discipline on an argument, but D's informal reasoning may still outperform it, by taking more of his knowledge into account (explicitly or implicitly). There is no assurance that a decision tool will contribute *anything* (Brown, in press). A decider with sound intuition may consistently hit on close-to-ideal choices but get led hopelessly astray trying to apply a quantitative tool. However, properly done, quantitative decision tools can be most useful and

---

[11]An approximate model can be made exact by adding an error term. The model may also be an upper or lower bound, as in: total sales > (is greater than) sales in North America + sales in South America.

I believe, potentially at least, outperform unaided intuition (and probably qualitative tools, too).

4.4 PERSONAL DECISION ANALYSIS

Personal decision analysis (DA, for short) is a class of decision tools based on a quantitative *model* of the judgment used by a single decider, whether as a private person or as a professional. DA is the primary tool developed in this book, and may be the most promising. It reflects D's personal judgments of options, outcomes, and goals (or, at least, judgments that D accepts, if not originates). Its main purpose is to save D from the major pitfalls of confused thinking that can result from unaided decisions, in a way that makes the logic clear to, and reviewable by, others—friend or foe.

In essence, DA represents quantitatively the three universal components of logical decision making noted in Chapter 1—goals, options, and outcomes—and specifies how to infer the logical choice they imply. *Options* are the set of alternative actions to be compared. *Outcomes* are possible results of options, whose uncertainty is expressed in probabilities. *Goals* are represented as quantified preference judgments—"utility functions"—that translate outcomes into numerical *utilities*.

4.4.1 Utility

Utility, as used here, is any numerical measure of welfare, satisfaction, etc., such that D would prefer more to less. Among a number of interpretations proposed by economists, philosophers, etc., an interpretation of special interest to us is *gamble-defined utility*. Option utility is measured, somewhat awkwardly, by the probability of winning a *gamble* between a "good" and a "bad" outcome, suitably defined. This meaning of utility has the nice property that D should logically prefer whatever option has the highest *average* utility.

D would normally *want* to pick the option with the most utility to produce an *optimal* choice, in which case D is *optimizing*. In practice, it will often make sense for D to *satisfice*; that is, to settle on the first satisfactory option identified.

4.4.2 Maximizing Average Personal Utility

The conceptual core of statistical decision theory (of which DA is the practical application) is roughly as follows. D's uncertainty and preference are characterized with a probability and utility, respectively, for each option. (*How* to characterize these to properly reflect what is in D's mind is discussed in Chapters 10 and 11.) D's best option is the one with the highest average personal utility, *APU* (commonly referred to as "subjective expected utility"[12]).

---

[12] I prefer the more precise term APU, for reasons given in Brown (2004).

APU can be described briefly as follows. D has a number of options, each of which leads to one of several outcomes, characterized by probabilities. D values each outcome as a utility. Based on these judgments, D's preferred option is the one with the greatest *average (probability-weighted)* utility.[13] For example, Tex has two options, business and academia, whose outcomes could be:

- *Business:* success probability 10%, utility 80; failure 90%, utility 15
- *Academia:* success 40%, utility 70; failure 60%, utility 40

Their APUs are:

- *Business:* $(0.1 \times 80) + (0.9 \times 15) = 21.5$
- *Academia:* $(0.4 \times 60) + (0.6 \times 25) = 39$

Since $39 > 21.5$, academia is to be preferred, at least on these numbers.

Statistical decision theory develops the logical norms of rational behavior (Savage, 1954; Raiffa and Schlaifer, 1962). DA is the application of the theory to practical purposes, that is, combines it with realistic appreciation of human behavior to produce implementable tools (Raiffa, 1986).

However, the most appropriate practice of DA is by no means yet settled (Brown, 1992; Howard, 1992). Indeed, I have had to recant much of the conventional DA wisdom on best practice that I and colleagues published in an earlier textbook (Brown et al., 1974), even though some of the old methods are still widely taught (in otherwise excellent texts: Clemen, 1996; McNamee and Celona, 2001). DA is certainly a work in progress. It is still often difficult and uncomfortable to do it right (although many find it stimulating), but I am convinced that it is well worth the effort. However, if not done right, it may leave D worse off than before (Brown, in press).

4.5 QUANTITATIVE SUBSTITUTION OF JUDGMENTS

Substitution is a central decision analysis concept. It consists of replacing one judgment (of possibility or preference), or set of judgments, by another in an analysis, usually because the **substitute** is easier to work with. *Substitutes* can be either judgmental or logical equivalents.

4.5.1 Judgmental Substitution

If D is *judgmentally* indifferent between the substitute and the original judgment, it is a *judgmental equivalent*. For example, some certain (sure) outcome might be

---

[13]The practical value of the maximum APU rule is limited by the fact that Ds are *not* perfectly rational (if they were, DA would serve little purpose). In the inevitable event of D's judgment on the best option being inconsistent with the component judgments in the decision model, there is no sure guide about which should be changed to ensure consistency. Nevertheless, this test of consistency should *help* identify the best option.

judged to be an *equivalent substitute* for a real but *uncertain* gamble among several outcomes, in which case it is a ***certain equivalent***.

Hypothetical Example. I offer you a choice between two deals:

- A 50:50 gamble between gaining $20 or losing $10
- A certainty of gaining $5

The *average* value of the gamble is (50% × $20) + (50% × −$10) (i.e., $5), so you *might* be equally happy with one deal or the other. If so, $5 is a *certain equivalent* for the gamble. ♦

However, the average value is not always a certain equivalent. If I am ***risk averse***, I might prefer having the certain amount to the average of an uncertain amount. My certain equivalent will be conservative (i.e., less than the average of an uncertain prospect). The difference is a ***risk penalty***. If D is risk seeking, as presumably gamblers are, the certain equivalent will be *better* than the average value.

Hypothetical Example *(cont.).* I offer you a different (but seemingly similar) gamble, with a 50:50 chance at gaining $20,000 or losing $10,000. It has an average gain of $5000 (comparable to the preceding example), but $5000 might *not* be a certain equivalent to this gamble. Think for a moment. Would you really hesitate between accepting a sure thing of $5000 and a gamble that has the same average but you risk losing $10,000? If you are an impoverished student who can ill afford such a loss, I doubt it. You might accept as little as, say, $2000 in place of the gamble, which would then be your certain equivalent (not $5000). ♦

A ***present equivalent*** is a single quantity, realized now, that is judgmentally equivalent to one or more quantities realized in the *future*, say a stream of money.[14] If we prefer money, etc. today to money tomorrow, the *present equivalent* will be a smaller amount than the sum of future moneys.

If a substitute is not exactly equivalent to a set of judgments, but good enough, it is an ***approximate equivalent***. (For example, $5000 would not be an approximate equivalent to the second gamble above.)

4.5.2 Logical Equivalence

If a judgment is implied *logically* by a set of other judgments, it is a ***logical equivalent***. How substitution works in decision analysis practice is illustrated below in the context of the decision tree, a widely used decision analysis tool.

---

[14]In economic texts, it is typical to *calculate* (rather than judge) the present equivalent (usually called "present value") by means of a yearly *discount rate* (e.g., 5%). It is a judgment, but usually set at some available actual interest rate.

4.5.3 The Decision Tree: Simple Example

The *decision tree* is the graphic version of a model of the average value of options, commonly used for choices involving major uncertainty. The average value is derived from processing analytically certain factual and preference judgments, in unfolding sequence (according to when D takes action and learns facts).

The specifics can be communicated with an example. Figure 4.2 shows basic decision tree mechanics in the context of a simplified interpretation of Tex's career decision, where Tex is supposed only to care about (peak) income and is *risk neutral* (i.e., not averse to risk). Disregarding for now the two quantities in ovals, the decision tree in Figure 4.2 is a model of Tex's perception of his career problem. It follows common decision tree conventions:

- Two immediate options, business (BUS) and academia (ACAD), are represented as branches of a *choice fork* with a square at the base and are labeled in capitals.
- After making the choice, D will learn whether he succeeds or fails (two factual possibilities). They are shown as branches of a *possibility fork* with a circle at the base and labels in lowercase. Branch probabilities (shown in parentheses) depend on the preceding option, shown to the left. Thus, if Tex opts for BUS, his probability of success is 10%.

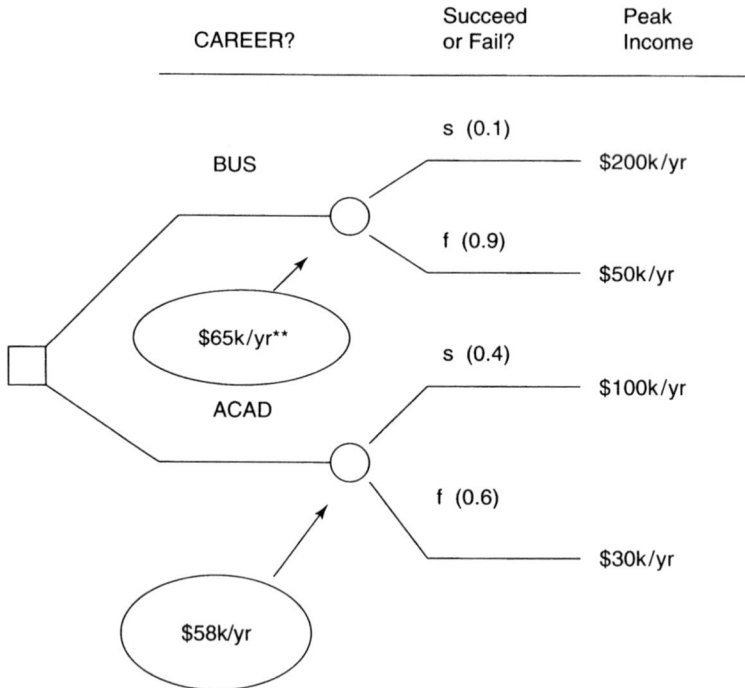

FIGURE 4.2 Tex's decision tree: income only.

- The outcome of any sequence of option and possibility, in terms of D's criterion (peak income, here) is shown in a column to the right of the corresponding two-segment tree *sequence*. Thus, the "BUS → succeed" sequence results in a yearly income of $200,000.

Although he would, in fact, still be uncertain about the outcome of going into business and succeeding, Tex accepts the $200k/yr income as a *certain equivalent* for the actual income. In other words, he is prepared to act as if he were sure that the "BUS → succeed" sequence would result in exactly $200k/yr—and similarly for the other three income figures on the right. Calculating the choice that is logically equivalent to the initial decision tree by successive substitution is known as *rollback*.

The tree (i.e., *model*) as a whole is treated as a *judgmental equivalent* for Tex's real, more complex perception of career choice considerations. That is, Tex considers the best choice according to the tree also to be the best choice according to all his real judgments. If he considers the tree close enough to be useful, it will be an *approximate substitute*.

Tex's preferred option, implied logically (not judgmentally) by the tree/model, is derived as follows. The *certain equivalent* income from each option is calculated as the probability-weighted *average* income, because Tex is neutral toward risk. This average is shown in an oval at the base of the *possibility fork* for each option. Since option utility for Tex is measured by income (for now), his certain equivalent income (average) for going into business is $65k/yr [(0.1 × 200) + (0.9 × 50)] and for going into academia is $58k/yr [(0.4 × 100) + (0.6 × 30)], so business is preferred and is marked as such by a double asterisk.

4.5.4 Inclusion of Multiple Criteria

The example in Figure 4.2 unrealistically assumes that Tex cares only about economic outcomes of his career choice, and of these only peak income [which has a convenient *natural metric* (see Chapter 5), dollars]. In reality, Tex has a number of other relevant criteria. Noneconomic criteria include quality of life, prestige, and work interest. Economic criteria include final wealth as well as peak income (see Figure 5.2).

To account for other criteria, Tex can adjust his values for peak income by the equivalents[15] in peak income of these other criteria (see Figure 4.3). For example, the impact of the "business, then succeed" sequence could be increased from $200k to $230k to account for other criteria. Thus, Tex is indifferent between the original $200k peak income plus other impacts, and $230k peak income plus *no* other impacts. The difference of +$30k is a "bonus" peak income equivalent to the impact on other criteria. This is a form of equivalent substitution, where two (or more) criteria are reduced to one. The other three adjustments in the rightmost column, for other criteria, are interpreted the same way. Thus, the $50k following

---

[15]Treating criteria scores as approximately additive.

64 QUANTITATIVE AID TO RATIONAL CHOICE

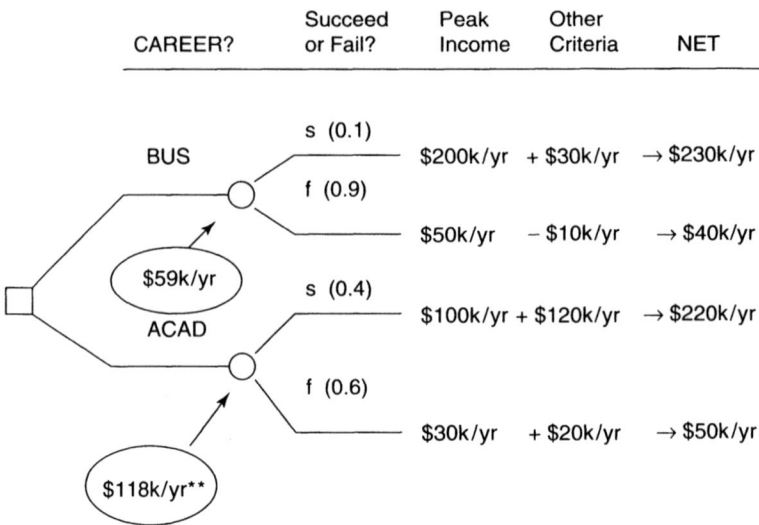

FIGURE 4.3 Tex's decision tree: adjustment for criteria other than peak income.

"business, then fail" is reduced by $10k. This is the peak income equivalent of other criteria values.[16]

Taking into account the probabilities for the four substitute outcomes, we have equated Tex's choice to a 10:90 chance at $230k and $40k for business plus a 40:60 chance at $220k and $50k for academia. The averages of these two gamble options are $59k and $118k respectively. If Tex is *risk neutral*, these will be certain equivalents for his career options.[17] The choice can now be analyzed *as if* the option outcomes of business and academia were *certain* to be $59k or $118k, and the real uncertainty can be ignored thereafter. Since 118 > 59, academia is the clear winner.[18]

The real-world complexities of multiple criteria and uncertainty in these two cases have been substituted by a simpler equivalent problem, where there is only a single, certain criterion, in this case peak income. Taking other criteria into account in this way has reversed Tex's career preference (not necessarily for the better, since the substitution may be flawed).

The substitution process need not stop there. There is at least one more substitution implicit in the Figure 4.3 model. It treats Tex's prospects as limited to either success or failure. In actuality, his career outcomes would be more finely distinguished and have many possible values. If he is indifferent between his real uncertainty and a world where success and failure were the only possibilities (with those probabilities), the situations are *judgmentally equivalent*. He can analyze the simpler case and should arrive at the same choice.

---

[16]Criteria other than peak income are compared with some level taken to be "normal" (see Chapter 5).
[17]The procedure is called *grouping* by Schlaifer (1978, pp. 248–254).
[18]If Tex were risk averse, his certain equivalents would be less for both. Risk aversion would hurt BUS more than ACAD, and academia would still be preferred.

4.6 A DA TOOL KIT

Decision analysis models comprise a number of distinct **methods**. This book is designed as a minimal "tool kit" of DA methods, selected to be useful to nonmathematical people on a wide variety of judgmental tasks involving choice and uncertainty. The tools may be a bit blunt, but they can be used right away and they can do the job.

4.6.1 First Steps of 1000 Miles

My position is that most of the contribution that DA can make can usually be achieved with half a dozen very spare and structurally simple modeling tools. This is not to say that effective DA is easy—far from it. But most of the art comes from knowing how to use tools cost-effectively (i.e., producing maximum benefit with minimum effort) in a way that brings an improvement (much as Michelangelo using a simple chisel to improve on a block of stone).

Any option that D is considering can almost always be reasonably modeled, at a first pass at least, by one of the model types presented here, which correspond to common lines of reasoning. One of our model types, for example, is oriented toward evaluating options with conflicting criteria (Chapter 6), and another toward decisions where uncertainty dominates (Chapter 7). Which model to use depends on which aspect of the problem D most wants help with. More complex models can combine two or more aspects (see Figure 7A.3).

A distinctive feature of these tools is that they are *judgment intensive*. This means complex reasoning is broken down into a few pieces. Each piece still requires difficult informal thinking, but this thinking is less difficult than for the unaided choice. By contrast, many other decision science approaches are more *structure intensive*: that is, the modeling is complex, calling for many inputs, each requiring relatively simple judgments. The more structure, the more inputs. DA can be made progressively more structure intensive, and that may often be useful, but we will stay with judgment-intensive models in this book.

4.6.2 Universality

Is DA universally applicable to all decisions? In principle, I say yes. Any choice that is well-defined (i.e., where the options have been specified; see Section 4.6.3) can always be modeled, at least to a good approximation, with DA (whether it is worth doing or not).

It is sometimes argued that it *not* appropriate to model the *factual* component of analysis if you *don't know enough*. "We don't have the data" is a common objection to using DA. However, I maintain that if you have *any* view on a question of fact, however tentative, you always have *some* supporting reasoning for that view that can be decision analytically modeled (not necessarily with the DA tools in this book). Ask yourself if there is *any* outcome of a given uncertainty that would surprise you. If there is, you know enough to model that implicit judgment.

Modeling value judgments is a somewhat special case. Like uncertainty and factual judgment, preferences can *logically* always be quantified. It may, however, be morally or philosophically objectionable to some to do so explicitly, say with "sacred" entities such as the value of life. In fact, D may not accept our help at all if it involves disclosing sensitive or embarrassing value judgments. However, it may not be necessary to quantify values for analysis to be useful. D may only want help in understanding outcomes (see Chapter 5), not in putting a value on them (Chapter 6).

4.6.3 Dangers of Overreliance on DA

It may be true that an *ideal* analysis will always outperform D's unaided judgment. However, no real analysis ever manages to be ideal, and any particular analysis may fall so far short that its results are actually less sound than unaided judgment (Brown, in press).

Example. A short introductory text on DA for business that I coauthored (Brown et al., 1974) was used in executive training programs. A frustrating but common aftermath of this course was that students who mastered the basics felt that they now knew how to do decision analysis effectively. Then they would come back a few months later to say, "I tried it, but it doesn't work." I hadn't made sufficiently clear to them that in a two-week course they could only expect to appreciate principles, not to apply them successfully to live decisions. ♦

Analogy. To return to the musical analogy in Section 1.1.2, it's like mastering the basics of musical theory and then being surprised when your attempt to play Chopin sounds terrible! ♦

Decision analysis contributes to only part of the decision. It does not directly address the critical task of identifying promising options. That can be done either informally or with the help of other structured approaches.[19] DA is instead concerned primarily with *comparing* identified options. DA may, indeed, impede the creative option-generation process by diverting attention from it. Therefore, I suggest you avoid using DA on decision problems where the major challenge is to develop options rather than to choose among them (e.g., when designing a marketing strategy or an anticrime program). On the other hand, DA can sometimes stimulate the search for alternatives by clarifying the strengths and weaknesses of existing options.[20]

4.6.4 Decision Analysis Activities Developed Here

Several core activities of decision analysis are developed in subsequent chapters:

- Formulating D's choice, that is, specifying options to compare (Chapter 8)
- Translating D's relevant knowledge about option outcomes—or at least part of it—into a predictive model (Chapters 5 and 7)

---

[19]See Klein (1989) on "recognition primed decision making" or Keeney (1992) on "value-focused thinking."
[20]As Ford Autolite did when considering whether to go into the tire business (Brown et al., 1974). The verbal variant of decision analysis developed by Russian colleagues operates primarily to help define improved options in this way (Flanders et al., 1998).

- Completing the model with D's evaluation of option outcomes (Chapters 6 and 11)
- Enriching the model with additional analysis or knowledge (Chapter 10)
- Integrating model results with D's judgmental processes to make a choice (Chapters 8 and 12)
- Adapting *private* analysis to *professional* decisions (Chapter 9)

Appendix 4A gives a fairly straightforward hypothetical example of DA in a business context. Appendix 4B gives a more ambitious example, again hypothetical, in a personal context. It anticipates methods covered later, and so its assignment would be delayed (until, say, Chapter 7).

ASSIGNMENTS

Prepare for Discussion After Reading

Running Exercise-Civic Choice

1. If you were a legislator, would you vote to legalize assisted suicide? What arguments would you take into account favoring yes or no? How strong is each argument? Express this by one to three pluses or minuses for each option–argument pair. Add them up. Does this tally fully capture your preference between options? Why might it not?

Motivation for Rationality

2. "Lucy is the rational one in the family. Sam, on the other hand, is the emotional one with strong feelings." Comment on whether you have to be one or the other.

3. Does your own experience support the view that greater rationality would do people good? Do you know people who have consistently messed up because they made dumb choices (rather than simply being unlucky)? Should they have known better?

Prepare for Later Discussion or Submission

Features of Rationality

4. In the Olympic trials in Barcelona, pole-vaulter gold medal hopeful O'Brien opted to delay his first jump until the bar had been raised dangerously high. He failed at his first try and so did not qualify. Was his delay decision subrational or simply unlucky in hindsight?

5. The U.S. government is spending billions of dollars to find a technically and politically acceptable U.S. site to dispose of high-level nuclear waste. It has been proposed that the U.S. government offer nuclear waste to Ethiopia for

enough money to eliminate starvation in Ethiopia in the foreseeable future. Under what circumstances might this be a responsible and rational decision for the U.S. government?

Substitution

6. "If I have to work this hard serving burgers, I'd just as soon stay at home and draw an unemployment check." Is this a logical or judgmental equivalent substitute?

7. Consider the following.
   (a) I offer you a deal. I will toss a coin. Heads, I give you $2; tails, you give me $1. Do you take it? Draw and analyze a decision tree that confirms your choice.
   (b) Now I offer you a new deal. Heads, I give you $10,002; tails, you give me $10,000. Do you take it? Draw and analyze a tree for this deal.

8. In France, residents living close to a new nuclear power plant are compensated by a tax reduction. Under what circumstances might a resident consider such compensation an equivalent substitute?

APPENDIX 4A

BUSINESS DECISION TREE EXAMPLE

(Hypothetical case adapted from Brown et al., 1974)

ORE BROKER: I have an opportunity to buy 100,000 tons of ore from a Far Eastern government for $5 per ton. If I am allowed to import it, I expect to be able to sell that ore for about $8 per ton. But if the government refuses to grant an import license, the sale will be canceled and I get my money back, less a penalty of $1 per ton. I will thus either make $300,000 profit or suffer a $100,000 loss. Please help me decide whether or not to buy.

DECISION AIDER: We can start the analysis by drawing a simple decision tree. A decision tree is rather like a road map. It is a map of your decision problem, and it includes only the events and your actions that are relevant to the problem. We will start the tree with a *choice fork* that we represent by a small box with several branches emanating from it. Each branch represents one of the possible courses of action available to you now. In this case it appears that you only have two acts available: to buy the ore or not to buy the ore. Let the upper branch represent the decision "buy ore" and the lower branch the decision "don't buy ore." I use capital letters to label the act branches (see Figure 4A.1).

Now start moving along the option branch that indicates that you buy the ore. We will use a *possibility fork*, which has a circle rather than a box at the node, to represent the relevant outcomes of that option. One possibility is that your

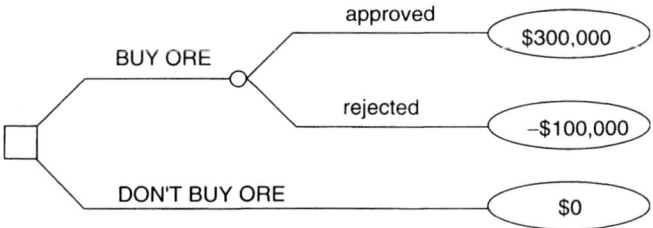

FIGURE 4A.1 Broker's decision tree: structure.

application for an import license will be approved and you will then be $300,000 better off than you presently are. The upper branch of the possibility fork represents that potential. I will label it with lowercase letters. The other possibility, represented by the lower branch, is that your application for an import license will be rejected and you will lose $100,000. This too will be labeled with lowercase letters.

Finally, consider the other option branch, the one that corresponds to a decision not to buy the ore. Then there is only one event, and it represents neither a profit nor a loss. Thus, its outcome is zero. Notice that I am using your present position as a base of zero (see Section 5.5) from which to measure the outcomes on each of the end-points of the tree.

Your initial decision tree is now structured. The next step is to estimate a few probabilities. Do you think it is more likely that your application for a license will be approved or rejected?

BROKER: That's a tough question. I've had considerable experience in these matters, but it seems to me that such requests are rejected just about as often as they are approved.

AIDER: Does that mean that you don't favor either outcome, not even by a little bit?

BROKER: I know which one I want to happen, but I can't decide which one is really more likely to happen. It's not that I don't know anything about it, but I honestly think that the government rejects about as many of these applications as it approves.

AIDER: Fine. All I need is your carefully considered opinion. We will now assume, at least for a start, that the probability is 0.5 that your application will be approved and 0.5 that it will be rejected.

BROKER: Is that the same as the probability that I will get heads when I toss a coin?

AIDER: Yes. You have said that if you apply for the license, you would be no more surprised if the government approved it than if it rejected it. Also, of course, if I were to toss a coin, you would be no more surprised if it came up heads than if it came up tails. We are going to use this 0.5 in analyzing the decision tree in the same way that we would use the same figure of 0.5 if a coin toss were really part of the problem we were analyzing.

Now that the decision tree is structured in terms of choice and possibility forks and evaluated in terms of both dollars and probabilities, we need to figure out the implication of these evaluations for the two initial courses of action. We call this process of evaluation *roll back*. We have labeled each of the end positions with what it is worth to you, with the net profit or loss that it represents. The goal of rolling the tree back is to calculate what each of the initial acts is worth. It is rather easy in the case of the lower branch, where you don't buy the ore. Not buying is followed only by a single possibility branch, so the outcome of $0 can be rolled back and labeled on the branch of not buying the ore. On the upper branch, where you do buy the ore, things are not quite so simple. The *value distribution* in Figure 4A.2 displays your estimated probability distribution over the possible values that can result from buying the ore. Obviously, buying the ore must be worth some value that is between the two equally likely values, a $300,000 profit for the "approved" branch and a $100,000 loss for the "rejected" branch. The question is then to know what that value is.

We will use the concept of an *average value* as a first approximation of what it is worth to buy the ore, that is, to represent with a single value what

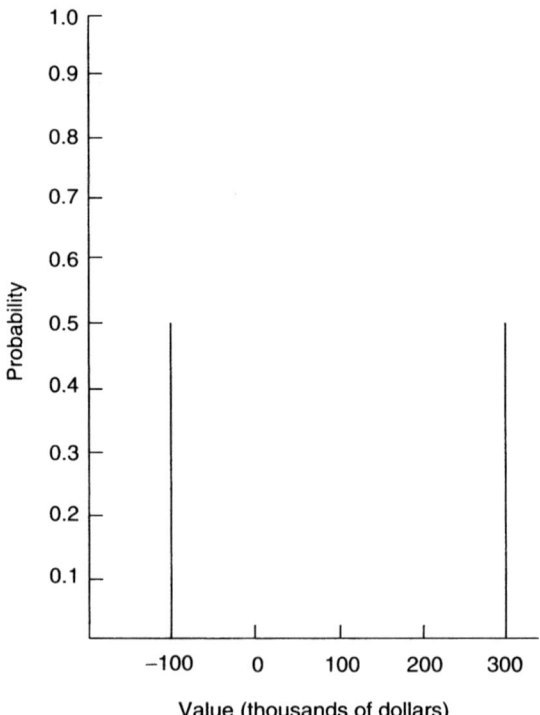

FIGURE 4A.2   Value distribution.

the entire value distribution in Figure 4A.2 is worth. First, each possible value of the value distribution is weighted or multiplied by its associated probability and then these weighted values are summed. Thus, $0.50 \times -\$100{,}000 = -\$50{,}000; 0.50 \times \$300{,}000 = \$150{,}000$; and the sum = $\$100{,}000$. The sum of $100,000 is thus the average value of the distribution. Of course, if someone else made different probability judgments from yours, his average value would differ from yours. For example, if he estimated that the profit were more likely than the loss, his average value would be greater than $100,000.

BROKER: But what does it mean to calculate an average value of $100,000?

AIDER: We are after a single number that will represent the attractiveness of two numbers. Here we are interested in a single measure of profit or loss that will represent both the $300,000 profit and the $100,000 loss. Average value is a probability-weighted value in which each of the profits or losses is weighted precisely by its probability of occurrence. It is a number somewhere between the possible outcomes of $300,000 profit and $100,000 loss. The reason that the average value of $100,000 is exactly midway between the profit and loss is that your probability estimates in Figure 4A.3 indicate that it is just as likely that the license will be approved as rejected.

Look at the scale in Figure 4A.4 while I try to explain just how the probabilities influence an average value. The scale extends from $-\$100{,}000$ to $\$300{,}000$, the two possible outcomes if you decide to buy the ore. The average value that we calculate on scale A is $(-\$100{,}000 \times 0.50) + (\$300{,}000 \times 0.50) = \$100{,}000$. Suppose that the probability you had estimated were different. Note what that does to the average. Suppose, for example, that you had estimated a probability of 0.75 for approval of the license and a probability of 0.25 for rejection. Now we are on the value distribution of scale B. The average is $(0.75 \times \$300{,}000) + (0.25 \times -\$100{,}000)$, for a net of $200,000. This average is 75% of the distance away from the loss toward the profit because the profit is being weighted by probability of 0.75. On scale C we will assume that you were much more pessimistic and had estimated only a 10% chance of a profit. Then the average value would be $(0.1 \times \$300{,}000) + (0.9 \times -\$100{,}000)$, for a net of

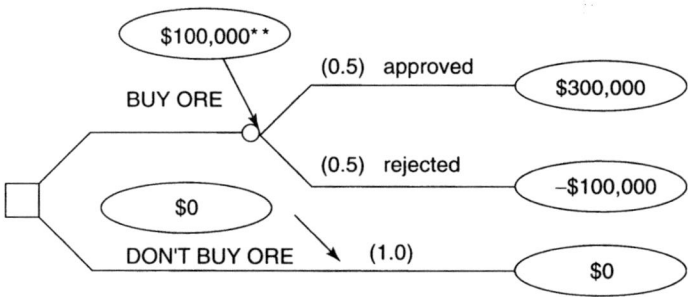

FIGURE 4A.3 Broker's decision tree: evaluation.

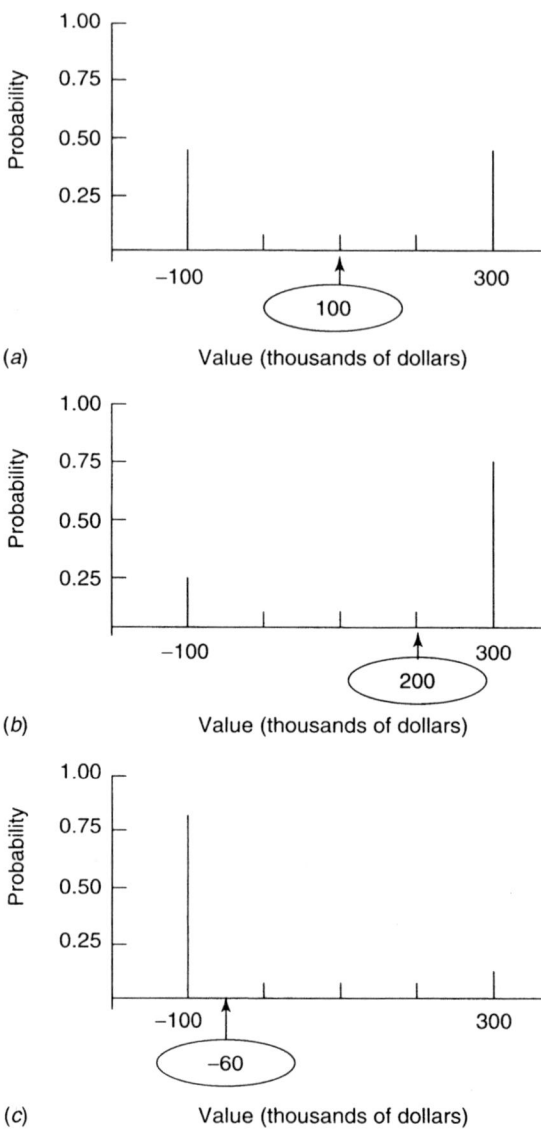

(a)

(b)

(c)

FIGURE 4A.4 Influence of probability on average.

−$60,000. The $60,000 average loss is exactly 10% of the distance away from the $100,000 loss in the direction of the $300,000 profit.

This is what is meant by a probability-weighted average. *Each of the dollar amounts entering into the average is weighted precisely by its probability of occurrence.* At this point, I would like you to figure out the average value associated with your other course of action, where you do not buy the ore.

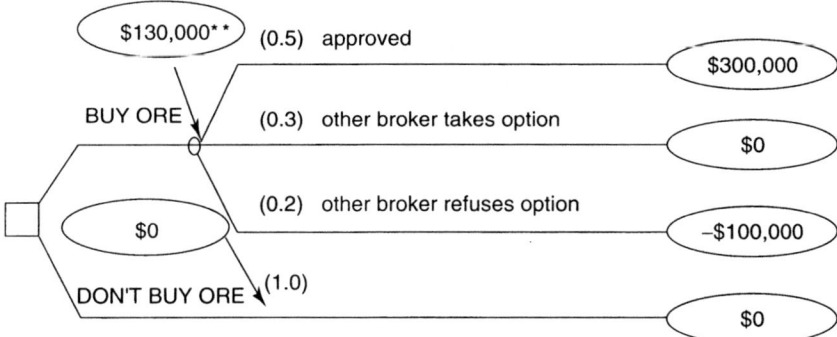

FIGURE 4A.5 Average value: three hypothetical events.

BROKER: But there are no profits or losses if I don't buy the ore. And there are no probabilities except... wait a minute. There is a probability of 1 that I will make $0 profit. If a multiply 1 by $0, my answer is $0. Is that the average value?

AIDER: Correct. The average value of not buying the ore must be $0 because you are sure to make no profit.

Try a hypothetical example for practice to make sure that you understand what this average is. Imagine that you have the same 50% chance that you'll get the license and earn a $300,000 profit, but that if the government rejects your license application, there is a chance that another brokerage firm would find the option attractive enough to be willing to take the deal off your hands, in which case you would not be penalized the $100,000. Just imagine that there is a 30% chance of ending up with $0 profit (in the event that the other firm will assume your option) and a 20% chance of facing the $100,000 loss, and we still have the 50% chance of the $300,000 profit. Can you calculate the average of this more complex set of profit possibilities? The decision tree is sketched in Figure 4A.5.

BROKER: We now have three different things that might happen. I guess that I just multiply each possible outcome by its probability and add up the products. That gives me $150,000 + $0 − $20,000 and the expected value should be $130,000 (see Figure 4A.5).

AIDER: Fine. This is probably a good time to stop doing arithmetic. Do you think the actual average value figure of $100,000 that we calculated for your problem can help determine your decision?

BROKER: The $100,000 is a number that seems to be the right distance in between my profit or loss, assuming I buy the ore, but it is certainly not an amount of money that I will actually make. The average is a probability-weighted profit, but it isn't a number that is like an actual net profit, is it?

AIDER: Your question shows a lot of insight. But I want to delay answering it. I would like you to assume, uncritically for now, that an average value is a good measure of the attractiveness of an act and that it is a good policy to select whichever act has the highest average value.[21] Technically, you are following the policy of *maximizing average values*. Thus, you would buy the ore rather than not buy it because the expected value of $100,000 is more than the expected value $0.

BROKER: I guess that makes sense.

ASSIGNMENTS

Prepare for Later Discussion or Submission

1. Consider the decision tree displayed in Figure 4A.5. Calculate the average value associated with buying the ore under the assumption that the broker changes his probability assessment to 0.2 for "approved," to 0.3 for "other broker takes option," and to 0.5 for "other broker refuses option."

2. The three probabilities must sum to 1. Find a combination of probabilities for the three events mentioned in assignment problem 1 such that the average value associated with buying the ore is exactly $0.

APPENDIX 4B

PERSONAL EXAMPLE: STUDY OR PLAY?

This appendix describes an *example*, not a *case study* (as I use the terms), because although the problem was real, the analysis was not used to aid the decider. It anticipates some material covered in later chapters.

On TV's *60 Minutes*, Ali, a 14-year-old black boy, was reported to be spending six hours a day practicing basketball instead of attending school. His reasoning, as he explained to interviewer Dan Rather: "I want to grow up like Michael Jordan and earn a million dollars a year." The boy was short and overweight.

4B.1 Need for Decision Aid

I believe, like most, I expect, that Ali was making a bad (subrational) decision, even in the light of his own limited knowledge of relevant considerations. A moment's reflection should alert him that only a few hundred among tens of thousands of basketball hopefuls get to make a living in the game, let alone achieve the success of a Michael Jordan. Given his present physique, Ali surely cannot expect even an average chance of making it, certainly no more than a fraction of 1%. If he doesn't make it, he has only to look at what careers other school dropouts in the past have had, and to compare them with careers of school graduates otherwise similar to himself, in order to reasonably conclude that his career prospects are much dimmer if he doesn't study. Play will certainly be more fun in the next couple of years. However, mature

---

[21]Subsequent chapters in Brown et al. (1974) relax this and other simplifications in this example.

reflection would probably persuade him that the rest of his life deserves more attention, even bearing in mind the uncertainty about what it holds in store for him, and that study is the more promising option.

On balance, by the foregoing judgments of possibility and value, Ali should surely conclude that play is subrational. If, however, he does not adopt these judgments, it could be quite rational for him to continue playing rather than studying (ill-informed though his own judgment may be). He may believe unshakably that he will grow up to be a superathlete and that the gods are looking out for him. He may also not care what becomes of him after adolescence. Then play might, after all, be the right choice for him, *based on his own underlying judgments*.

4B.2   Initial Model Structure

Figure 4B.1 organizes the foregoing reasoning into goals, options, and outcomes, and takes the first step toward quantification, by assigning pluses and minuses to the possible outcomes, to reflect their significance as pros or cons. Summing pluses and minuses as a rough evaluation measure gives the edge to study. (Study nets one plus, as against play, which nets zero.) To help Ali make up his mind, it may not be necessary to go any further if his preferred choice is now clear.

4B.3   Quantifying Possibility and Preference Graphically

Ali's judgments above—if he thought seriously about them—*could* be characterized more quantitatively, to make the conclusions firmer or more persuasive.

	OPTIONS	
GOALS	STUDY	PLAY
Reward now	Boring (−)	Fun (+)
Reward later (more important)	Good (++)	Great if I make it (but unlikely); rotten if not (−)
Overall outcome	Pretty good (+)	Not worth the risk (0)

IMPLIED CONCLUSION: STUDY!

> Pluses and minuses are compared with "OK" outcomes

FIGURE 4B.1   Prognosis for Ali's study–choice.

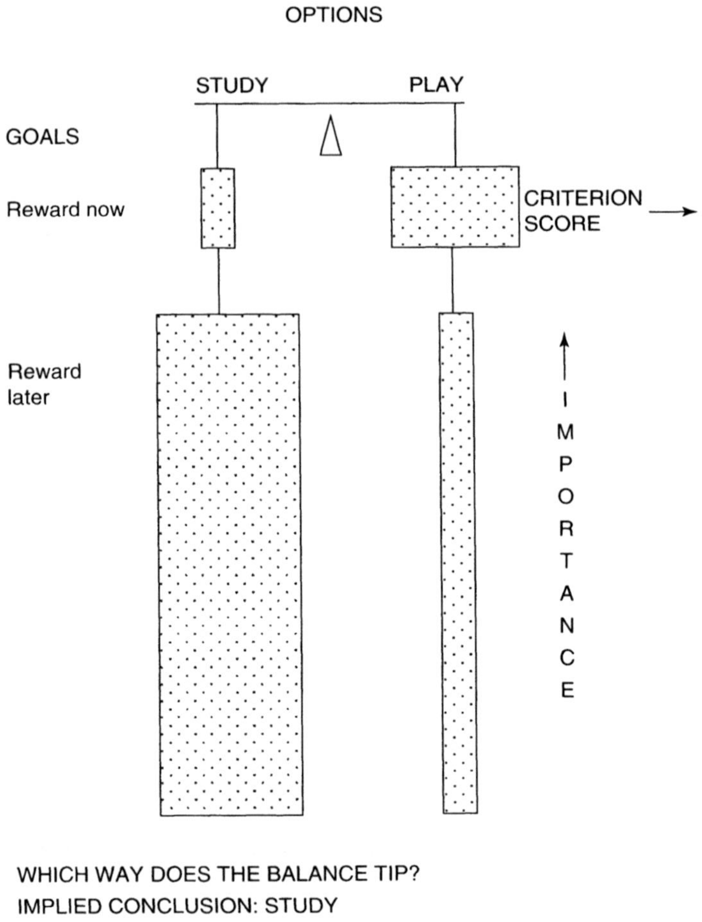

OPTIONS

```
         STUDY      PLAY
GOALS       ┌───△───┐
Reward now  │ ▫ │ ▫ │  CRITERION SCORE →
```

```
Reward later  │ STUDY │ PLAY │   ↑
                                 │
                                 I
                                 M
                                 P
                                 O
                                 R
                                 T
                                 A
                                 N
                                 C
                                 E
```

WHICH WAY DOES THE BALANCE TIP?
IMPLIED CONCLUSION: STUDY

FIGURE 4B.2 Criterion scores and their importance in Ali's choice.

Figure 4B.2 shows how these judgments can be expressed graphically in a way that indicates a preferred choice. Each option, "study" and "play," can be evaluated as the total area of boxes that reflect quantitative judgments of both possibility and value (see Chapter 6).

The top two boxes compare study and play on "reward now" (i.e., the *short-run* implications of each option). The width of the boxes predicts how much reward there will be now (in the form of having fun). Play clearly promises the greater reward now. The height of the boxes indicates how important "reward now" is relative to "reward later" (see below). This importance does not depend on the option and so is the same for both options.

The lower part of the figure evaluates "reward later" (i.e., the *long-run* implications of the options). Study has a wide box because it yields a good deal of "reward later." The play box is narrower, corresponding to a prediction of less reward later. This is because although success would be much more fun, failure (and attendant lack of fun) is overwhelmingly more likely. Since "reward later" is considered much more important than "reward now," the height of both "reward later" boxes is much greater, which magnifies any difference in width between them.

This advantage in "reward later" for study more than offsets play's greater "reward now." In fact, the total area under study is several times that of play. (Total area is a measure of preference.) So study should be decisively preferred, at least on the judgments reflected in Figure 4B.2. Note that the case is much stronger than with the plus–minus tally, where the measurements are less precise. The distances shown can be measured numerically (see below), although here just looking at the diagram should be sufficient.

4B.3.1 Cognitive Fit For this tool to help Ali make up his mind, he must understand its message and believe it reflects his best judgment. A jumble of numbers, let alone a mathematical formula, may confuse him fatally. I believe that box areas would communicate better to Ali than logically equivalent numbers. Even more effective might be to imagine the boxes composed of metal sheets of the same shape, and judge which side would tip down.

4B.3.2 Sensitivity Alternative views on importance and criterion score in the short and long term would be reflected in rectangle areas and therefore in implied choice. Considering additional criteria ("bucking the establishment"?) would result in additional boxes, favoring either study or play. One can see by eye that disagreements with inputs shown would need to be implausibly large before play was preferred over study.

4B.3.3 Refining the Input Assessments Box comparison is a very simple model structurally, but this does not mean that it is easy to get right because it may be very difficult to get sound inputs. Indeed, the simpler the input structure, the more difficult it is to make sure that those fewer inputs accurately measure the decider's judgment. Measuring the relative importance of criteria is particularly difficult (see Chapter 11).

Making numerical rather than geometric assessments may facilitate refining input. Suppose that on a scale of 0 to 100 (from misery to bliss), Ali assesses "rewards now" for study at 10 and for play at 50 (corresponding to box widths in Figure 4B.2).

If criterion importance is also measured numerically, say on a scale of 0 to 10, with 1 for reward now and 8 for reward later, and the "reward later" effects of study

Criterion	Importance	Study	Product	Play	Product	Difference (Study − Play)
Reward now	1	10	(10)	50	(50)	(−40)
Reward later	8	60	(480)	10	(80)	(400)
Weighted sum			490		130	360

and play are 60 and 10, respectively, the following arithmetic again shows study well ahead (490 vs. 130).

4B.3.4 More Modeling?

The overall choice judgment between play and study has been broken down into only a few input judgments. Each of these could be broken down further by finer modeling, to get a better "fix" on some part of the argument. Further modeling could be appropriate (but again not likely to change the choice). For example, uncertainty could be addressed explicitly. In Figure 4B.2, the impact of play on "reward later" is represented by a single quantity (i.e., the width of the bottom right box). This representation summarizes and combines arguments about the chances of success in basketball and the utility of success and failure. If modeling stops here, that quantity is the result of intuitive or informal judgment.

That judgment might be improved by more detailed modeling, which could be done formally with an additional step.

Suppose the utility of playing and *succeeding* at basketball is valued at 100; playing and failing (say, having to pump gas), at 10. Chances of success are 0.1%. Quantitative analysis of these evaluations might be as follows: Importance weighted value of play in the successful case is $(1 \times 50) + (8 \times 100) = 850$; and in the unsuccessful case is $(1 \times 50) + (8 \times 10) = 130$. Incorporating uncertainty, the overall value for play is $(0.01 \times 850) + (0.99 \times 130) = 137.2$. The importance weighted value of study is still 490, indicating that study should be preferred. Figure 4B.3 shows how the problem might be modeled in tree form.

The improvement from finer modeling may not be worth the trouble if (as here) it is most unlikely to shift the conclusions from the coarser model.

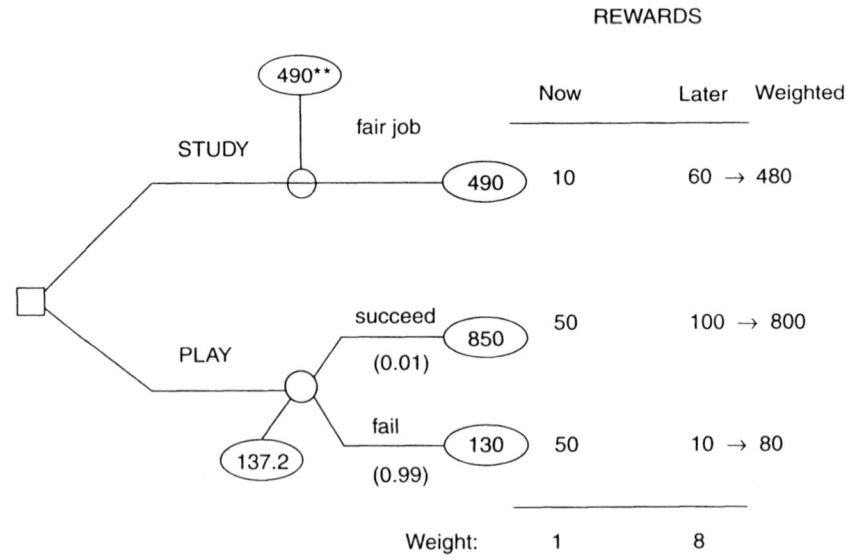

FIGURE 4B.3 Tree for Ali's choice.

ASSIGNMENTS

Prepare for Discussion After Reading

Rationality Tested by Outcome?

1. In the study–play case above, suppose that while Ali was cutting school, a terrorist breaks into school and guns down all Ali's classmates, and he is spared. Would you then think his choice to play rather than study was rational? Why? Conversely, suppose that you had persuaded him to return to the classroom and he was among those who were gunned down. Was your advice proven to be irrational? Why?

Sensitivity

2. What plausible changes in the problem as described could make play the rational choice for Ali?

Chapter 5

Describing Consequences

This chapter is concerned with identifying, defining, and measuring option *consequences* (however intangible) and quantitative or specified *outcomes* in particular. In Chapter 6 we address how D evaluates these consequences. Taking account of uncertainty about them is addressed in Chapter 7[1] and deriving their probabilities in Chapter 10.

Some parts of this chapter may be hard work. However, failure to master them will make successful use of the prescriptive tools that follow almost impossible. Unless the possible consequences of contending options are communicated accurately, you cannot say which you prefer. To really improve on unaided judgment, "the devil is in the detail!" Nitpicking may be critical.

5.1 TYPES OF POSSIBILITY

There are important distinctions to be made among possibilities related to option–consequences. Figure 5.1 displays diagrammatically these distinctions and the standard terms for them. *Possibilities* are the most general type of fact, including events, propositions, and *attribute values*. *Prospects* are future possibilities. In Figure 5.1 the oval labeled "prospects" is completely contained within the "possibilities" oval, since prospects are one kind (subset) of possibilities. To illustrate, suppose that Tex

---

[1] In Chapter 7 we address the uncertain impact of an option on a criterion. In this chapter I treat all impacts as certain, substituting a *certain equivalent* for uncertain impact, if necessary. The uncertainty about a criterion can ordinarily be ignored if D is not concerned about risk.

Rational Choice and Judgment: Decision Analysis for the Decider, by Rex Brown
Copyright © 2005 John Wiley & Sons, Inc.

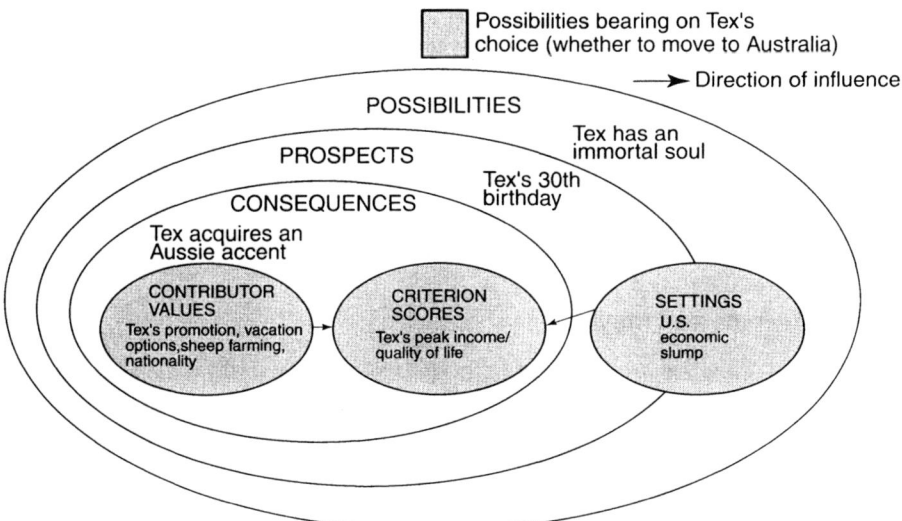

FIGURE 5.1 Hierarchy of possibilities.

has settled on a business career and is now considering moving to Australia on an attractive job offer. Tex's having an immortal soul is a (present) possibility, but not a prospect, so it appears in the figure as an example inside the "possibilities" oval but outside the "prospects" oval.

Regardless of whether Tex moves, his *prospects* include his thirtieth birthday (which will not be affected by the choice). *Consequences* are prospects that *are* affected by the choice (e.g., for Tex, homesickness, or an Aussie accent). *Outcomes* are identified consequences; Section 5.1.1 describes attributes of outcomes. *Settings* are possibilities (including *prospects*) that are not themselves outcomes but do affect outcomes (so their oval overlaps prospects, but does not outcomes). For example, a future U.S. economic slump is a setting and is out of Tex's control, but could affect his peak income if he does *not* move.

5.1.1 Criteria and Contributors

Criteria are outcome *attributes* that D ultimately cares about and which are a part of his/her *goals*. For Tex they include peak income and quality of life. Criteria have **scores** (to underline their essentially **evaluatory** nature). Tex's final wealth is an example of a criterion score in the Australia choice. Since criterion scores are essential to Tex's choice, their oval is shaded.

Contributors are outcome possibilities that influence criteria, but are not themselves criteria. *Contributors* can be events, such as future promotion (affecting income), or *attributes*, such as vacation options (affecting quality of life). Contributory attributes have **values** (for which Tex has no direct preference). Getting a job in sheep farming would be a contributor[2] to quality of life. Tex's vacation options are contributor options, which could be affected by his changing from U.S. to British Commonwealth nationality, as a result of the move option. Nationality change is thus itself a contributor to vacation options.

Although Tex does not *have* to consider any contributors (he can relate options directly to criteria), they may help him evaluate criteria, especially if the criterion *scores* are very uncertain. On a decision tree (Chapter 4), criteria will go at the end of a tree sequence. Contributors would appear in the body of the tree.

5.1.2 Outcome and Impact

Impact is the change in an outcome (e.g., *criterion score* or *contributor value*) due to an option, compared with doing nothing.[3] The option *impact* of Tex's move on his peak income (criterion) might be large (compared with his low income if he does not move).

5.2 HOLISTIC VS. MULTICRITERIA CONSEQUENCES

Consequences can be described ***holistically*** (i.e., as a whole), or as a set of attribute values, that is a ***multicriteria*** description.

5.2.1 Holistic Qualitative Description

A holistic description can be qualitative (e.g., "If Tex goes into business, he will meet with only fair success"). This approach is usually, in fact, a useful first step in description, which D may not need to go beyond (although the primary thrust of this book is the *quantitative* "beyond").

One useful qualitative way to describe outcomes is *storytelling*, where one or more possible representative outcomes of each option is described as a plausible narrative scenario, much as in a novel. The more richly textured such a scenario is, the more readily and soundly can its utility be evaluated (see Chapter 6).

In the Tex case, a scenario might be a detailed career path, with good and bad intermingled (and possibly uncertain). The description could be Tex's interior monologue, along the following lines: "If I go into business, I would probably be my own boss. I might struggle financially for the first five years or so, and then make a go of it. But if I did come a cropper, which I well might, I suppose I would take a salaried job and still not be far behind my classmates who took salaried employment all along. Unlike them, however, I will have had a valuable personal experience."

Uncertainty could be addressed by adding wording like: "I may not follow exactly this career path, but I'll probably do something equally appealing, or at least something not a lot better or worse." Tex might conceivably specify a single scenario

---

[2]It is a *possibility*, even though it could be a Tex *choice* subsequent to the target choice (whether to move to Australia).
[3]"Impact" has no meaning when the null-option is not a realistic option, as in Tex's career choice, since he must choose *some* career.

(e.g., the most likely) to represent that uncertain future and then evaluate the option as if this outcome were sure. Alternatively, he could specify two or more scenarios (e.g., optimistic and pessimistic) and consider them together to be a judgmental equivalent to his real messy and complex prognosis.[4]

5.2.2 Holistic Quantitative Description

A holistic description can also be *quantitative* (e.g., "Tex will end up a third of the way from abject failure to glittering success"). Such extreme **anchors** can be interpreted as 0 and 100, on a *scale* with specific outcomes interpolated between them. (See Section 5.6 for more discussion on the use of *anchors*.) Anchors can be defined quite briefly, provided that their appeal is clear and every relevant criterion is covered implicitly. For example, in the above example, "abject failure" could be the worst job anyone you know ever had, and "glittering success" could be the best. If the scale has a *range* too narrow to include all the possibilities of this job (e.g., if your option could be much better than any job you know about), you could instead specify historical characters with better or worse jobs. Such a scale could help Tex evaluate a new career option other than business and academia (e.g., law, where the range of outcomes could be wider).

Beware of defining holistic anchors as the case where *everything* is good (or bad), since this may imply an implausible combined scenario, which cannot be realistically imagined and therefore evaluated. For example, financial success in a career may not plausibly coexist with unlimited free time. The current Harvard president could be a realistic high (good) anchor for Tex, although no doubt there are unsatisfactory aspects even to the president's life.

5.2.3 Multicriteria Description

Holistic evaluation requires somehow taking conflicting criteria into account implicitly. They can also be taken into account explicitly as multiple criteria.

Prolog Example. In the baby delivery case in the Prolog, there were three possible outcomes of the mother's delivery choice (see Figure P.2): double caesarian (for "caesarian first" option), two naturals and natural-then-caesarian (for "natural first" option). Each possible outcome was evaluated *holistically* as a single number on a scale of 0 to 100: 0 = natural-then-caesarian; 100 = two naturals; 20 = double caesarian (i.e., double caesarian was closer to the worst than the best outcome).

The mother could instead have *disaggregated* this holistic metric of utility into two (or more) criteria; for example:

- *Baby's health, measured on a scale of 0 to 100:* from 0 = lifelong disability to 100 = no health problems. (For example, "double caesarian" might score 40 on baby's health.)

---

[4]Ideally, they would constitute a representative or random sample of possible consequences, as in Monte Carlo simulation.

- *Mother's health on a scale of 0 to 100:* from 0 = long, painful recovery to 100 = no health problems. (For example, "double caesarian" might score 25 on mother's health.) ♦

Similarly, in the GOO analysis of the Tex case in Chapter 3, overall utility of the two career options was disaggregated into economic and noneconomic criteria. Any criterion can be subdivided further (such as the economic criterion into peak income, final wealth, other economic and the noneconomic criterion into prestige, fun, other noneconomic).

There are various ways of disaggregating utility, both as multiple *tiers* in a hierarchy and within each tier. For example, Tex's total utility could be disaggregated first into criteria that do or do not have a natural measure, such as money, rather than economic (which could have nonmonetary subcriteria) vs. noneconomic; and each of these can be further disaggregated in a second tier. Disaggregation into criteria taps the same totality of D's judgment as does holistic evaluation. Because the focus is sharper, disaggregation may uncover additional insights, prompt deeper examination of what counts, and break the problem down into more manageable pieces. However, it also requires more judgmental effort and is not necessarily more accurate. Knowledge may "slip between the cracks" when separating criteria (and subcriteria in a hierarchy), and important criteria may be omitted entirely.

5.2.4 Completeness vs. Complexity

Everything important to D needs to be accounted for if the model is to compare options realistically. The disaggregation must be **complete** in this sense, but not necessarily **complex**. An evaluation can be complete at any level of disaggregation. Indeed, the coarser the disaggregation, the easier it is to achieve completeness. A holistic criterion can avoid the risk of disaggregated criteria being incomplete.

5.2.5 Characterizing Criteria (and Other Quantities)

Characterizing criteria precisely enough to be usable involves two steps, which are elaborated in succeeding sections.

- *Identifying criteria.* What part(s) of the world may be affected by the choice that is to be characterized? How should that world be subdivided by criterion (e.g., how finely should items within it be defined or grouped)?
- *Measuring criteria.* How should each criterion be measured? Including: What zero? What units of measurement? Do criterion scores have a real interpretation (like money) or artificially constructed scales (0 to 100)?

5.2.6 Danger of Criterion Overprecision

The more precise and measurable the scale definition, the greater the risk that some important consideration connoted by the broader term (e.g., "economics") may be missed (e.g., "income stability"). A narrow target is more difficult to hit than a broad target. [Buede (1986) and Keeney (1992) treat specifying criteria helpfully.]

Example. If you state your criterion for choosing a wife as "quality of omelet she cooks" rather than the broader "general quality of cooking," you may undervalue a lady who knows how to cook everything *but* an omelet. ♦

5.3 IDENTIFYING CRITERIA

Identifying criteria for a choice hinges on what may be affected significantly by the target choice. This may emerge from an informal discussion of why D tentatively likes one option more than another.

Example. What public policy should a British voter support? If a drastic initiative that could affect all aspects of British life is being considered (e.g., opting out of the European Union), the entire state of the nation might be affected. Such a choice thus has very broad outcomes. [The outcomes need not be characterized in detail. "A return to the England of Thatcher" (Conservative prime minister in the 1980s) might be a specific enough description of a possible outcome.] A different British political decision, on the other hand, might affect only one or two aspects of British life. If the choice is whether to raise taxes on the rich, the only relevant criteria considered might be social equity and national wealth. ♦

5.3.1 Differentiating Criteria

In the Tex case so far, much of our exposition has been in the context of just two criteria: economic and noneconomic. Two criteria are usually sufficient to make a methodological point. In practice, however, it is typically useful to break out more criteria. The outcomes of Tex's choice can, for example, be disaggregated as two economic criteria ("peak income" and "final wealth") and three noneconomic criteria ("prestige," "quality of life," and "work interest"). Up to a dozen criteria are usually manageable. Finer differentiation than that can be handled by grouping criteria in a hierarchy, or simply bearing them in mind informally when assessing higher-order criteria.[5] Within, say, quality of life, as one noneconomic criterion, you might distinguish: location, sports facilities, social contacts, and "anything else."

Hierarchical listing can clarify the *meaning* of the main criterion or help assess the effect of options on it. The hierarchy of criteria can have several *tiers.* The highest tier of the hierarchy might consist of two or more interested parties, such as the "selfish" interests of Tex and those of his parents, and the lower tiers may consist of criteria

---

[5]Criterion hierarchies can be addressed through multiple tiers. Each main criterion can be expressed as a function (e.g., a weighted sum) of lower-order criteria, but there is no space to pursue that here.

relevant to each interested party, such as "proximity to grandchildren" under "parents' interests."

Finer differentiation is particularly useful where different subcriteria favor different options. For example, noneconomic criteria may be split into the group of those that tend to favor academia (such as intellectual challenge) and the group of those that tend to favor business (say, international experience).

5.3.2 "Anything Else" Criterion

It almost always makes sense to allow for a residual "anything else" criterion, even if you can't think at the moment of any criteria omitted.[6] It is dangerous if the criteria specified include all those that D *can think of*, but make no allowance for the possibility (or even D's conviction) that some unnoticed attributes may also be important. Leaving these attributes out of the model amounts to D asserting with certainty that there are none, which is rarely the case.

Even if you do have an idea of what other criteria might be, you may not want to take the trouble to disentangle them (see Chapter 6). Additional criteria nearly always surface before the decision is made, and "anything else" guards against the temptation to relax and assume that there *is nothing* else to be taken into account. In my experience, the most common source of an unrealistic analysis is overlooking some critical criteria when the problem is first formulated.

It is difficult to measure an "anything else" criterion. If it is likely to be minor, you can disregard it for now and adjust for it informally when the time comes to make a choice. A very useful question then to ask is: "Could taking anything else into account change the best choice?" If not, "anything else" need not be of too much concern. If yes, try to make "anything else" small, by breaking off as many specific criteria as possible. Alternatively, leave the higher tier criterion aggregated, so as to automatically include anything else (see also Section 11.4.3).

In the Tex case, "other" noneconomic subcriteria might include "power" (which would presumably favor business). We could add this in explicitly as an additional subcriterion; or, when making his final choice, Tex can bear in mind that the calculated comparison of utilities improperly favors academia over business, and take that informally into account.

5.4 METRIC VS. RATING SCALES

Once the number and general nature of criteria are settled, a method for measuring each criterion must be devised. Failure to define and use ***measures*** carefully is a major cause of distorted evaluation. The insidious danger (difficult to detect) is that the measurement may be logically coherent but not fit reality.

---

[6]In this book, any disaggregation of a high-level criterion should always be taken as including "other," even if it is not mentioned.

5.4.1 Natural Metrics

The most straightforward but not very common decision situation is where the only outcomes D cares about are one or more *natural metrics*, such as dollars in a bank account for the criterion "money," or votes for popularity in an election (i.e., the criterion score exists as a real quantity). Then the appropriate characterization of outcomes is a *metric*: say, how much money D makes after he has taken one business option or another, or the votes lost if a legislature takes an unpopular action. A metric scale has units of measurement that have a real-world interpretation and is easy to visualize and understand.

However, the outcomes of most decisions do not lend themselves to characterization by simple measures. In general, a broad criterion, even if largely quantitative, such as economic welfare, cannot be captured completely by a single quantity (or even several). It all depends on just what D understands by the criterion. Tex's economic interest *could* be interpreted as net worth at retirement (i.e., "final wealth"), but that would fail to distinguish two careers: one that was mainly poverty stricken until Aunt Louise left him her fortune, and another that gave him a good life from the start and let him accumulate the same fortune by the time he retired. Presumably he would greatly prefer the latter.

The risk of incomplete description by natural metrics is greatest for criteria that, unlike economics, are not inherently quantitative. If "prestige," as a noneconomic criterion, had as **surrogate** the number of citations in publications such as *Who's Who*, it would fail to distinguish different levels of prestige, for example, among people who did not get any citations at all.

In the Tex case, the "economic" criterion might be (or include) something intangible, such as standard of living, or be a large set of metrics, such as all cash flows, year by year, over his lifetime (i.e., no single metric captures the criterion). Even if the criterion *can* be interpreted in purely numerical terms (e.g., the stream of income), quantifying it may be so complex as to be impractically burdensome.

Some simpler or more compact feature can sometimes be an adequate surrogate to describe economic outcomes, but in my experience this adequacy is rare.

In the Tex income stream case, the surrogate metric could be accumulated income over Tex's lifetime, or income's present value, or average income per year,[7] or peak annual income (which was used in a Tex example). However, as is common for surrogates, peak income suffers by being an incomplete description of all economic outcomes of Tex's option. What if his peak year is much greater than the other years for one option but not for another? The business option may produce a freak peak income one year, but do worse than the academic option in every other year, and be worse economically overall. Peak income would then appear to favor the option (business) that is, in fact, economically inferior.

---

[7]A common alternative is a composite criterion, which is more comprehensive but also more complex. For example, cash flows over time can be taken into account, by "present equivalent." Present equivalent is cognitively uncomfortable, since it requires imagining some, typically implausibly large, lump sum now, so "equivalent steady stream" might be a better surrogate.

5.4.2 Surrogate Metrics

To help solve the incomplete surrogate problem, two or more surrogates may measure one criterion (e.g., average and peak income, for economics, in the Tex case). Where the incompleteness of surrogates is not too serious, D can take into account what has been left out by an informal adjustment at decision time. However, where the incompleteness is major or the criterion is inherently nonquantitative, like prestige, surrogates may need to be abandoned entirely. Surrogates may also be dangerously misleading: for example, by measuring "environmental quality" as "undisturbed land area." One urban renewal option effect may score higher than another on undisturbed land area but have lower overall environmental quality, because of other undesirable impacts, such as increased water pollution.

The relative ease of estimating surrogates makes them tempting to use, especially in public policy subject to outside scrutiny, even if they are measuring the wrong thing. (This approach is similar to looking for your keys under the street lamp rather than in the shadows where you lost them, because the light is better there.) Ease of measurement may conflict with accuracy. High body count in Vietnam was a poor indication that we were winning the war. The army was motivated to inflate body count and ignore more relevant metrics of success.

5.4.3 Artificially Constructed Rating Scales

If there is no natural metric, or suitable surrogate, you can construct an arbitrary *rating scale* to characterize either individual criterion scores or holistic outcomes (see Section 5.2.2). Each such scale has to be defined operationally. Defining the scale for measuring the option effect of a criterion includes two related issues.

- *Base:* What is the zero from which an attribute is measured?
- *Units:* How is distance from that zero measured?

5.5 RATING SCALE BASE

The *base* of a scale is the interpretation of zero in relation to which a criterion (or other attribute) is rated.

5.5.1 Fixed Base

A *fixed* base is not related to any particular choice. For a *natural metric* such as temperature, the scale chosen could be Celsius, whose zero base is freezing point, or Kelvin, whose base is absolute zero (corresponding to $-273°$ Celsius). Cash in the bank would be a fixed-base metric scale, with zero base being an empty bank account.

For a criterion without a natural metric, such as environmental quality, where zero has no obvious meaning, you can pick some arbitrarily dreadful state, such as wall-to-wall industrial slum. If you are working with a single holistic criterion, such as Tex's entire life, this state could be misery on all fronts: for example, corresponding to some tragic character in literature. This base is easy to understand but may include elements not affected by the target choice (and therefore superfluous).

Standard Base A variant of fixed base is where zero is some "normal" or average state. Examples include the usual temperature for this time of year, the average health of a given population, and the beauty at the 50th percentile of girls you have known. A fixed base need not even be explicit. An *implicit* scale is often used in everyday speech (e.g., "On a scale of 1 to 10, I'd give her an 8 on charm"). More specificity may be desirable, but not always essential.

Current Base It is sometimes useful to treat option impact as the difference between criterion option effect and the criterion's current score (which may not be the effect of any actual option). Current bases include the present balance in a bank account or the current state of the environment. Examples of using a current base include: "How much richer or poorer (or happier) will Tex be *than he is now* if he goes into business?" Or, "Will opting out of the European Union make life in England much worse than it is now?"

An advantage of current base is that you don't need to evaluate what the current state actually is, only changes to it. On the other hand, you need to hold more considerations in your head, at least implicitly. Current base thus economizes assessment effort, but it may also lose some information relevant to option evaluation. For example, a decline in fortunes due to an option may be worse if the fortunes are already low. It may also be hard to give a precise quantitative interpretation to option impact (i.e., to the change that the option produced) in terms of current base, if the attribute is not metric.

5.5.2 Option Base

Option base is more compact than *fixed* base, although more complex to evaluate. It sets zero at the outcome value of a particular option, so that option effect is the difference in outcome between one option and another. The easiest base option to handle is the **null option** (i.e., do nothing). For example: "How much more or less money will the investment option leave D with than he would have if he does nothing?" However, if the null option has no useful meaning (as in Tex's career decision, since he must follow *some* career), the base could instead be one of the real options (e.g., academia *or* business; see Figure 5.2). This approach is particularly compact, since one of the options is by definition zero and does not have to be evaluated *explicitly*. Thus, if only two options are being compared (as with Tex), only one set of outcomes (i.e., for the other option) needs to be assessed.

Be careful to get the signs right with option base, where the base option is one of those being compared. The rightmost column is labeled "academia − business," meaning that if academia is better, you will see a plus. (The same principle applies to

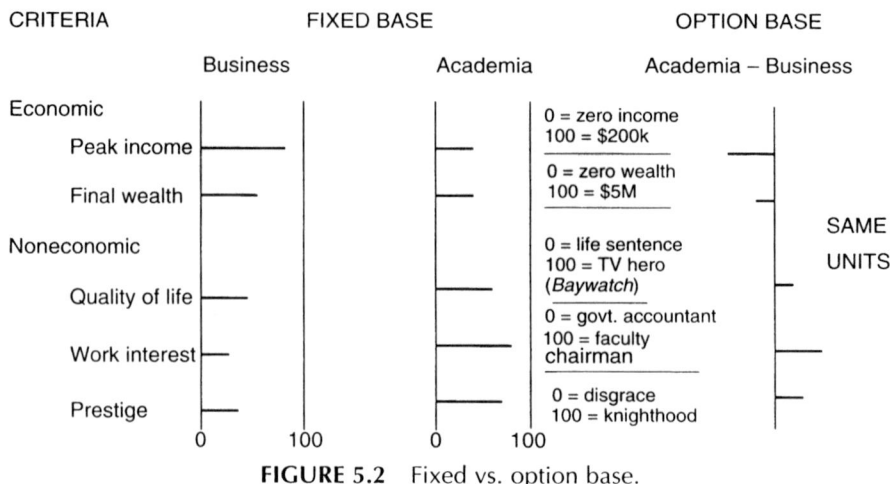

FIGURE 5.2 Fixed vs. option base.

plus–minus tally.[8]) If the null option preserves the status quo, current fixed base and null option base are the same. However they are not if the null option is accompanied by improvement or deterioration from *causes unrelated to the choice* (and which we may not need to know about to make this choice).

Example. A ship has just been hit with a cannonball, causing a leak in the hull just below the waterline, and is beginning to sink. Relative to the current base, in which the ship is afloat, the option "throw all ballast overboard" would have a zero impact on the score for the criterion "flotation of ship" if that option results in the ship remaining afloat (its current status). Relative to the null option base, however, the same option will have a very high option impact on flotation, since the ship will be significantly more afloat than if it were allowed to continue to sink unimpeded. ♦

Dummy Option. The base option may also be a *"dummy" option* (i.e., a handy option not actually being considered), some hypothetical option that is easy to visualize and compare with. It should be some option that you can readily imagine D choosing for comparison purposes on a specific criterion, but not necessarily a realistic option (e.g., "do nothing, *now or ever*," even if this is not something D would consider if there is no need to make a final commitment now). In the Tex case, opting for a lifelong business career, without the chance of changing his mind ever, would be a dummy option. ♦

5.5.3 Correspondence Between Bases

Example. Suppose that D has $3k in the bank now but will get another $4k in salary next week. He is considering an investment that will net him $2k. Figure 5.3 shows monetary outcomes of investment or not, measured with three bases.

---

[8]See instructor comment on sample student report in Appendix 12A, where there is just such an error in a plus–minus tally.

	FIXED BASE		OPTION BASE
OPTIONS	Empty account	Current balance	Null option
A. Invest	$ 9 k	$ 6 k	$ 2 k
B. Don't invest	$ 7 k	$ 4 k	0

FIGURE 5.3 Alternative scale bases for "invest?" choice (tabular).

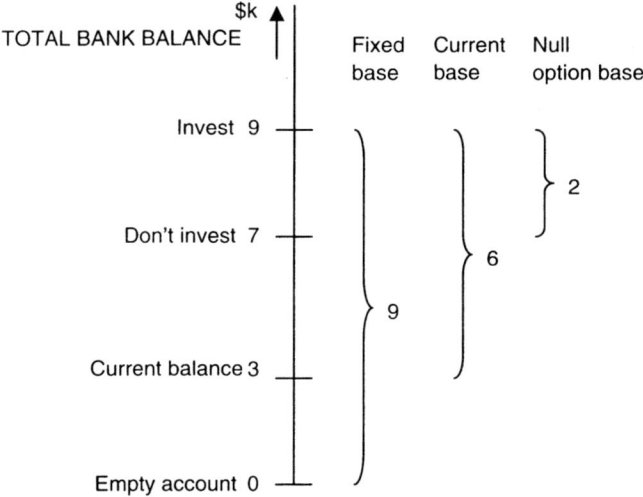

FIGURE 5.4 Alternative scale bases for same "invest?" choice (graphic).

Note that the difference between investing and not is $2k in each case, but measured from a different base. Figure 5.4 shows the same information graphically, noting the three metrics for the invest option only. ♦

Suppose that Tex's economic criterion were defined as "ending net worth at retirement."[9] Then alternative bases could be as follows:

absolute fixed = zero net worth at retirement
standard fixed = average net worth of Tex's peers
current fixed = ending worth is the same as present net worth

---

[9] A more complex, multicriteria metric of money may be life stream of cash. Then, fixed base, absolute: 0 = no cash ever, or crippling debt.

Example: Whether to Install Air Conditioning. A criterion may be the effect on temperature during a heat wave. With a fixed base we may look at the absolute temperature; with an option base, the difference in temperature (a drop of 5°); and with a current base, that the temperature will rise only 2° from today's (when a heat wave hit). ♦

Environmental Example. The choice is whether to pass some clean air legislation. One criterion is "aesthetic appeal to landscape." Zero on a null option-based scale might be defined as "no impact on aesthetics," but aesthetics could deteriorate (for other reasons) to the same extent as if the legislation were not passed. Absolute fixed base might be 0 = "aesthetics are everywhere as bad as now in LA." ♦

5.6 RATING SCALE UNITS

The ends of the scale, or *anchors*, normally corresponding to defined good and bad contingencies, are labeled 0 to 100. Options or possibilities are *rated* on this scale. Normally, *anchors* for attributes can be defined simply as *hi* or *lo*, or in the case of a criterion, *good* or *bad*. The anchors are arbitrary and set, for example, by the aider. Illustrative specific examples, or anchor scenarios, are helpful to make clear what they mean.

5.6.1 Anchor Scenarios

One anchor point marks off 100 *units* from the base. Option outcomes are interpolated, (judgmentally or otherwise) between 0 and 100.[10] Thus, the usual metric scale for temperature is base 0 = water freezing point, and it is usually measured in number of degrees Celsius above freezing point (e.g., 30°). Anchors can be any characterization that D can readily evaluate. They can be compact, like the careers of real or fictional losers and winners, whose utility can readily be understood (e.g., "a career as satisfactory for D as Ronald Reagan's"), or they can be detailed descriptions of disastrous and idyllic careers.

There may be any number of equally appropriate equivalent "anchor scenarios," real or imaginary, that can be interpreted as 100 or 0, but just one of them is sufficient to define that anchor. For example, Bill Gates and Croesus (of Greek mythology) might be considered equally successful materially and both score 100 on an economic criterion, but either alone could be chosen to fix the definition of 100 for the criterion "economic success." The other would be *assessed* as 100 on that scale, and could be reassessed (e.g., if Gates went bankrupt).

Any memorable and well-understood specific scenario that exemplifies a good or bad value of the criterion would be a logically acceptable anchor, provided that it

---

[10]In principle, additional intermediate points are needed to specify scale, but in practice D can usually adequately interpolate where options lie on the two-anchor scale using informal direct judgment.

unambiguously defines the criterion in question. Practically, however, the definition of the anchors needs to be treated with much care, so as to assure that *outcomes* are interpolated accurately and used properly in subsequent analysis (if any). "Very good" on athletic talent is less useful than "comparable to Michael Jordan." A good operational definition of the anchors is valuable in facilitating intercriterion comparisons (see Chapter 6) or inter-evaluator comparison. Ideally, anchors need to be described in as much detail as will make clear their appeal, but be compact enough to communicate conveniently.

Negative Scales A zero base will sometimes be the *upper* anchor of the scale (e.g., if more of the criterion is *undesirable*, as with cost). In that case, -100 to 0 might be a more convenient scale than 0 to $+100$. Although the scale could logically be either from $+100$ to 0 or -100 to 0, only one of $+100$ or -100 can be specified in scale *definition*. If both are specified, the implication is that the *range* in criterion score (or attribute value) between the defined -100 and 0 must be the *same* as between 0 and $+100$, which won't normally be the case.

Fixed vs. Option Base Option bases are often difficult to handle with rating scales because of the difficulty of describing usefully the incremental units (which are obvious with metric scales). How do you describe some major effect on national health that will be defined as 100 units? This is relatively straightforward with an explicit fixed base—you just describe a particularly good (or bad) situation (say, no one is sick). For this reason, normally I recommend using a fixed base for rating scales unless a convenient option base is evident.

5.6.2 Plausible Range Anchors

It is generally better to have anchors that closely bracket possible option outcomes. Otherwise, a scale may be too extreme to permit sharp differentiation among options. If zero is bankruptcy and 100 is Bill Gates on a "financial outcome" scale, it will be difficult to discriminate among the outcomes of minor investments (e.g., buying a lottery ticket). "Institute head" would be a better high anchor than rock star Mick Jagger for status in the Tex career choice, because it is less remote. Similarly, "low-level corporate staff" might be a better low anchor than "unemployed clerk" (which may be unrealistically pessimistic).

When an outcome measure is to be used subsequently in a quantitative evaluation of options[11] (see Chapter 6), a *plausible range* scale often make sense. The anchors could be some interpretation of "as good or as bad as it normally gets," possibly

---

[11]The definition of an appropriate criterion measure may depend on the use to which the measure is put. If the outcome description is to be digested and acted upon *informally*, it needs to be communicated clearly to D. However, if the outcome description is subsequently to be incorporated into an algorithm for evaluating choice, refinements in how scales are defined can substantially enhance the choice process (see Chapter 6).

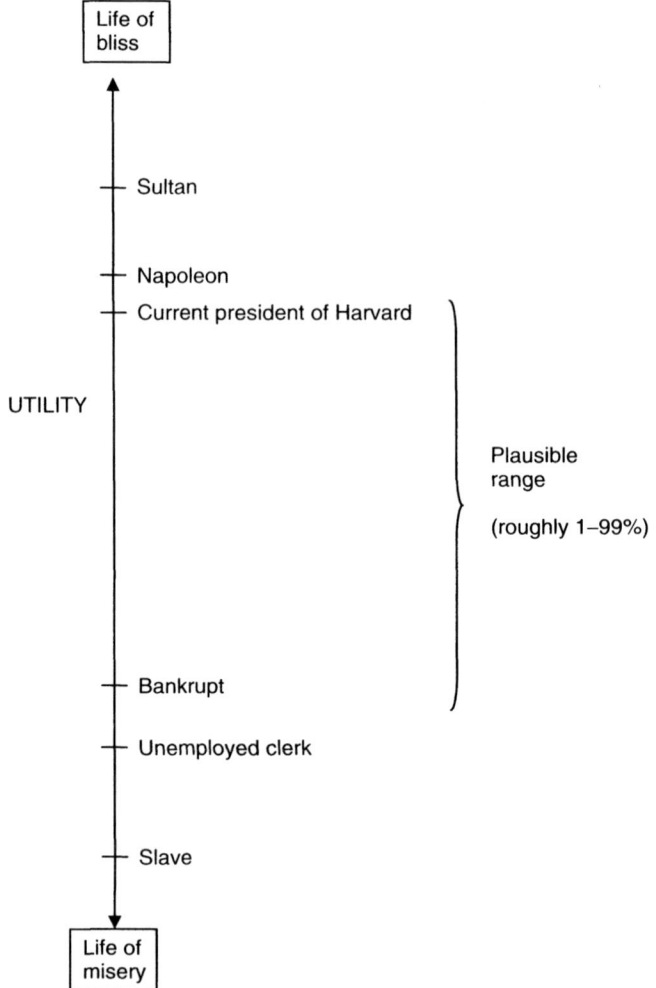

FIGURE 5.5 Alternative scales for total utility of Tex's options.

typified by specific outcomes to fix their desirability.[12] Figure 5.5 shows alternative anchors for the Tex case, including plausible range. Thus, among people Tex knows, almost none of them have done better (in terms of appeal to Tex) than the president of Harvard, and almost none have done worse than being bankrupt. Outcomes of his own career choices (not necessarily restricted to business or academia) will probably be somewhere within that range. (If an outcome happened to fall outside the plausible range, it is acceptable to give it 110, etc.) Plausible range can usually correspond fairly closely to what D has intuitively in mind when he says, say, "on a

---

[12]If more specificity is needed, anchors can be operationalized as the 1st and 99th percentiles (best and worst 1%) of some appropriate reference population (e.g., situations D has come across).

scale of 0 to 100, I'd give it 45." Plausible range also helps to give the right technical interpretation to D's answers to general and undefined questions such as "How important is criterion A compared to B?", which is discussed in Chapter 6.

Interpolating values on a rating scale can be helped by *assessing* easy-to-understand marker points, such as where on the scale the current situation is located, or some standard value.

5.7 COMPARISON OF SCALES

5.7.1 Illustrations of Scale Alternatives

The following statements illustrate different scale types presented above. The format followed below is: "Statement." (Criterion. Base type; unit type.)

- "I expect to lose $1000 if I go into business with my nephew." (Money out of pocket. Null option base; natural metric.)
- "It is a couple of degrees Fahrenheit colder than usual for this time of year." (Temperature. Fixed base, standard; natural metric.)
- "Acquiring the more expensive weapon system will accomplish 80% of the mission; the cheaper one, only 60%." (Degree of mission accomplishment. Fixed base, current; 0 = no mission accomplishment, 100 = full mission).
- "Poor Fred is on his last legs. His health is at 20, where 0 is death and 100 is normal good health." (Health. Fixed base; rating units.)

5.7.2 Choosing Among Scales

Which of the foregoing scaling methods you select depends on:

- Your preference for ease of application vs. efficiency. Usually, there is less cognitive challenge in approaches that are more laborious (e.g., fixed base is more straightforward than option base, but requires more assessments).
- The importance of the problem to D. The higher the stakes, the more effort is worth spending on scaling for a given degree of enhancement.
- Whether any convenient set of disaggregated criteria misses important considerations. If so, a holistic scale is favored.
- How easy it is to specify units. Usually, it is difficult to define 100 as an increment from an option base.

There is no need to use the same scales for all criteria, provided that differences are taken into account in option evaluation.[13] However, using metrics for some criteria and

---

[13] Avoid mixing anchor types on the same scale. A common mistake is to make 0 null option, but 100 fixed base.

ratings for others can be confusing unless the metrics are converted into ratings by defining anchors as particular high and low metric values.

5.8 WHEN DESCRIBING OUTCOMES IS SUFFICIENT

Decision aid will often go no further than *projecting* option outcomes, and the decider will make a choice without any formal attempt at evaluating those outcomes (covered in Chapter 6).

Example. In selecting among alternative weapon systems, military authorities will typically take great trouble and effort to assess individual performance criteria, such as "survivability" in battle, and then present their criterion-specific findings to the deciding general, who bases his decision on that basis. For political reasons, however, the general may wish to preserve discretion: not to disclose all the considerations that enter into his decision nor the importance he attaches to them. ♦

Deciders' reluctance to let their precise decision process be known is particularly strong where there is a question of "conflict of interest." The "revolving door" phenomenon, where grateful contractors offer lucrative positions to retiring government officials with purchasing authority may motivate those officials to fudge their criteria.

ASSIGNMENTS

Prepare for Discussion After Reading

Scope

1. List the relevant criteria that might be affected by a student choosing whether to drop out of school. Group as coarsely as you like. Use two to four words per item.

Prepare for Later Discussion or Submission

Outcome Distinctions

2. List the following terms in order of inclusiveness:[14] consequence, criterion value, prospect, and possibility. Give an example of each in the context of whom to vote for as U.S. President.

3. In Figure 5.1, "Tex acquires an Aussie accent" is classed as an *outcome* that is neither a *contributor* nor a *criterion*. If Tex's wife Dolly couldn't stand being around someone who sounded Aussie, how would that change the classification of that possibility?

---

[14]Candy is more inclusive than chocolate.

4. Which of these statements involve fixed or option bases?
   (a) "If Britain leaves the European Union, exporting will be harder than it would have been."
   (b) "If Britain leaves the European Union, it will become a third-rate power."
   (c) "If Britain leaves the European Union, exporting will be harder than it has been."
5. In the Tex career choice, suggest two *setting* possibilities (not appearing in Chapter 5), one that is and one that is not a *prospect*.

Completeness

6. Which statement in each of these pairs is more *comprehensive* (regardless of accuracy)? Explain.
   (a) "American elections are not corrupt" vs. "America is democratic."
   (b) "This stream is polluted" vs. "This stream has unacceptable levels of fecal coliform bacteria."
   (c) "Microsoft is getting less profitable" vs. "Microsoft is losing sales."

Specifying Criteria

7. Suggest in no more than one line a surrogate metric to represent the U.S. average material standard of living for purposes of describing the impact of a federal law to require employers to give three months' notice of terminating employment. (Don't say anything about *what* that impact might be.) How might that surrogate be inadequate for comparing the effect of such a law on the standard of living? Use no more than three lines.

"Anything Else" Criterion

8. In the Ford example in Section 2.2.2, the original model that favored retaining convertibles only took certain financial criteria into account. When decision time came, the vice-president judged that "anything else" was significant enough to switch his decision on retaining or dropping convertibles. What different judgment about that effect would have led him to prefer retaining convertibles?

Rating Scale Base

9. What kind of scale base do these statements refers to? (If any question seems ambiguous, say)
   (a) Adding salt to water reduces its freezing point from 0° Celsius to −4°.
   (b) It's 10° Celsius colder than usual for this time of year.
   (c) If you turn on the oven in the kitchen, it will raise the present temperature by 5° Celsius.

(d) If the Kyoto protocols are strictly enforced, they should reduce global warming by $\frac{1}{2}$ degree Celsius for each of the next few years, although global warming will still be higher than now from other causes.

10. Illustrate fixed and option base for predicting what will happen to next winter's average temperature in U.S. homes that install central heating for the first time. No need to be too realistic. Use a maximum of one line for each base.

Scale Definition

11. (*Continuation of assisted-suicide exercise*) Suggest scales to describe the following three possible criteria affected by a choice as to whether to legalize assisted suicide: criterion a, freedom of choice; criterion b, reducing suffering; criterion c, "saving" lives. State what the base is (e.g., "fixed base, standard") and the anchors, if appropriate. Define (or describe) anchors so that it is clear what you mean by 0 and either $+100$ or -100 (good or bad anchors) for rating scales, or base and units for natural metrics. (Do not address how important the criterion is, only how it is measured.)

12. In the familiar Fahrenheit scale for temperature, water freezing scores 32°, and boiling, 212°. What base and units does this scale use?

13. Suggest scales (base, plus units or anchors), including definitions or interpretations, for the following choices and a selected criterion:
    (a) Should I gamble at a casino? Criterion: wealth
    (b) Should I have hip surgery? Criterion: physical mobility
    (c) Should I marry my partner? Criterion: total outcome, including all dimensions
    (d) Should the UK abandon the European Union? Criterion: economic welfare
    (e) Should Abzania increase taxes? Criterion: standard of living over next five years. (The economy is currently collapsing rapidly from other causes.) Use current base.

Interpreting Assessments

14. Tex is reviewing Uncle Albert's past career to get insight on the economic prospects of his own choice. Albert went to work for a retailer out of grade school, rose rapidly to be manager of the company's warehouse, and stayed there until he retired. If Tex were to replicate Albert's career, he would rate his economic fate halfway between the best and the worst economic scenarios that Tex could plausibly envisage for himself. If Tex were to opt for academia, he predicts he would fare economically appreciably worse than Albert, but still a lot better than Tex's worst scenario. What scale could Tex use to rate his academic option on the economic criterion? Suggest a plausible numerical rating on this scale.

Recognizing Scales

15. Characterize the following statements by criterion, base and unit type (as in Section 5.7.1).

  (a) "Too many cooks spoil the broth. Adding cooks will make the broth worse than it is now."

  (b) "Building the Three Gorges Dam will turn that region from mostly untouched wilderness now to ecological disaster approaching that of the Aral Sea in Russia. However, that region of China will deteriorate somewhat anyway from industrialization. Impacts of building/not-building dam are, respectively, -95 and -20 on a scale from untouched wilderness (0) to Aral condition (-100)."

  (c) "The United States will have a major recession if the Federal Reserve does nothing. If it tightens the money supply, there will be only a mild recession. No recession = 0. Full-scale depression, such as the 1930s, = -100. Outcome of no Fed action = -45."

  (d) Tex: "I judge both career options to be about a third of the way, in utility, from the life of an unemployed clerk to the president of Harvard, with business at 35 a little higher than academia, at 30."

16. D, owner of ABC football team, is deciding whether to fire the head coach, C, for making a racist remark. He wishes to take the following judgments into account:

  (1) D thinks it would be unethical to fire C on racist grounds; C has a right to his opinion.

  (2) If D does not fire C, the local press will probably attack D, unless something like a war in the Middle East diverts their attention.

  (3) Bad press will probably reduce game attendance (which is not important to D in itself), which will cause D painful embarrassment and make less money for D.

  (4) If C is fired, it may break ABC's winning streak.

  (5) Winning boosts ABC's standing (national ranking), which D cares about greatly.

  (6) National standing increases attendance, which makes more money for D.

List all D's *distinct* choice criteria (i.e., not overlapping any of the other criteria and no redundancy) corresponding to D's *ultimate* goals (i.e., not just *contributing* to an ultimate goal) suggested by the preceding statements.

Write a label (one to three words) for each criterion, and state which statement(s) suggest it. Propose a scale for any **ONE** of these criteria specifying:

  (a) Whether fixed or option base

  (b) Description of 0 situation (base)

  (c) Whether metric or rating scale

(d) **Either** units of measurement (metric), **OR** a description of the +/−100 anchor point (rating), as appropriate.

17. This assignment involves evaluating holistically a possible career you might have over the next 20 years or so. Among people you know well from your parents' generation, describe briefly (in not more than two lines each), the careers of two people[15] that appeal most and least to you (the careers, that is). Their appeals will be 0–100 anchors for your own prospects. Outline, in not more than three lines, a most likely career path (scenario) for yourself from now on, including significant education and job steps. Rate the appeal to you of that career path on the scale defined above, and discuss briefly.

---

[15]Camouflage the identity of people, to the extent you feel you need, to protect their privacy.

Chapter **6**

Taking Value Judgments into Account

In Chapter 5 we proposed how to describe the consequences of an option both holistically and by criteria. In this chapter we address how to evaluate the utility of or preference for those consequences, in order to compare options. We introduce quantitative *multicriteria* models that incorporate D's preferences and indicate a favored option.[1] How best to elicit the preference judgments needed is covered in Chapter 11.

6.1 DISAGGREGATING UTILITY INTO MULTIPLE CRITERIA

As noted in Chapter 5, description can be *holistic*, where each option's outcome is evaluated as a single number. If that number varies with desirability (e.g., utility), it indicates the preferred option directly. Although such holistic evaluation is difficult to do in your head, you know it is addressing the right question. By contrast, *disaggregated evaluation* may have easier assessments but be incomplete.

The description of outcomes can be disaggregated into two or more criteria and simply presented to D. In this case, D's preference among options is not directly indicated, although D can judge informally which option, as described, s/he prefers. This approach does not go beyond anything in Chapter 5. Alternatively, disaggregated descriptions can be evaluated by applying a formal procedure to incorporate D's preferences.

---

[1]Commonly referred to as "multiattribute utility analysis" (MUA).

Rational Choice and Judgment: Decision Analysis for the Decider, by Rex Brown
Copyright © 2005 John Wiley & Sons, Inc.

6.2 PARTITIONING CRITERIA

Partitioned evaluation by criterion disaggregates total utility into the sum of two or more *components* due to different criteria.[2] The size of each component is affected implicitly both by the size of the option's score on the criterion (a factual judgment) and the importance of that criterion (a preference judgment).

6.2.1 Plus–Minus Tally Revisited

The simplest case of partitioned evaluation is *plus–minus tally*, introduced in Chapter 4. D notes which option performs best on each criterion and whether the difference in performance is small, medium, or large, in terms of significance to the overall evaluation of options. These differences are turned into one, two, or three pluses or minuses, respectively, and netted out to compare options. Figure 6.1 is based on Figure 4.1, which favors Tex's academic option by one plus.

Plus–minus tally may sound simplistic, but the thinking involves the same tough elicitation issues as more "sophisticated" quantitative methods. The *difference* in methods is the relatively straightforward question of scaling. As noted in Chapter 5, a scale may have a *fixed* or *option* base. In Figure 4.1, a fixed base was used, interpreted as some kind of *normal* criterion value (summarized on right side of Figure 6.1). Academia and business options were each compared with that base and the option with the highest net of pluses (or fewest minuses) is favored. In this example, both academia and business are favored over *normal*. Academia's improvement over normal is given as twice as great as business's (as shown by + + and +, respectively).

If one of the options, say, academia, had been taken as the *option base* (instead of a *fixed base*), the net difference in +/− would be the same, but there would only be one option column (as on the right of Figure 6.1), because all entries for the base

TEX'S CAREER CHOICE	IMPLICIT FIXED BASE*		OPTION BASE
	Business	Academia	Academia (− Business)
Economic	+ +	0	− −
Noneconomic	−	+ +	+ + +
NET +/−	+	+ +	+

* Compared with some interpretation of a *standard* career

FIGURE 6.1 Plus–minus tally as partitioned evaluation.

---

[2]Provided that D judges the components to be additive. This will not be the case if the score of one criterion affects the preference for another.

option are zero by definition. Thus, if the base is the null option (do nothing) and there are just two options, the +/− entries will correspond to the difference between taking an option and doing nothing, that is, the option *impact*. In an analysis where there are more than two options, there will be one fewer columns than with fixed base[3].

A critical requirement of plus–minus tally is that the pluses/minuses for each criterion must be measured from the same base of comparison, which can be *either* fixed *or* option defined. A major but common error is for the *judger* to confuse the bases. In particular, in a two-option problem, the judger might specify two option columns; one would be option based, with the other option as base, but that option would also have entries as for fixed base. This seriously distorts the comparison of options.

For example, in Figure 6.1, the evaluation of the business option might be taken from the left side (fixed base) and the evaluation of academia from the right side (option base). This would make the options misleadingly appear equally attractive (both with one net plus). Proper use of bases in Fact favors academia (two versus one plus for fixed base, or equivalently one plus for option base). This potential base confusion also applies to more quantitative variants of partitioning (see 6.2.2.) Although option base is more compact than a fixed base, there is more to think about when eliciting the +/− inputs[4], so I recommend fixed base unless you are very confident of your elicitation.

6.2.2 Numerical Partition

Plus–minus tally is intrinsically a quantitative approach, since you could score an option's utility components as +/− 3, 2, 1, 0 (equivalent to +++, ++, +, etc.) and sum the scores. A simple elaboration along these lines is to rescale to +/− 10, etc., using additional fractions for even finer distinctions. However, people seem to find it easier to understand what you want if you ask for +/− without much explanation than if you ask for a number (which they may misinterpret as only the *size* of an effect, disregarding its *importance*, which +/− incorporates).

A variation of partitioned evaluation is to convert several criteria to one criterion, usually a natural *metric* such as money. In particular, **monetary conversion** reduces differences among options on several criteria to an equivalent difference in a monetary metric. Figure 6.2 illustrates monetary conversion in the Tex exercise. Suppose that Tex's primary criterion is monetary: specifically, his peak income, which he estimates at $70k/yr for business and $40k/yr for academia. Business, on this basis, is preferred by $30k/yr (the difference, A − B, is −$30k/yr).

The other economic criterion is Tex's final wealth, which he estimates at $500k for business and $300k for academia. The difference, A − B, on final wealth is thus −$200k. If Tex considers $10 of final wealth[5] equivalent to $1/yr of peak income,

---

[3]Unless the base is a *dummy* option, i.e., not an option being considered (see Chapter 5).
[4]That is, more *judgment-intensive* and less *structure-intensive* (see Chapter 4).
[5]This is a special case of constant conversion rate.

TEX'S CAREER CHOICE

	Business	Academia	A – B	Conversion rate to $k/yr	A – B ($k/yr)
Economic					
Peak income	$70k/yr	$40k/yr	–$30k/yr	—	–30
Final wealth	$500k	$300k	–$200k	$10k → $1k/yr	–20
					–50
Noneconomic					
Quality of life	50	60	10	1 → $2k/yr	+20
Work interest	20	80	60	1 → $0.5k/yr	+30
Prestige	25	70	45	1 → $0.2k/yr	+9
					+59
				NET	**+9**

Implies: *Academia* is preferred (since net A–B is positive)

FIGURE 6.2 Monetary conversion.

the $200k difference in final wealth would equate to $20k/yr of peak income. With both these economic criteria taken into account, B is the equivalent of $30k/yr + $20k/yr = $50k/yr in peak income better than A (on economics alone).

Monetary conversion can be done to other criteria, including those that do not have natural metrics. Suppose, as in (the "noneconomic" part) Figure 6.2, that the subcriterion ratings for A – B are:

Quality of life: 60 – 50 = 10
Work interest: 80 – 20 = 60
Prestige: 70 – 25 = 45

Suppose further that the conversion rates of peak income per unit rating are $2k/yr, $500/yr, and $200/yr, respectively. This implies peak income equivalents for each criterion A – B difference will be: quality of life = $20k/yr; work interest = $30k/yr; prestige = $9k/yr. The total of the A – B differences on these noneconomic criteria will be 20 + 30 + 9 = $59k/yr. This analysis implies that academia is favored over business by the equivalent of $59k/yr (for noneconomic criteria), less $50k/yr (for economic criteria), making a net difference of $9k/yr peak income equivalent in favor of academia. We can now ignore all criteria other than peak income, since they no longer distinguish among options.

Be careful not to confuse the real monetary impact of an option and *equivalent* money that another criterion impact has been converted into. Figure 6.2 shows the "quality of life" effect of the business option to be $20k/yr in equivalent dollars, but it is not a market value, just a preference judgment. The more important "quality of life" is to Tex relative to real money, the greater is its monetary equivalent.

6.3 DECOMPOSING UTILITY COMPONENTS INTO IMPORTANCE AND CRITERION SCORE

A next step in model elaboration is to express the criteria components in the partitioning of an option's utility and as a function of two factors: size of option effect on the criterion score and the importance of that criterion.

6.3.1 Importance-Weighted Criteria Evaluation

The prime example of this more decomposed method is the *importance-weighted criterion evaluation* (ICE) model. The net option utility is calculated as the sum, across all criteria, of the products of weights and criteria scores.

The main steps in ICE are:

1. Select the criteria affected by the choice.
2. Score the various options on each criterion, either in natural units (such as money) or on a scale of 0 to 100 (defining the scales, either fixed base or option base).
3. Weight the scores by the relative importance of criterion ranges.
4. Choose the option with the highest total importance-weighted criteria score.

With the illustrative numbers of Figure 6.3a for Tex's choice, the results are:

Business: $(0.3 \times 60) + (0.7 \times 20) = 32$
Academia: $(0.3 \times 30) + (0.7 \times 60) = 51**$

A double asterisk indicates the option preferred, in this case, academia. So if this model is an *equivalent substitute* for D's realistic perception of the real choice, D would opt for academia. Figure 6.3b elaborates this model.

The ICE procedure often yields valuable insights into the roles of fact and value in how the options compare. But it can be dangerous to rely on the output of such a model as a substitute for unaided judgment, without a great deal of care and hard thought. In the sections below we look at some of the major issues that need to be dealt with.

6.3.2 Importance Weights

Importance weight compares the *ranges* between the high and low anchors of each criterion scale (or equivalently, between single units on the scale, which may be easier to visualize) in terms of the importance to D of moving over that range.

Thus, suppose that initially, Tex sets the importance of the economic criterion as 5 and of the noneconomic criterion as 10 (or, equivalently, $\frac{1}{3}$ and $\frac{2}{3}$). He is saying that the difference in "economics" between the bottom and top of the economic

(a) Coarsely grouped criteria

		Business		Academia	
CRITERIA	W T	SCORE	PRODUCT	SCORE	PRODUCT
Economic	0.3	60	18	30	9
Noneconomic	0.7	20	14	60	42
Totals			32		51**

(b) More finely grouped criteria

		Business		Academia	
CRITERIA	W T	SCORE	PRODUCT	SCORE	PRODUCT
Economic					
Peak income	0.2	80	16	40	8
Final wealth	0.1	60	6	40	4
Noneconomic					
Quality of life	0.3	50	15	60	18
Work interest	0.2	30	6	80	16
Prestige	0.2	40	8	70	14
Totals			51		60**

** = Preferred option

FIGURE 6.3 Importance-weighted criteria evaluation (Tex choice).

scale, is half as important to him as the difference in "noneconomics" between a miserable and blissful career (if those were his anchors). Equivalently, D likes a change of one unit of "noneconomics" as much as a change of two units of "economics."

This importance elicitation procedure can be very awkward and burdensome to do with adequate precision (and is frequently not achieved). Both the range of the scale and how much it matters to D must be determined *together*. All too often, importance weights are assessed intuitively ("money is only half as important as fun"). This appears much simpler but can lead to misleading option evaluations unless the criterion scales are defined correspondingly. Option evaluations for given importance weights are very sensitive to how scales are defined, particularly how widely or narrowly (see Figure 6.4). The wider the range, the larger the 1% units, and therefore the greater the importance attached to them. An advantage of using a *plausible range* (see Chapter 5) is that then intuitive weights seem to be more or less what they should be.

In *private* decisions, this issue does not matter too much, since the same person assigns the weights and defines the scale (provided that s/he is consistent in his/her anchors, whether corresponding to a plausible range or not). In *professional* decisions (see Chapter 9), however, several people will often contribute input, and they may not mesh properly.

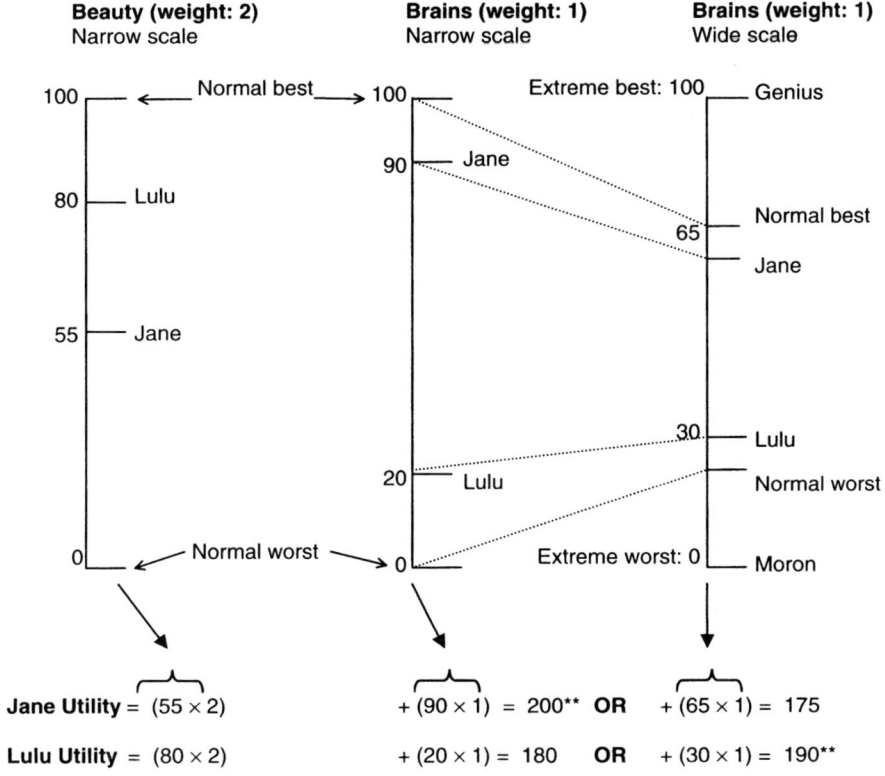

FIGURE 6.4 Changing scales without changing weight (choice of date).

6.3.3 Application to Metrics

Where criteria include both metric and rating scales (see Chapter 5), I recommend turning metrics into ratings by setting plausible good and bad values of the metric at 100 and 0.

Take money, the most common case. At first sight, it would appear a natural choice to choose $0 as the low anchor (0). However, for an importance weight to correspond to D's intuitive sense of a criterion's importance, the range of the scale should span plausible criterion scores. Zero income, etc. may not be a plausible criterion score for an option. If the plausible range on money for the choice in question is entirely above zero, then even if the 100 anchor is chosen to be plausible, the entire range will be too large for sound weight evaluation. D might not care a lot about money, but if the distance between 0 and 100 on the scale is large, D should assign more weight than s/he might intuitively be inclined to assign.

6.3.4 Demonstrating Effect of Range on Importance

Example. D is to decide whether to invite Jane or Lulu to the commencement ball. He judges that they differ in brains and beauty, and that is all D cares about. Intuitively, he values beauty "twice as much as" brains (i.e., importance weights of 2 and 1, respectively). What exactly he means by those weights, however, depends on the ranges that define the weights, which in turn can switch the implied choice.

On beauty, he rates Jane 55 and Lulu 80, on a scale where 100 is the prettiest 1% of girls in his circle and 0 is the least pretty 1% (left scale in Figure 6.4). On brains, he has a choice of scales. One is comparable to the beauty scale: anchored to the smartest and dumbest 1% of girls in his circle (middle scale). Jane scores 90 and Lulu 20 on this scale. Accordingly:

- Jane's ICE utility score is $(55 \times 2) + (90 \times 1) = 200**$.
- Lulu's ICE utility score is $(80 \times 2) + (20 \times 1) = 180$.

So Jane appears to be preferred.

Suppose, instead, that he uses the scale on the right. This other scale is twice as wide, anchored to 100 = genius and 0 = moron, on which the other brains scale's anchors would correspond to 70 and 20 (i.e., that scale has a range half as great). Accordingly, on the new scale, Jane scores 65, and Lulu scores 30.

If the same intuitive weights are used as before (2:1), ICE evaluation of the ladies is now:

- Jane: $(55 \times 2) + (65 \times 1) = 175$
- Lulu: $(80 \times 2) + (30 \times 1) = 190**$

D's apparent choice is reversed: Lulu now appears to be preferred. This anomaly occurs because there is less difference in brains (a criterion that favors Jane) on the new scale, but it is weighted the same (whereas to be consistent, the weight should be doubled). This is a good illustration of the rule that weights should reflect both the range of the scale and how much the criterion matters to D. ♦

Case Study. A U.S. presidential commission was considering lifting an embargo on exporting high-powered computers to the Soviet Union. Our decision analysis required as input two types of evaluation: a description of the outcomes of lifting the embargo, such as the *impact* on military threat; and a value judgment (preference), such as the relative *importance* of military threat compared with other criteria. However, the colonel who was to estimate only the impacts mistakenly also incorporated *importance* (which someone else supplied). When both types of input were combined in the analysis, this had the effect of double-counting threat importance (relative to economic criteria) and exaggerating the role of threat. This tilted the choice toward retaining the embargo. Fortunately, we caught the error by also analyzing the choice in a different way ("plus–minus tally"; see Chapter 4), and catching the discrepancy. ♦

6.3.5 Nonmonotonic Measures

Sometimes a measure that looks promising as a criterion is not "monotonic," in the sense that more is not always better (or conversely).

Example. More tartness in a dessert may be desirable up to a certain point, beyond which it is increasingly undesirable. The criteria used in ICE should be monotonic, converting original scales if necessary. This may be achieved by defining a higher-order criterion that is monotonic (e.g., good taste, which includes both tartness and sweetness). Alternatively, the original scale can be graphed against a rating scale of 0 to 100. Thus, if tartness is measured by pH (a standard metric of alkalinity), a pH of 6 might be set at 100 and pHs of 4 and 8 could both be zero (i.e., equally unappealing). ♦

6.4 GRAPHIC REPRESENTATION

6.4.1 Utility Component Boxes

The ICE model can be represented graphically by boxes, as in Figure 6.5. The utility component due to each criterion is shown as a rectangle, where the height

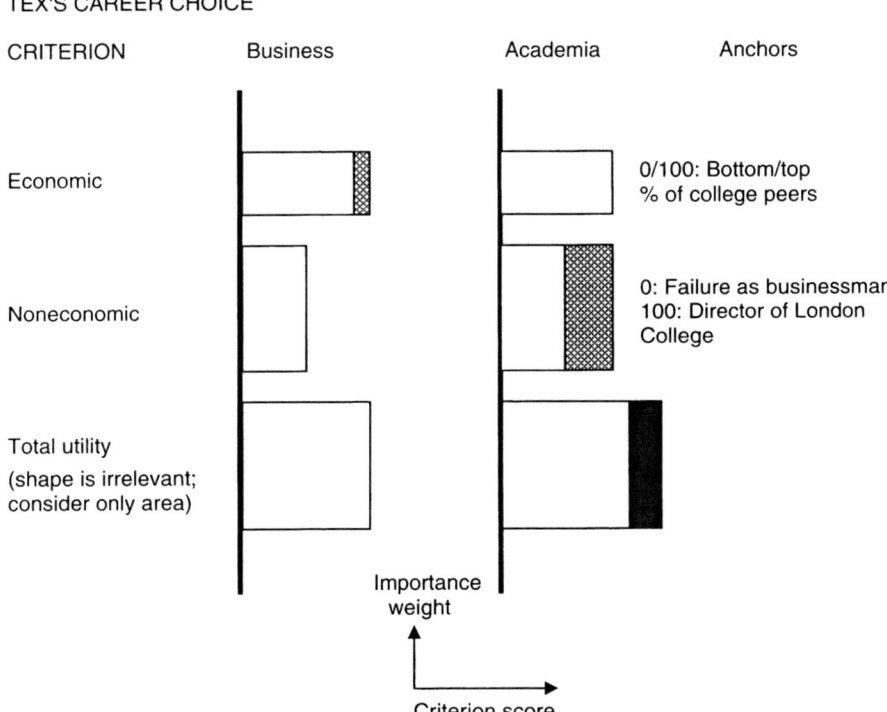

FIGURE 6.5 Sum-of-boxes ICE format: fixed scale.

is the importance weight for that criterion and the width is the criterion score, positive or negative, of the option on that criterion. The difference between options on a criterion, in the same row, is shaded gray. The net ICE difference between the options corresponds to the net of the shaded areas and is shown in black on the bottom row. (This is a kind of partitioning.)

6.4.2 Numerical vs. Graphic Format

Visually locating a point on a line, for impact or importance, may or may not be easier than estimating a number. People may or may not be able to judge by eye which column of boxes has the greater total area. The main advantage of using boxes is probably in ease of doing sensitivity analysis (i.e., seeing what happens when input numbers change if the analysis is implemented on computer graphics).

Three cognitive issues that may determine the choice between the approaches are:

- To which format can you more readily supply input? Probably numbers, unless you have good computer graphics.
- Which lets you understand the message better? I originally thought graphic, but student feedback seems to say that this is not necessarily the case. It may depend on training and practice by user. (Some users improperly visualize the boxes as plates whose *thickness* is greater for the wider plates, and which therefore in their imagination carry more weight than they should.)
- On which can you better judge the result of changing inputs? A computer is needed either way. I suspect graphic wins, and the case gets stronger the more practice the user has.

6.5 OTHER PREFERENCE ISSUES

6.5.1 Caution on Summing Utility Components

Any disaggregation into criteria (e.g., partitioning or ICE) that involves subsequent reaggregating by *summing* the pieces is strictly sound only if the total utility is really the *sum* of individual utility components. This will not be true if criteria are *preference covarying* (i.e., the score of one affects the preference for another). If the score for one criterion has a positive effect on the utility component due to another, you have **synergy**, and the joint component due to the two together will be greater than their simple sum. Conversely, a greater score on one criterion may *reduce* the utility component due to another, because of **redundancy** (e.g., if Tex has more power, he may value increments in his income less).[6]

Mishandling this issue can have major consequences.

---

[6] A distinction is made between **preference dependence**, which has to do with value judgments, and *covariation,* also known as "probabilistic dependence," which has to do with factual judgment (discussed in Chapter 10).

Example.[7] During the World War II battle of Stalingrad, left and right boots were flown in by Germans in different planes. The plane with left boots was shot down, making the other plane's cargo useless. The importance of criterion R (right shoes) depends on the value of L (left shoes). If $L = 0$, $R = 0$. Otherwise, R will have some positive value. This is choice-relevant to Soviet deciders. If they knew of the German practice, they wouldn't bother to attack the R plane if the L plane was gone. ♦

Example. Suppose that D has to choose among getting a guard dog, a burglar alarm, or a tropical fish. If he can only afford one, he may prefer them in that order and so pick the dog. However, if he can afford two of them, he may add the third-ranked fish to the dog, because his home protection needs are covered by the dog. The second-ranked alarm doesn't add much, and now he also has the ornamental appeal of the fish.[8] ♦

There are alternative ways of handling criterion scores and importance in cases where the ICE "sum of products" does *not* adequately represent D's preferences. Different combining formulas can be used, such as multiplicative rather than additive (although this by no means exhausts common interactions). D can also directly evaluate a "package" of scores, as in holistic evaluation (Chapter 5). Also, if the criteria are arranged in a hierarchy, as discussed in Section 5.3.1, corresponding preference judgments are needed (but there is no space to address that here).

If two (or more) criteria overlap and tend to cancel each other out (redundancy), D can judgmentally readjust the net evaluation of options to account for this overlap (if the criteria are positive, the adjustment will be downward). Conversely, if the criteria interact positively or synergistically, D can augment their effect.

6.5.2 Tailoring Criteria to Evaluation Approach

If the decision analytic task ends by displaying criterion scores, and that is sufficient analysis to make a choice, the choice of criteria is fairly straightforward. Specify whatever criteria will convey relevant outcomes of choice most clearly and efficiently. A certain amount of *redundancy* or *synergy* among criteria is tolerable, in this case, since D can take this into account informally, when making his informal evaluation of option impacts. However, if ICE or another formal evaluation method is used, other considerations come into play. Redundancy or synergy among criteria must either be avoided or handled explicitly.

6.5.3 Handling Unmodeled Uncertainty

Although we are not modeling uncertainty in this chapter, Ds will usually have some uncertainty about the outcome of an option. If they are *risk averse*, they may not want to ignore it. However, if all options are comparably risky, uncertainty will not affect the

---

[7]Example contributed by student Mike Veneri.
[8]A special case of nonadditivity is "decreasing marginal utility," where the more D already has of a good, the less value any more of it adds. D values his first dollar more than his millionth. Two guard dogs are not twice as valuable as one.

choice much, particularly if one option is clearly leading, so uncertainty can be ignored.[9]

On the other hand, if the leading option has a significantly uncertain outcome, and its lead on *average utility* is small, its greater riskiness could switch the best choice. This can be handled in one of several ways.

- A direct judgment by D of whether the extra riskiness of one option outweighs the higher average utility of the other.
- Reanalyzing the problem with an uncertainty model (see Chapter 7) and merging the results.
- Elaborating the multicriteria model to include uncertainty (see Appendix 7A). This is difficult to do right, and I do not usually advise it.
- Reducing average utility by a *risk penalty* to produce a *certain equivalent* (see Chapter 4).

ASSIGNMENTS

Prepare for Later Discussion or Submission

Holistic Evaluation vs. ICE

1. Instructor Drown has two options in grading students in his rational choice course:
   (a) Holistic: Consider informally all that he has learned about each student's mastery of course material, and issue an "impressionistic" grade.
   (b) ICE: Grade all evidence on a student, grouped under classroom performances, homework assignments, project contribution, midterm quiz, and final exam. Score these five criteria and weight them by importance. Assign grades according to scores.

   Compare the two grading practices on how appropriately they measure mastery of course material.

Legalization of Assisted Suicide

2. (*Continued from assignment problem 11 of Chapter 5*) Develop an ICE table for the public policy decision of whether to legalize assisted suicide, with about 6 to 10 criteria, defining scales (fixed or option base). How does your real preference correspond to this analysis, if at all?

Car Tax Abolition

3. Governor D of the state of Utopia is considering abolishing the state car tax, which he predicts will save an average of $300/yr per state resident. To make up that loss

---

[9] One exception could be where D's subsequent action depends on where in its uncertainty range some contributing value happens to fall.

in state revenue, he sees himself having to abandon temporarily a major environmental protection program, saving the state about the same amount of money as would be lost annually in car tax revenues. D judges that the environmental program represents a value to residents of $500/yr each. However, abolishing the tax will be politically more popular. Should the governor abolish the tax? Why? What does it depend on?

ICE Logic

4. Choice Consultants, Ltd. has just lost a major contract. President Innes must decide whether to fire the project manager. If he does, he thinks the morale of CCL will drop halfway toward "rock bottom." If he doesn't, he expects to lose a third of his influence with the owners of the company. Losing all influence is twice as bad for him as hitting rock-bottom morale. Analyze his decision, based on these and any other plausible judgments needed.

Career Choice

5. Mary is considering whether to train as an accountant or a dancer. She cares somewhat about income and a great deal about fulfillment. The many other careers she had considered promise average incomes of between $10k and $100k. Dancing is near the bottom of that ranking and accounting is near the top. She hopes her career will be more fulfilling than her father's dead-end job in government. She would love it if she could have a career as fulfilling as that of her aunt, who is a world-famous poet. She expects dancing to be very fulfilling, and accounting to be only modestly fulfilling. Determine Mary's preferred option, using hypothetical judgments where needed which are consistent with the above.

Formulating a Multicriteria Model

6. You are a black juror in the trial of a black athlete accused of murdering his wife and a friend. You have to vote to acquit or convict. The black majority of the jury wants to acquit. You are convinced "beyond reasonable doubt" that he is guilty. However, you have conflicting concerns. You want to:

   - Get home to watch the Superbowl.
   - Send a message to the LA police that irresponsible treatment of evidence ("framing a guilty man") does not pay.
   - Avoid hassle from aggressive fellow jurors.
   - Avoid hostility from neighborhood supporters of the accused.
   - Show racial solidarity with the accused.
   - Show that rich defendants who can hire pricey lawyers don't always get off.

Making any *necessary* plausible judgments consistent with these statements:
- **(a)** Construct a plus–minus tally table (noting the type of base). Determine the option preferred.
- **(b)** Construct an ICE model/table (noting the type of base). Determine the option preferred.

Are parts (a) and (b) consistent? If not, in which would you have more confidence? If the juror is employed at minimum wage, imagine how much would she need to be bribed to change her vote (if bribery didn't bother her ethically)? Be consistent with judgments in a plus–minus tally.

Chapter 7

Choice Under Uncertainty

As discussed in Chapter 5, an option has outcomes that affect its utility and therefore D's choice among options. In general, these outcomes will both be uncertain and have conflicting criteria scores. Either or both considerations—uncertainty and criteria—can be modeled, in order to make option evaluation more precise. The more important the precision of each aspect is to achieve, the stronger the case for modeling it. We want to model most thoroughly the issues that matter most (i.e., where D's unaided intuition is most likely to lead to costly errors). In this chapter we address situations where uncertainty is the most important to model.[1]

Examples. The soundness of a foreign policy decision about whether to invade Islamia would depend on whether all the different types of outcome have been taken into account (national security, international approval, lives lost, morality, oil supply, regional influence, etc.). This would be a reason to model *multiple criteria* carefully. On the other hand, in a security decision about whether to cancel a Superbowl game threatened by a terrorist attack, it would be more valuable (and perhaps sufficient) to analyze *uncertainty* about the threat. ♦

Any decision consideration can be modeled to any degree of thoroughness, but for most purposes, and for reasons of simplicity, I favor choosing *either* a model addressing multiple criteria (as in Chapter 6) *or* a model addressing uncertain outcomes (covered in this chapter) or possibly both in different models, rather than

---
[1] Useful supplementary material on probabilistic modeling can be found in Clemen (1996, pp. 219–middle 221; bottom 226–middle 230; middle 236–end 237; end 239–midddle 241).

Rational Choice and Judgment: Decision Analysis for the Decider, by Rex Brown
Copyright © 2005 John Wiley & Sons, Inc.

a hybrid model that covers both aspects. All three cases are discussed and diagrammed schematically in Appendix 7A.

7.1 TYPES OF UNCERTAIN POSSIBILITY

Factual possibilities differ from one another in significant respects that affect how they are treated in DA. As shown in Figure 5.1, possibilities can be successively narrowed down to *prospects*, *consequences* (*contributor* values or *criterion* scores), and *settings*.

Examples. Should D take an umbrella to work? Comfort is the *criterion*. Wetness and perspiration are *contributors*. Rain is the *setting*. Should D go into a business venture? Profitability is the *criterion*. Sales demand is a *contributor*. Economic climate is a *setting*. ♦

7.1.1 Form

Any of these levels of possibility can take on different forms. A possibility can be either ***discrete*** (few alternatives) or ***continuous*** (a ***quantity***, with infinitely many values possible). If *discrete*, it can be ***binary*** (two alternatives) or multiple (three or more). It may also be theoretically discrete but ***quasicontinuous***, with more possibilities than are worth distinguishing (such as the U.S. population) and therefore treated as continuous.

7.1.2 Probability Distribution

D's uncertainty about possibilities can be expressed by a ***probability distribution***, where each specific possibility[2] is associated with a chance or ***probability***.[3] If the possibilities are binary or multiple, each possibility is characterized by a single probability number from 0 to 1. If the possibilities are continuous or quasicontinuous, the uncertainty of each can be expressed as a *continuous* distribution, which specifies a probability for each ***range*** of possibilities, usually in the form of a graph.

7.2 CHARACTERIZING UNCERTAINTY: PERSONAL PROBABILITY

D must adopt and accept elements in the analysis, including probability assessment,[4] even if it originally came from another *informant*. Therefore, for our purposes the interpretation of probability has to be *personal*.

---

[2] The term "possibility" here is used to refer both to specific possibilities, such as "Ford," and to the broader concept of a set of possibilities, such as "make of car."

[3] A probability can also be expressed as "odds" (e.g., "D would give odds of 3 : 1 the Redskins will win" implies that his probability of a Redskins' win is 75%).

[4] D can be treated as the *assessor*, even if someone else originally provided the assessment, because D must adopt the assessment as his own in any DA that he is to accept.

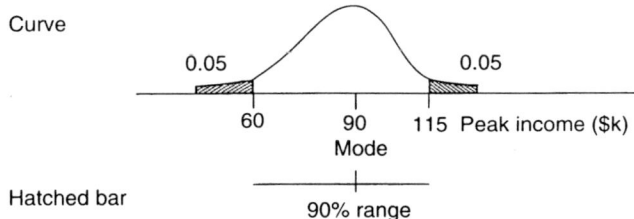

FIGURE 7.1 Representing an uncertain quantity (Tex).

7.2.1 Discrete Possibilities

Discrete possibilities and their probabilities (whether personal or not) have some formal properties:

- Possibilities are exclusive and exhaustive (i.e., one, and only one, of the possibilities can occur).[5]
- The probability of any one possibility in a *set* of possibilities is measured on a scale between 0 and 100%. [For example, a 20% probability that my next car will be a Ford is represented as P(car is a Ford) = 0.2].
- The probability of one of two exclusive possibilities in a *set* is the sum of their individual probabilities [e.g., P(My next car will be a primary color other than red) = 0.1 and P(My next car will be red) = 0.2; therefore, P(My next car will be a primary color) = 0.2 + 0.1 = 0.3].
- Alternative possibilities in a set are exhaustive—together, their probabilities total 100% [e.g., P(My next car will be red, another primary color or not a primary color) = 100%].

7.2.2 Continuous Possibilities

A choice may involve a continuous **uncertain quantity**[6] or **UQ**, which may take on any value in a range (rather than two or more *discrete* possibilities). The UQ may be a natural metric, like height or cash, or a constructed rating, 0 to 100. Continuous probabilities also have formal properties. However, in this book they will normally be approximated by *discrete* probabilities, for analysis purposes, or summarized otherwise by simple numbers or lines.

Representing and Summarizing Uncertain Quantities An uncertain quantity is often represented graphically as a curve[7], often bell-shaped (see Figure 7.1), where the probability of the quantity falling within a given range corresponds to the area

---

[5]Including perhaps a residual "anything else" (i.e., some contingency that D has not thought of in advance or not explicitly specified).
[6]Often called a "continuous variable."
[7]Called a "density" curve to distinguish it from a "cumulative" curve, but we will not use the latter.

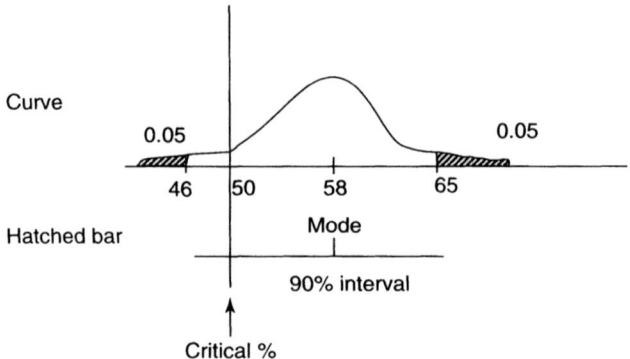

FIGURE 7.2 UQ with critical percentile (percent note for candidate).

under the curve. A compact way to summarize a UQ is as a point estimate, which can be one of several measures of central tendency. For example:

- The *mode* is the most likely value.
- The *median* is the value such that there is an equal probability that the true value is above or below.
- The *average* (or mean) is an average of all possible values, weighted by their probabilities.

If the uncertainty is bell-shaped and symmetrical, these three measures are the same. Otherwise, they are different, but often close to each other. The *mode* and *median* are good as inputs to be judged intuitively, since they are easier to think about than *average* (which is usually more appropriate logically).

A 90% *plausible range* is the UQ range within which the assessor is 90% confident (i.e., assesses 90% probability) that the true value lies. Thus, I might express my uncertainty about your weight as: "Your most likely weight is 160 pounds, but I am 90% confident that it is between 150 and 175 pounds." Figure 7.1 shows a possible state of Tex's uncertainty about his peak income, which he believes will most likely be $90k, and is 90% "confident"[8] (probability) that it will be between $60k and $115k. This UQ is represented by both a continuous curve and a **hatched bar** (with a hatch at the *mode*[9]).

Figure 7.2 shows the probable percentage of vote for a candidate. The curve here includes an extra piece of information: the critical 50% proportion of votes the candidate needs to be elected. The probability of getting more than 50% is equal to the area under the curve to the right of 50%. The figure says that the most likely vote percentage for the candidate is 58%, with a 90% probability that the percentage will

---

[8] Not to be confused with its sense in "confidence interval," which has a special meaning for statisticians, not relevant here.

[9] Standard deviation is another measure of range used by statisticians. I use plausible range here because it is easier to understand, and its width is usually in fairly constant ratio (about 4 : 1) to the standard deviation.

be between 46% and 65%. The probability that the candidate will win the election (that the vote percentage will be above the critical 50%) is 90%.

I generally use a 90% plausible range rather than, for example, a 98% range, on the arguable grounds that we can more readily assess a possibility that has a 1:20 (5%) chance of being exceeded, etc. than one with a 1:100 (1%) chance. Plausible range can be expressed in several ways: the edges of the range (e.g., 10 and 30); the separation between these two (e.g., 20); or an estimate +/− a number or percentage if the distribution is symmetrical (e.g., 20 ± 10 or 20 ± 50%).

7.2.3 Making Assessments

In Chapter 10 we address how to best assess probability input to uncertainty models. It includes both eliciting judgments directly and inferring probabilities from other probabilities that may be easier to judge. There are invariably several ways of making probability assessments of possibilities, whether *discrete* (e.g., a person's race) or *continuous* (e.g., temperature).

7.3 AVERAGE PERSONAL UTILITY FOR OPTION EVALUATION

Evaluation of the utility of contending options is a major end product of a choice *uncertainty model*. A common way to compare options where the critical issue is uncertainty is to derive each option's *probability-weighted average* utility or **average personal utility** (APU).[10]

Where utility is measured by (or converted to) a natural metric (such as money), its average value is a sound measure of option *utility* for a D who is *risk neutral* (i.e., is prepared to "play the averages").[11] For example, Tex can evaluate career options by assigning probabilities and utilities to binary success possibilities and calculating an average utility (see Figure 7.3a). Academia comes out top at 37 (vs. 29.5 for business).

As noted in Chapter 4, choices involving uncertainty are often represented by decision trees, where a fork, whose branches correspond to all possible outcomes, represents uncertainty. Figure 7.3b gives the same analysis as the table in Figure 7.3a, but in decision tree form. The (probability-weighted) evaluation of each option is circled (29.5 and 37, as before).

7.4 SIMPLIFIED SUBSTITUTIONS FOR COMPLEX UNCERTAINTY

No feasible analysis using our tools can hope to represent exactly numerous and complex outcomes. More substantial model simplification is needed, by *substitution*. Many uncertain possibilities can be replaced by one or a few.

---

[10]Often referred to as "subjective expected utility (SEU)."
[11]If, on the other hand, D is risk averse and is specially concerned about extreme outcomes, the appropriate metric of option preference is average gamble-defined utility defined in terms of a "reference" gamble. Utility is equal to the probability in an equivalent gamble between arbitrary "good" and "bad" (see Appendix 7A).

(a) Table format

OPTIONS	BUSINESS			ACADEMIA		
OUTCOMES	PROB	UTIL	PROD	PROB	UTIL	PROD
Lower success[1]	0.9	25	(22.5)	0.8	30	(24)
Higher success[2]	0.1	70	(7)	0.2	65	(13)
			29.5			37**

[1] Humdrum job, or no tenure
[2] Hit big time, or get tenure
** Indicates preferred option

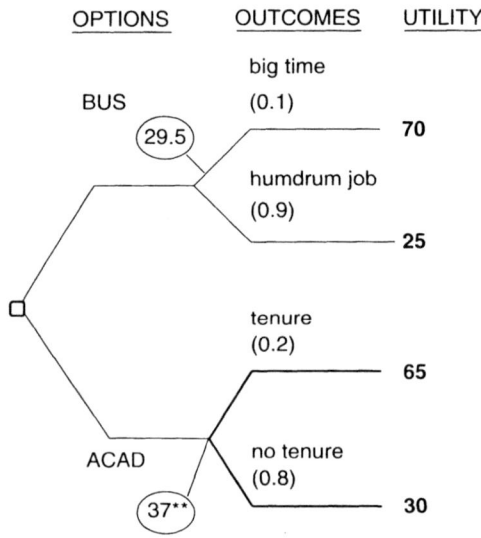

FIGURE 7.3 Probability-weighted utility (Tex).

7.4.1 Uncertain Scenarios

The uncertain outcomes of an option may be numerous *scenarios* (not quantities). *In theory*, all detailed possible scenarios (often numerous) *could* be assigned a probability and a utility, and the option then evaluated with a probability-weighted utility, to be compared with other options (see Figure 7A.2). More convenient substitutes can themselves be one or more scenarios. If the substitute is a single sure scenario, it is a *certain equivalent* scenario. Two or more scenarios associated with probabilities, would be a ***multipossibility*** equivalent substitute, as in Figure 7.4.

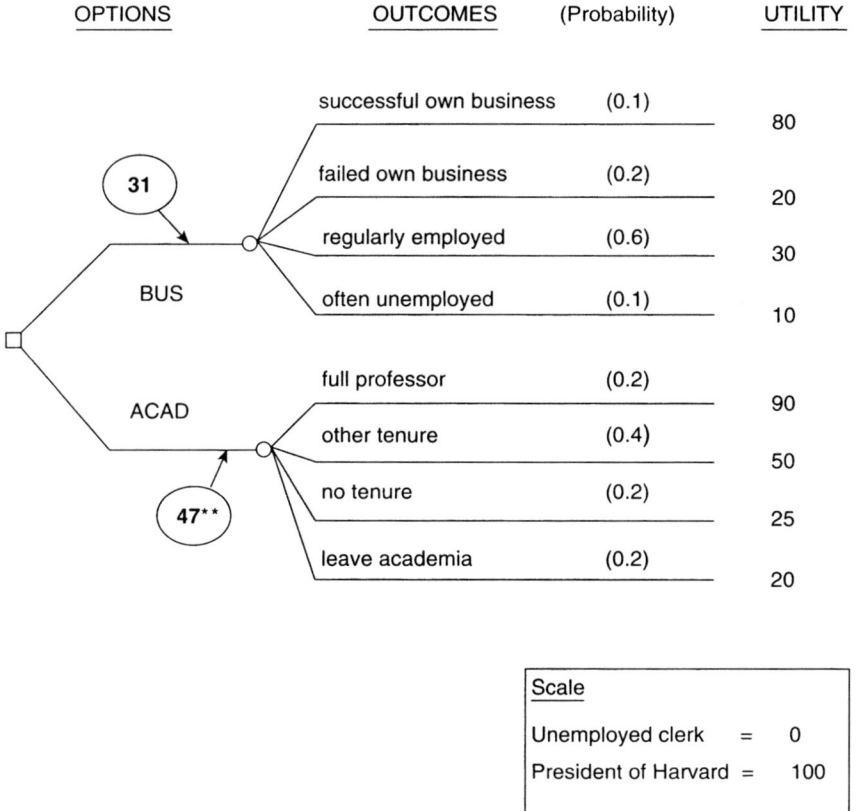

FIGURE 7.4 Multipossibility tree (Tex).

Hypothetical Example. If D is uncertain what an upcoming blind date will be like, s/he can substitute for that gamble some particular person or past experience that *if it were sure*, D would equate with *this* date gamble.[12] That substitute would be a *certain equivalent* blind date. If *this* blind date prospect seems comparable to D's past five blind dates, s/he might attach equal probabilities to each of them as a multipossibility equivalent gamble.[13] ♦

To make the main methodological points clear in the Tex case, I substituted *binary* gambles (e.g., "big time" and "humdrum job" in Figure 7.3) for the much richer realistic outcomes of each career option. Modeling these two outcomes as the only ones possible may not equate *successfully* with reality. Instead, a *multipossibility substitute* may be necessary. Accordingly, Figure 7.4 models four outcomes for

---

[12]Taking due account of any risk aversion (i.e., dislike for uncertainty about the real blind date).
[13]If D, on the other hand, thought this was an unusually promising blind date, the equivalent gamble might be made more appealing by putting higher probabilities on the best past experiences.

each option (instead of two), producing a richer equivalence to the real outcome complexity of Tex's choice. APU (average personal utility) is calculated by obvious extension of the binary case.

7.4.2 Acceptable Equivalent Substitution

These four possibilities per option would, of course, still not exhaust the many realistic career outcomes for Tex. However, this model (or even the binary outcome model) could still be an acceptable judgmental equivalent substitute, if the following conditions applied:

- All realistic possible outcomes to an option were partitioned into exclusive and exhaustive groups.
- The substituted outcomes are *representative* of these groups.
- The probabilities are treated as referring to the groups (not just the specific representative outcomes within the groups).

7.4.3 Discrete Substitutions for Uncertain Quantities

An equivalent multipossibility discrete distribution is a more informative *judgmental equivalent* for a *quantity* distribution than a *certain equivalent* (see Chapter 4) but is more convenient to analyze than the original distribution. It involves dividing the continuum into subranges, noting the probability of falling within each, and treating each probability as if it applied to a representative value within the subrange. A discrete distribution has now replaced a continuous distribution.

The more subranges, the closer the equivalence, but a three-possibility substitution is often adequate, at least for a bell-curve shape. It can be based directly on the information contained in a hatched bar representation (see Figure 7.1). The three possibilities are the ends of the bar (marking off 5% and 95% of the curve), which each take 0.1 probability, and the central hatch (usually corresponding to the mode), which takes the remaining 0.8 probability. In essence, the UQ distribution is cut into three segments, representing 10%, 80%, and 10% of the total area under the curve, as in Figure 7.5. The representative values are taken to be the 5th, 50th, and 95th percentiles, respectively. The original curve is now replaced by the three black vertical bars in Figure 7.5.[14]

In summary, the substitute distribution is:

Percentile of Curve	Substitute Probability
5%	0.1
50%	0.8
95%	0.1
	1.0

---

[14]There are other methods of substituting discrete for continuous distribution, such as *grouping* (Schlaifer, 1978), but the three-possibility substitution is adeqate for our purposes.

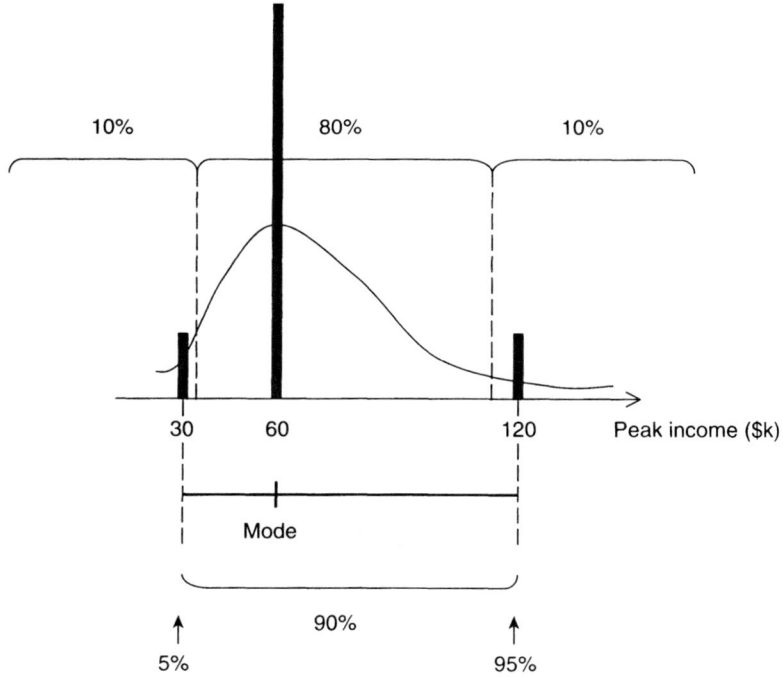

FIGURE 7.5 Three-possibility substitute for a UQ (Tex).

7.4.4 Analytic Use of Substitution

A choice involving continuous, or quasicontinuous, UQs can now be analyzed as if these UQs were three-possibility distributions (Figure 7.6).

In Section 7.2.2 we used, as an example, an uncertain estimate of a person's weight: "Your most likely weight is 160 pounds, but I am 90% confident it is between 150 and 175 pounds." The three-possibility representation allows us to derive a three-possibility distribution as a fairly good equivalent to the UQ. Probabilities are attached, according to the substitution rule above, to the three summary numbers above as follows:

Mode:	160 pounds	0.8
Lower end of 90% range:	150 pounds	0.1
Upper end:	175 pounds	0.1

We can now analyze any choice that involves your weight as if it could only take those three values with those probabilities. This substitution is one step more informative than a *certain equivalent*. If the CE is the average value (for a risk neutral D), it is

$$(160 \times 0.8) + (150 \times 0.1) + (175 \times 0.1) = 128 + 15 + 17.5 = 160.5$$

124   CHOICE UNDER UNCERTAINTY

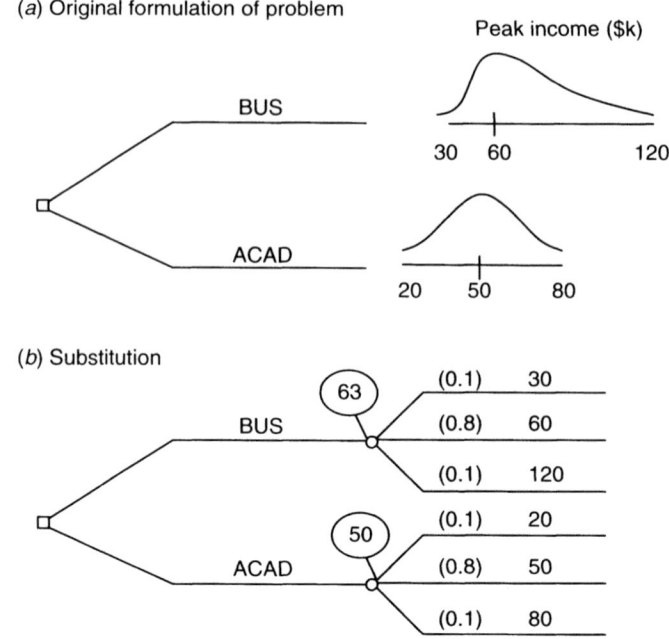

FIGURE 7.6   Use of three-possibility substitution (Tex).

Figure 7.6 illustrates the use of three-possibility substitution in an example using Tex's peak income uncertainty.

7.5   BALANCE OF CONFLICTING CRITERIA AND UNCERTAINTY IN MODELING

Since any choice will normally have significant aspects of both uncertainty and conflicting criteria, both issues must be modeled either explicitly or implicitly.

7.5.1   Two Single-Aspect Models

So far we have looked only at explicit choice models of either criteria (Chapter 6) or uncertainty (Chapter 7). Whichever *aspect* is *not* modeled explicitly has been represented by an equivalent substitute. Thus, in a *multicriteria* model, uncertainty is incorporated through a certain equivalent; in an uncertainty model, criteria are incorporated through a single aggregate utility.

7.5.2   Models Combining Both Aspects

An uncertainty model can incorporate preference by disaggregating the utilities of each option into utility components from several criteria. Figure 7.7 shows how the

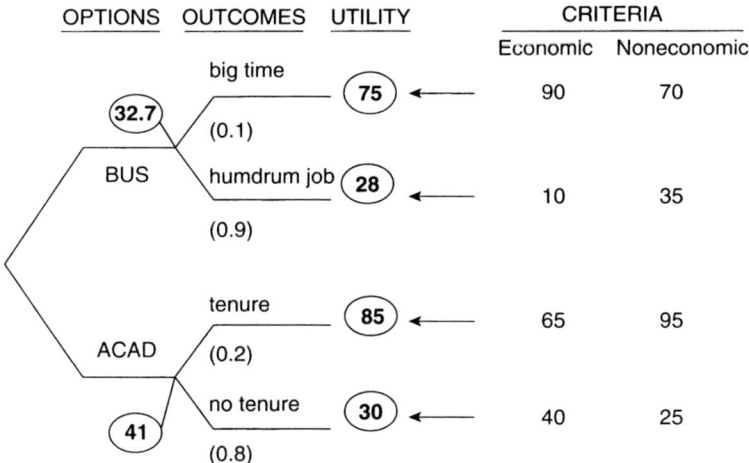

FIGURE 7.7 Uncertainty plus multiple criteria (Tex).

four outcome utilities in Figure 7.3*b* could be assessed by evaluating the economic and noneconomic criterion *components* that go into these utilities. As usual in *plural evaluation*, the elaboration produces a somewhat different evaluation of the career options from that derived earlier (academia is still preferred to business, but now 41 to 32.7).[15] In general, I have found combined models cumbersome to work with; I generally prefer to pursue separate models of each aspect for a given choice and reconcile or pool any conflicting results.

ASSIGNMENTS

Prepare for Discussion After Reading

When to Model Uncertainty

1. For which of these choices would you favor modeling uncertainty or multiple criteria and why (or is that unclear)?
   (a) Whether a corporation should buy out its competitor
   (b) Whether a corporation president should leave business and become a Buddhist monk
   (c) Whether the Federal Drug Administration should approve for sale a new drug claimed to cure Altzheimer's disease
   (d) Whether the U.S. president should launch a conventional nonnuclear attack on North Korea if it does not dismantle its nuclear weapons program

---

[15]If importance weights had been specified (see Chapter 6), the four utilities could have been derived explicitly by ICE.

Prepare for Later Discussion or Submission
Modeling Exercises

2. Suppose that I offer you the following gamble:
   You pay me $200 to play a game. The result depends on how the maximum temperature next Monday compares with the maximum temperature today. If the temperature is higher next Monday, I pay you $2000; if it is lower, you pay me $1400; if it is the same, measured to the nearest degree Farenheit, you pay me $600. Would you play? Why?

3. I am convinced that tomorrow, Dostoyevsky will pay me the $1200 he owes when he cashes his uncle's check, but only if he survives Russian roulette that he is going to play tonight.[16] Before he plays, he offers me the $900 he has in his pocket if I will cancel the debt. (Unless I accept this offer, I will not get anything before he plays, and nothing afterward if he "loses.")
   (a) Making any necessary additional assumptions, but accepting as true everything stated above, calculate whether I should accept the $900 now or wait until after the Russian roulette plays and hope to collect all $1200 (which I will do only if Dostoyevsky survives).
   (b) Which of the original assumption(s) above, if wrong, might change my decision? Why?

Making Assessments

4. Assess your probability that the candidate who won the previous presidential or comparable election in your country will do so again at the next election. Draw your distribution of his/her percent of the total vote—like Figure 7.2. Use only the knowledge you already have. Be prepared to discuss your reasoning in class.

Discrete UQ Substitution

5. D estimates that last year, there were in Slobovia 100,000 deaths due to air pollution, plus or minus 20% (with 90% probability).
   (a) Draw a bell curve consistent with these assessments and use it to estimate D's probability that there were more than 110,000 deaths due to air pollution.
   (b) Specify a three-possibility distribution that D might consider an equivalent substitute.

6. I am uncertain about Lulu's cooking. On a scale from 0 to 100, I'd give her cooking 40 ± 10, with 90% probability. In deciding whether to propose marriage to her, specify a plausible three-possibility probability distribution that I could use as an equivalent substitute for my real uncertainty.

---

[16]In Russian roulette, the player shoots himself with a revolver that has six chambers, only one of which contains a bullet.

Two-Aspect Model

7. Identify a local parking or traffic restriction (e.g., high-occupancy-vehicle-only lanes) that you might be tempted to violate when you are running late. You are sure that you won't be late if you're not stopped, but you wonder if it is worth risking a $25 ticket.
   (a) What significant criteria (maximum three) and possibilities (maximum two) would you bear in mind?
   (b) Define the criterion scales.
   (c) Draw a decision tree to help you decide.
   (d) Make plausible any numerical judgments that the tree calls for (e.g., probabilities, impacts, weights).
   (e) What does this model indicate that you should do?

APPENDIX 7A

TECHNICAL NOTES

7A.1 Major Elements of DA

The theory and practice of personal decision analysis as an instrument of rational choice has the following interlocking components:

1. The normative foundations (i.e., the logic and mathematics of statistical decision theory)
2. Specific procedures that adapt these foundations for practical use (the core of this book)
3. The descriptive foundations (i.e., the behavioral science of how people do think, including their reasoning shortcomings and limits on their ability to use procedures)
4. The applied art of putting procedures productively to work
5. Research to advance the state of the art of components 1 to 4

The book focuses mainly on components 2 and 4. In this appendix we discuss component 1, some normative issues.

7A.2 Decision Theory as a Test of Coherence

Decision theory is normative in that it adheres to well-established logical norms in producing models by which some judgments (of choice, uncertainty, and preference) can be inferred from other judgments. These models are not *prescriptive* in the sense that they *prescribe action* that is necessarily closer to a rational choice for the decider. DA is rather a test of coherence: it tells you whether various related judgments are consistent with each other (according to some set of fairly uncontroversial logical rules). The test does not say how judgments should be changed if they are found to be inconsistent. On the other hand, a rational choice does have the property that *all* D's relevant judgments cohere with each other. Any given DA model tests a *subset* of D's judgments for coherence, which is only a step on the road to making *all* judgments cohere.[17]

Example. Social surveys invariably estimate that American men average many more extramarital relationships (i.e., a relationship with someone of the opposite sex to whom they are not married) over their lifetime than women do. Statistics (a form of coherence) requires that the *averages* be essentially the same if each relationship accounts for one man and one woman. Then total number of relationships can be expressed either as number of men times average relations per man, or number of women times average relations per woman. If there are as many men as women, the averages should be the same. A tempting explanation for this incoherence would be that the men in the survey overcounted and/or the women undercounted their adventures. (The *distributions* for men and women may be quite different. There could be a lot of moderately promiscuous men and a few very busy women—or the reverse. The averages will still be the same.) ♦

I believe, although I do not know of a proof, that coherence among judgments is a good thing in that it advances rationality, and rationality advances D's welfare. Coherence among a given set of judgments is not, however, enough to assure decider rationality in its broadest sense (i.e., *all* D's judgments, explicit or implicit, cohere with each other, not just those needed for a particular modeling exercise).

7A.2.1 Ideal Rationality

Proponents of a flat earth have been known to put forward a supporting argument that consists of weird assertions perfectly coherent *with each other*. The "flat-earther," to be rational, would need to reconcile *all* his/her experience, for example of the rising and setting of the sun and the observation that he can fly east and end up where he started. He can't do it, so he is not rational.

An *ideal* judgment is the result of an impeccable rational analysis, whatever exactly that means, of all available evidence and indications of the judger's preference (in the case when the judgment involves preferences). Although practically unachievable, it is a useful construct, because it serves as a conceptual benchmark against which to measure the adequacy of any given attempt to improve judgment. D can evaluate a judgment aiding approach by how close D *anticipates* its results to come to the ideal (Brown, 1993).

---

[17] As an analogy, arithmetic provides simple examples of coherence tests. Say you believe simultaneously that there are 25 students in your class, 10 of them female and 12 of them male (implying 22 in total). The rules of arithmetic tell you that you are being incoherent, but not which judgments you should change. This is a special case of the coherence rules; decision theory has less obvious applications.

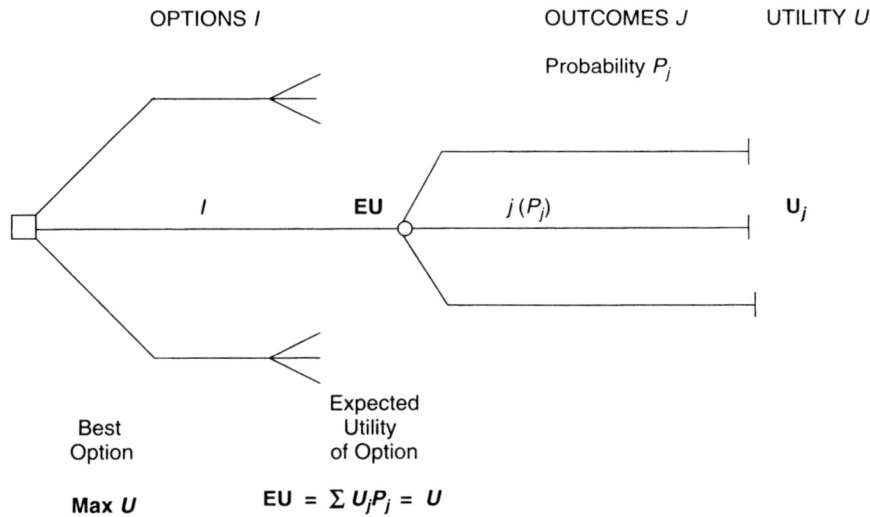

FIGURE 7A.1 Schematic Uncertainty model.

7A.2.2 Utility Although I have been interpreting utility as any metric where D prefers more than less, there is a very precise ideal definition such that if an option has uncertain outcomes, the utility of that option is always the average utility of outcome utilities. The ***gamble-defined utility*** of a prospect is the probability of good in an equivalent reference gamble between good and bad outcomes. The specification of "good" and "bad" can be more or less arbitrary—*relative* utility, and therefore comparison of options, will not be affected (see Schlaifer, 1978, Sec. 4.5.2).

7A.3 Schematic Representation of Models

7A.3.1 Uncertainty Models Figure 7A.1 shows schematically[18] a general framework for optimizing choice where only uncertainty is to be modeled (in this case, in the form of a decision tree). Options are shown as branches on the left-hand-choice fork. Each option has uncertain outcomes, also represented by a fork. Each branch has an associated probability, which corresponds to D's uncertainty, and a utility corresponding to the value D attaches to that outcome. The option logically preferred is the one whose average (i.e., probability-weighted) utility is highest.

Analytically practicable analysis cannot normally be in this graphic form. The uncertainty "fan" on the right would need to have as many branches as there are

---

[18]These schematic diagrams would need more complex notation (e.g., subscripts) to be mathematically complete, but should convey the concepts adequately.

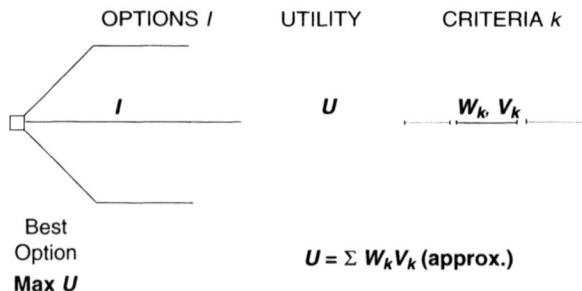

FIGURE 7A.2 Schematic multicriteria model.

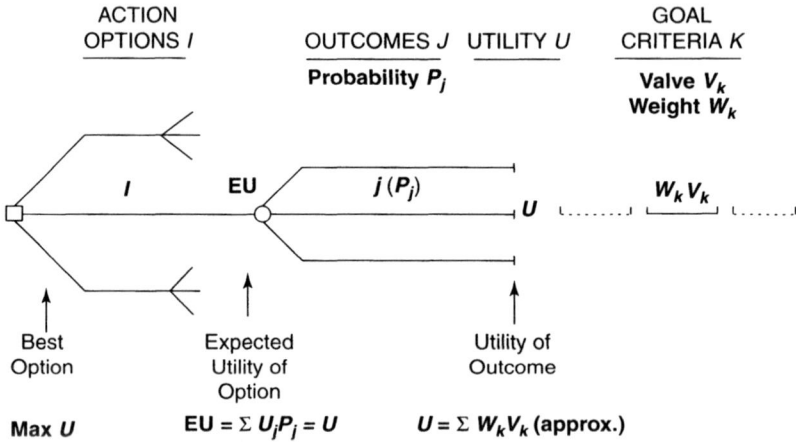

FIGURE 7A.3 Schematic two-aspect model.

discrete possibilities (including combinations of possibilities) or scenarios, which could run into thousands. We discuss feasible alternatives in Section 7.4.

7A.3.2 Multicriteria Models Figure 7A.2 shows schematically the general case of modeling conflicting criteria. The impact of each option on the value of each criterion k is derived, V_k. The V_k are combined into a single measure of utility for the option. The option with the highest average utility is preferred (see Chapter 6).

Overall ***gamble-defined utility*** is not necessarily equal to the importance-weighted sum of the individual V_k if D's preference for each varies with the value of others. For example, a multiplicative utility function implies that zero for any criterion score reduces the entire utility to zero, which is not an uncommon case. Other nonadditive functions may fit any given D's preferences better, although they may be difficult to formulate. I have used the additive form (importance-weighted) as a very convenient and usually quite adequate approximation in this book. Its value can be judgmentally adjusted up or down when the nature of any nonadditivity is well understood.

7A.3.3 General Form In fact, nearly every interesting choice has significant uncertainty *and* conflicting criteria issues. They can be modeled together. Professional decision analysts often do just that. However, the minimal kit of modeling tools presented here does not include (at least not explicitly) such *hybrid* models. Here, you must generally choose preference *or* uncertainty, whichever issue is most important or most amenable to improvement. Figure 7A.3 shows schematically in tree form a general-purpose decision analytic paradigm, according to which, in principle, the optimal choice among defined options can be derived in the light of any decider's judgment.

Chapter 8

Decision-Aiding Strategy

D wants to use DA efficiently; that is, to have it be as useful as possible while costing the least analytic effort. Decider and aider learn the analytic strategy needed to use DA tools efficiently mainly through practice, apprenticeship, and feedback from harsh experience. In this chapter we offer some parallel guidance, illustrated largely in the context of private decisions. (Professional decisions have some additional requirements discussed in Chapter 9.) A thorough grasp of the informal "smart choice" principles proposed by Hammond et al. (1999) should be very valuable and would usefully precede, or complement, any quantitative modeling presented in this book.

The strategic process of putting all these tools to use includes picking the right tools for the task and allocating the right amount of effort to each tool. D wants the DA to be improved progressively to the point where no further analytic effort is worth the trouble. The tools presented so far (and still to come) are developed and managed with this in mind.

8.1 REQUIREMENTS OF USEFUL DECISION AID

8.1.1 Tool Essentials

To help D manage his/her private and professional life more rationally, decision aid needs to meet some essential requirements. The analytic strategy needs to assure that:

- The aid addresses the right question, whose answer, if sound, will help D decide.

Rational Choice and Judgment: Decision Analysis for the Decider, by Rex Brown
Copyright © 2005 John Wiley & Sons, Inc.

- The aid makes use of all relevant knowledge available to D.
- Modeling is logically sound.
- The model input accurately represents the knowledge available.
- Output is in a usable, understandable, and timely form for D.
- The tool's cost is acceptable.

Unless *all* these requirements are met, the resulting "decision aid" is likely to be more harmful than helpful to rational action. Achieving balance among these requirements is a driving consideration in designing a decision-aiding strategy. All too often, the strategy is critically lopsided.[1]

8.1.2 Motivations for Aid Other than to Aid Decisions Directly

Decision analysis can have purposes other than making decisions more rational, which are sometimes at least as important. These include:

- To make it easier to defend and communicate the grounds for decision
- To advocate some choice to some other D (for selfish or altruistic purposes)
- To plan further information gathering or analysis
- To pinpoint sources of disagreement among adversaries

8.2 COMPONENTS OF AN ANALYTIC STRATEGY

Decision analysis strategy involves the following components, generally, but not necessarily, in the following sequence:

- Picking the right decision issue to attend to
- Taking account of D's knowledge of the issue
- Considering all plausible options on the issue
- Developing a choice model
- Developing alternative models/evaluations of same choice
- Integrating analyses into D's regular decision process
- Committing to a choice

Previous chapters have dealt largely with the fourth stage, developing a choice model. This is the step where aiding methodology is most critical, in the sense that it is easy to make errors serious enough to render the aiding effort useless. Cautionary tales abound of fatal modeling errors, for example, where the aider's model overlooks critical criteria and produces unsound or unacceptable

---
[1] Such "failure stories" are documented in Brown (2005).

recommendations.[2] It is thus critical that you master the modeling methodology before concentrating attention on strategy.

In this chapter we address how to incorporate decision analysis tools into an overall analytic strategy involving all the above steps. Additional decision analysis techniques are covered in later chapters (e.g., indirect probability assessment in Chapter 10), but the techniques already covered provide an adequate starter kit on which to develop strategy.

8.3 WHAT DECISION TO AID?

Before any specific decision issue is addressed, it must be identified as worth the use of DA. The effort involved in analysis must be justified by prospective gains. As Hammond et al. (1999) note in connection with their PROACT approach to decision making: "The worst thing you can do is to wait until a decision is forced upon you—or made for you." People don't always direct their attention where it is most needed, and failure to recognize that a deliberate decision has to be made is a serious source of poor decision making. Such misallocation of attention is due largely to the common human trait of accepting the status quo without challenge (Baron and Brown 1991). Say, D is in a job that is turning sour and just drifts on to retirement without considering whether s/he should try something else; or D sticks with a bad marriage. In either case, D may run an unnecessary risk of ruining his/her life. On the other hand, repeatedly agonizing ("Am I doing the right thing?") can be equally damaging, by wasting time and energy.

All that is needed may be for D to adopt the routine of "taking stock" of major areas of his/her private or professional life from time to time (e.g., every few months). D can simply ponder: "Is there an opportunity here to better myself or my organization that is good enough, or a problem serious enough to be worth thinking hard about now?" Moreover, an issue may be important and vulnerable to mistakes but still not be a strong candidate for DA. Inexperienced aiders working on a problem beyond their DA capability may go seriously astray. An *ideal* analysis (introduced in Chapter 1) should always outperform D's unaided judgment. However, any *particular attempt* at DA may fall so far short of ideal that D is actually worse off than had s/he used no aid at all.

Example. I have used a short introductory text on DA for business persons (Brown et al., 1974) in executive training programs. A frustrating but common aftermath of this course was that students who mastered the basics felt that they now knew how to do decision analysis effectively. They would come back a few months later and say "I tried it, but it doesn't work." ♦

To return to an earlier musical analogy, it's like people learning only the basics of musical theory and then being surprised at how terrible their Chopin sounds!

---

[2] See the parts depot example in Section 1.3.1.

8.4 BUILDING ON DECIDER'S THINKING

The first step in DA, I would argue, is always to start by building on what D already knows and judges. This is the *enhancement* mode for decision aiding, contrasted with the *emulation* and *replacement* modes (see Section 1.1.2). The following discussion is presented as if D has an aider, but it could be D's introspection.

8.4.1 Starter Questions

To begin, as suggested in Chapter 3, the aider engages D in a free-form conversation (taking care not to "lead the witness"). Questions might include:

- Who is to decide what, when, and how?
- What is the requirement, problem, or opportunity that motivates D to make a deliberate decision at this time?
- What is D provisionally inclined to do at this time, and why?

The aider probes D's reasoning, including any supporting and conflicting arguments.

8.4.2 Pilot Analysis and Feedback

An important check on whether D's thinking has been elicited adequately is for the aider to put together a very simple pilot DA, such as plus–minus tally, based on the aider's understanding of D's problem and perspective, using barely more than plausible inputs. The aider then reviews the implications with D, and in particular:

- Attempts to reconcile the analytic results with D's unaided evaluation.
- Seeks D's feedback on the formulation of the aiding task. Is it addressing the right question? This feedback can be in the form of a "thought experiment": Imagine that the output of this pilot analysis had resulted from a full-scale effort (rather than a "quick-and-dirty" one). Would D find it plausible and helpful?
- If *not* (as is typical in my experience), the aider resolves why. Has the pilot failed to capture some important element of D's judgment, such as a key but subtle criterion?
- Revises the understanding of D's perception of the problem.
- Uses this feedback to begin a more deliberate modeling process.

Some variant of this iteration is also useful at later stages of the modeling process ("build–test–build–test," in engineering design terms). That is, get decider feedback after each elaboration and consider whether to elaborate the model further, or to replace the model with another.

8.5 SPECIFYING OPTIONS

The aider should now be ready to develop a full-scale model to evaluate at least two realistic options for D. But first the options need to be identified and defined. Here are two useful guidelines in selecting options. Options should be:

- Exclusive (e.g., "follow strict diet" and "exercise daily" will not do as options, since one could do both)
- Clear-cut (i.e., unambiguous, and readily communicated)

Obviously, D cannot pick his/her best option if it is not among those considered. Nevertheless, D need not make the options exhaustive *at the outset*, provided that all promising options have been evaluated by the time D makes a choice. For now, then, for simplicity we focus on comparing only two options. The inclusion of additional options is usually a straightforward extension. For example, having compared two of the candidate options, one option can be eliminated and the remaining option now compared with a third option. Thus, options can be eliminated progressively by removing options by pairwise comparison.

Thus, initially, options and analysis do not need to be exhaustive. Your best option might prove to be something else that you are not yet considering. (For example, Tex's first two options might be business or academia, but if business wins this comparison, it can then be compared with, say, "join the army.") A more proficient aider will use more streamlined structuring than pairwise comparison in cases where there are many options of interest or they lie on a continuum. But walk before you can run.

8.5.1 Option Breadth

Options can be defined broadly or narrowly. The decision aider who concluded "Go West, young man!" might have phrased the option more broadly as "Seek fame and fortune!" or more narrowly as "Get a covered wagon!" or more narrowly still, "Buy a copy of the *Gold Prospector's Weekly!*" In a more realistic federal budgeting context, the choice might be formulated broadly as a prioritization of major objectives, such as deficit reduction, defense buildup, and holding down taxes; or as narrowly as setting each budget line item.

Options must be sufficiently narrow, however, that the subsequent action they entail is easy to envisage. This ease of imagining the option aftermath makes the null option, "Do nothing, leave things as they are," attractive as a *dummy* option. Narrow options, on the other hand, may exclude too many other promising options. A useful compromise is to compare broad options (e.g., "emigrate soon") by evaluating narrower options *representative* of those broader options (e.g., "join my uncle's firm in Australia as soon as I graduate"). *Different* narrow variants within the broad option (e.g., "work in Paris for a multinational company") can be considered later.

Thus, Tex could define his career options finely (e.g., choose a particular branch of business or academia); or broadly (as we so far have done) as academia or business, and leave unresolved for now exactly how he will implement this choice. In the broad case, he treats specific options within it as just another uncertain prospect to consider informally. In other words, leaving the options broadly defined means you have to bear in mind throughout that you're not yet sure what precise form each will take. This is difficult to do, especially for a novice decision analyst, so I recommend erring generally on the side of overspecificity, initially: for example, evaluate whether to go into business as an accountant or into academia as a public policy instructor, and consider business or academia more broadly later.

8.5.2 Incremental Commitment

Decision analysts know pretty well how to analyze **definitive** choices—ones where an irreversible commitment is made once and for all (e.g., declare bankruptcy). However, many interesting decision situations are essentially ones of **incremental commitment** (e.g., put off paying creditors in anticipation of possible bankruptcy). There may be many sequential choice points, each of which makes a partly irreversible commitment of resources (e.g., you test the temperature of the water with your toe, then the rest of your leg, before taking the plunge). The net effect of a succession of incremental commitments in the same direction is a cumulative commitment, or **culminating prospect**, which amounts to a *definitive* commitment (i.e., the ending position of a succession of incremental commitments).[3]

If aiders treat an incremental commitment option *as if* it were definitive (which they often do), they may fail to take into account the beneficial possibility of corrective action. That possibility would make the incremental option more appealing than a *really* definitive option. Treating as definitive an incremental option where D could abort a major project when the prospects start looking dim would undervalue the incremental option. For example, much of the projected investment in marketing new product may be saved if production is halted if early sales are disappointing.

Analytic Options Three possible strategies for handling the technically difficult problem of evaluating incremental commitment options are:

- Substitute *definitive* for *incremental* commitment, but adjust its evaluation upward judgmentally.[4]

---

[3]The prospect of a major cumulative commitment may never be addressed explicitly. No one person in the organization may be aware of, or charged with responsibility for, a major commitment in the making, and "creeping gradualism" may take over. The United States's progressive involvement in Vietnam and President Reagan's plaint that "dealing with the Iranian revolutionary regime ended up being an arms-for-hostages deal, but no one decided it that way" are poignant illustrations of that problem.

[4]Attempts to model this flexibility more explicitly have tended to deal with rather limited cases but provide promising generalized insights (Merkhofer, 1977). Approaches involving tightly specified strategies, such as dynamic programming and normal-form analysis, tend to require either unrealistic simplification or unmanageable complexity.

- Cautiously ignore the incremental feature if all contending options are incremental and comparably undervalued, since their relative evaluation will be unaffected.
- Treat as a definitive commitment some loosely worded dynamic strategy, such as "Head West until you see some reason not to, and use your best judgment along the way." The aggregate judgments this strategy calls for are by no means easy.

I have used the second strategy implicitly in the Tex career example. His choice is treated as if there were no going back, which is not the case. (He can reverse career direction if he learns of an unexpected problem or opportunity.) However, if any upward adjustment in option evaluation for disregarded flexibility would be similar for business and academia, it can be foregone.

8.6 CHOICE OF MODEL TYPE

From among the many variants of DA in use, I have put together in this book a small tool kit that should be helpful to a wide variety of decision types, aider and decider experiences, and problem contexts. What they all have in common is that the options to compare are few in number and clearly identified and use no mathematics beyond simple arithmetic.

The following tools have so far been presented:

1. Qualitative: "going through the GOO" (Chapter 3)
2. Quasi-quantitative: plus–minus tally (Chapter 4)
3. Decision trees (Chapter 4)
4. Characterizing outcomes without evaluating them (Chapter 5)
5. Partitioned utility (Chapter 6)
6. Importance-weighted criterion evaluation (Chapter 6)
7. Average value and utility based on personal probability (Chapter 7)

In addition, some refinements in the assessment of probabilities for tool 7 will be presented in Chapter 10.

As a general rule, I recommend always using 1 and 2. Then use either 3 or 7 for decisions where outcome uncertainty dominates; and 4, 5, or 6 where conflicting criteria dominate. These tools all lend themselves to being iterated at different levels of detail.

8.7 MODELING STRATEGY

Option evaluation can be structured by breaking the evaluation down into pieces that can be thought about separately and built back up. That is, analysis is followed by synthesis (Watson and Buede, 1987). A choice model can be structured in many different ways, appropriate in different circumstances. Strictly speaking, all models can be logically "correct" (in the sense that no errors can be detected just by examining the model itself). Distinctions have to do with how *useful* the structure is for the decision at hand.

8.7.1 Choosing Focus of Structure

Different structures can focus attention on different aspects of the choice. This focus permits analytic effort to be spent where it can do the most good. An excellent way to organize your thinking initially about what the key considerations are is with an *influence sketch* (shown in Appendix 8A).[5] The influence sketch lays out the salient causal connections between option and utility in a way that permits you to select a few to model explicitly. In particular, it provides a "menu" of items to choose among when constructing a decision tree. It displays the interplay of outcome possibilities that affect the impact of options on *criteria scores*. It draws on a menu of potential elements that are richer than one would normally want to actually use in a quantified model.

Bear in mind that some model structures are more difficult to elicit inputs for than others, which affects choice of structure. Although more nonbusiness decisions appear to be criteria focused than uncertainty focused, multicriteria models are often more difficult to do right, which tips the structure argument toward uncertainty models. In particular, as noted, the importance weights needed for ICE must be defined operationally in terms of scale units and not just gut feelings of importance, which often do not mesh.

In general, both uncertainty and conflicting criteria are significant. They *can* be modeled explicitly in the same model (see Figure 7A.3), but this makes for a rather complicated structure, and I prefer two single-aspect models. For example, in an Arctic oil construction case (described in Appendix 9A), we modeled an oil company's choice as to whether to build a causeway as an ICE model that trades off profit, environmental impact, etc. of oil company options. Although these effects were uncertain, they were replaced by certain equivalents.[6]

8.7.2 How Much of the Decision Process to Model?

Decision analysis *can* quantify just about any aspect of a decision-making process, but it does not have to. Some aspects are often left to informal reasoning. The role of DA may be solely to help D to describe and understand what the outcome of a choice may be (see Chapter 5), without attempting to evaluate the outcome. For example, what is generally known as "risk assessment" only quantifies uncertainty

---

[5] An influence sketch is a simple, qualitative version of the *influence diagram*, which is a well-established computerized device, logically equivalent to a decision tree, that deals more compactly and clearly with a complex representation of the problem, with many features of option outcome distinguished (Schacter, 1986).
[6] Initially assessed judgmentally, but potentially derived from an explicit probability distribution.

about a hazard; what to do about the hazard is usually handled informally. D may not need, or even accept, help in evaluating the outcomes (see Chapter 6), especially if this evaluation involves disclosing sensitive value judgments to others. Conversely, but less frequently, analysis may be limited to evaluating preference for possible outcomes, without explicitly addressing how likely they are.

Example. The U.S. Nuclear Regulatory Commission had us (DSC) construct an Index of Hazards for Radioactive Emissions, which only, for example, compared the social "disutility" of different risk criteria, such as infertility and mortality rates. ◆

8.7.3 Complexity vs. Completeness

It is sometimes taken for granted by decision scientists that subject to cost, it is always advantageous to elaborate models, say by substituting modeling for direct judgmental inputs. This belief only makes sense, however, if the inputs called for by the modeling are "better" than the direct judgment they replace, which is often not so. An appropriate model does not have to be *complex*. Paradoxically, the very proliferation of input judgments that a complex model requires may increase the danger that important judgments are overlooked.

Example. Take the measurement of ecological quality in the DA of a proposed environmental protection initiative. If an overall quality measure is disaggregated into a list of particular ecological dimensions, such as acreage of untouched forest and an index of water pollution, a multitude of less prominent effects may "slip between the cracks." The net effect is likely to be (and often is) to undervalue intangible outcomes of environmental regulation while leaving intact more readily measured cost outcomes, thus tipping the scales against regulation (see Appendix 9A). ◆

It is often fine for the model structure to be simple and to leave *implicit* much that *could have been* be modeled. This simplicity often makes the model more *complete*, as in the example above. A complete model is one that covers, at least implicitly, all considerations relevant to D. An incomplete model omits significant considerations, even if those it does consider are modeled in complex detail.

I generally favor completeness over complexity, where they compete, which usually means creating *coarse* models that are *judgment intensive* rather than *complex* models that are *structure intensive* (see Section 4.6.1). However, the downside of coarse models is that the inputs tend to be more challenging.

8.7.4 Sufficient Models

An extreme case of coarse modeling is where the only possibilities modeled are criterion scores themselves. If the criteria are exhaustive, such a model is complete, in that it is *sufficient* to determine choice.

Example. Chess player D is deciding whether to sacrifice her queen with a view to maximize her probability of winning. D could consider all possible game sequences for either option, with probabilities, each leading to D winning, losing, or drawing, from which overall probabilities of winning could be computed for each option. Such a complex model may be the basis for some chess-playing software, and some human players do something similar. On the other hand, an extreme *sufficient summary* model would be for D to assess the winning probabilities directly and sacrifice the queen if the probability of winning is judged higher.

Although just as complete (sufficient) as a complex model that includes many *contributors* to criterion scores, the coarsest model requires only two judgments (e.g., probabilities of winning with and without queen sacrifice). However, these two judgments will be far more challenging and, indeed, D may not have benefited much from the "divide-and-conquer" feature of DA. A more promising model of intermediate complexity might be to for D to assess the probability of capturing the opponent's queen if she sacrifices her own queen and then the probability of winning *if* the queen is captured, etc. Many chess players introduce (informally) *contributors*, such as the value of pieces captured, as another intermediate strategy. ♦

8.8 TAKING ACCOUNT OF HUMAN FACTORS

The aider's aim is *prescriptive*—to help determine what a decider *should* do. But to determine effectively what, if any, decision aid to offer D, the aider needs some *descriptive* understanding of D's mental processes and capabilities. Since the early 1950s (when the roots of prescriptive decision analysis were also being established), there has been a strong and growing line of academic research directed at describing human decision processes (Hogarth, 1987; Kahneman et al., 1982; Janis and Mann, 1977; Kahneman and Tversky, 2000). It has addressed several issues relevant to decision aiding.

8.8.1 Room for Improvement in Current Decision Making

As noted before, if D is fortunate enough to make informal decisions that are already ideally rational, prescriptions are the same as descriptions. For most of us, however, how we *should* decide differs from how we *do* decide. Were this not so, we would not need decision analysis to enhance our decision making (and I might be unemployed!). Informal appraisal of the world around us, plus some anecdotal evidence, suggests to me that there is much room for improvement in private and professional decisions. A difficulty in doing convincing research on decision quality is that we can never know for sure whether D would have been better or worse off had s/he taken a different action.[7]

---

[7]Promising but still inconclusive methods for monitoring decision quality are being explored (Brown, 1994).

8.8.2 Specific Defects in Human Judgment

Evaluating uncertainty assessment in decision making is easier than evaluating decision quality as a whole since we have observation and statistical inference rules to help us. The earliest work, spearheaded by experimental psychologist Ward Edwards, focused on apparent defects in how people draw inferences from evidence (Edwards, 1954). He found that subjects tended to pay too little attention to new evidence and fail to update their assessments enough, at least in highly structured laboratory experiments.

Mysteriously, other experiments involving the assessment of verifiable events (such as the population of Venezuela) found the opposite: People had too much confidence in their estimates.[8] Later work, notably by Tversky and Kahneman (2000) has identified many other types of mistakes (or at least conflicts with conventional interpretations of rationality). Ongoing research in this area is regularly reported in journals and at scientific conferences.[9]

My consistent experience is that almost all of us have great difficulty making sound *hypothetical* judgments, whether of fact or preference. This greatly impairs the usefulness of decision tools that rely on such judgments. Some, like a method for inferring truth from evidence (*assessment updating* introduced in Chapter 10), requires an assessor to answer awkward questions like, "If you happened to know that the truth were A, how surprised would you be to see this evidence?" Similarly, we have great trouble predicting how happy we would be (i.e., our utility) if some unexpected event were to occur (Carlin 2005).

8.9 MULTIPLE APPROACHES: PLURAL EVALUATION

In my considered opinion, as I have noted, the major flaw in much DA practice, responsible for many results that fail to outperform D's unaided judgment, is that decision models are used that do not take into account much valuable knowledge that D has access to and already uses implicitly. The often simple, but rarely used, device of *plural evaluation* is usually sufficient to avoid the most harmful failures.

Plural evaluation consists of trying several models or other approaches to evaluating a choice or assessing an uncertain quantity and combining any inconsistent results by either reconciling them (i.e., adjusting inputs so that outputs

---

[8]My own interpretation of the apparent discrepancy is that the first conservative finding is an artifact of the laboratory setting and probably should be discounted. People are not very good at unfamiliar tasks such as inference from random drawings from an urn (contrasted with assessing reality, with which they are more familiar).

[9]Main journals: *Organization Behavior and Human Decision Processes; Journal of Behavioral Decision Making*. Main professional societies: Society for Judgment and Decision Making; European Association for Decision Making.

coincide) or pooling them (i.e., averaging outputs in a way that takes relative confidence into account). Plural evaluation guards against serious, sometimes fatal flaws in analysis, by providing "defense in depth." Put another way, "Two half-baked approaches may be better than one $\frac{3}{4}$-baked approach." It is an analytic form of "not putting all your eggs in one basket" (Brown and Lindley, 1978), and applies equally well to formal and informal evaluations. I have found the practice absolutely invaluable, especially in catching gross errors in DA or other decision aid.

An essential and normally first step in plural evaluation is to check the findings of the first modeling approach attempted against D's unaided judgment. If the two evaluations differ, explore how the model and/or the judgment might be at fault.

I recommend approaching any major choice in at least three ways (e.g., models at different levels of disaggregation, not necessarily DA). The main exception is when the aider's time and budget are very limited, and the most promising approach needs all available resources to produce anything of value or the additional effort on a specific approach becomes increasingly valuable. As with the first paired comparison, combine conflicting findings (see Section 8.9.5).

8.9.1 Types of Single-Pass Evaluation

All of the alternative single-pass evaluations of a target judgment that constitute one plural evaluation would produce the same conclusion *if* the judger (e.g., D) were *logically coherent*.[10] However, as flawed humans, we never are fully coherent, which is why we turn to DA, etc., to help us. Candidate single-pass evaluations to be combined in a plural evaluation of a choice or judgment include:

- D's intuitive judgment
- One or more DA models (e.g., ICE and APU)
- Expert opinion
- Available independent studies of the issue (e.g., by Congressional Research Service on legislative proposals)
- Record of similar precedents (adjusted for any judged differences from this decision situation)
- Non-DA evaluations (e.g., "lateral thinking")
- Conventional wisdom on the topic

---

[10]Inputs to each single model should implicitly take into account the totality of the judger's knowledge. For example, certain equivalents in an ICE multicriteria model would be consistent with the explicit probabilities in an average utility model of the same choice. A judger would come up with the same "posterior" probabilities whether s/he assessed them directly or indirectly via "prior" and "likelihood" assessments (Raiffa and Schlaifer, 1962).

8.9.2 Plural Evaluation of Tex Career Choice

The following hypothetical alternative evaluations of the Tex career choice were previously presented:

- Unaided evaluation (Chapter 3) → **business** wins
- Multicriteria ICE model (Figure 6.3A) → **academia** wins, with 51 (vs. business 32)
- Average utility with binary outcomes (Figure 7.3) → **academia** wins, with 37 (vs. business 29.5)
- Average utility with multiple outcomes (Figure 7.4) → **academia** wins, with 47 (vs. business 31)
- Average utility combined with multiple criteria (Figure 7.7) → **academia** wins, with 41 (vs. business 32.7)

Four of these approaches favor academia and one favors business.[11] Tex considers his confidence in each approach and makes his overall evaluation. He has somewhat more confidence in the direct evaluation (favoring business) than each of the others on its own (favoring academia), but between them they are persuasive. He concludes from this that he favors **academia**, but only very slightly.

8.9.3 Non-DA Approaches

In the example above, Tex could have extended his plural evaluation with non-DA systematic approaches, such as lateral thinking (de Bono, 1970) and the analytic hierarchy process (Saaty, 1978). He could also consult with a career counselor or his best friend. Implicitly, he would weight his confidence in each approach in his final decision. This example illustrates a more general principle. D can consider as many and as diverse approaches as he wishes, including direct intuition and others' advice, provided that confidence in each is taken into account (see Section 8.9.5). It can be shown that confidence in a plural evaluation will usually be greater than in any single-pass assessment (Lindley et al., 1969) (see Figure 8.1).[12]

8.9.4 Multitier Plural Evaluation

Just as with the target evaluation, any *input* to a model, or intermediate calculation, can usefully be evaluated plurally. It is often useful to start DA with a simple *coarse* model that breaks down the original big problem into a few smaller problems. The

---

[11] Absolute numbers do not matter, since utility scales may differ comparison of options is what matter.
[12] If the discrepancy between individual distributions is great enough to cast doubt on their originally assessed uncertainty, plural evaluation would actually *increase* uncertainty, but the increase would be appropriate. If some of the single-pass evaluations share possible sources of error (as with ICE and the analytic hierarchy process), their role in the combined evaluation would be reduced.

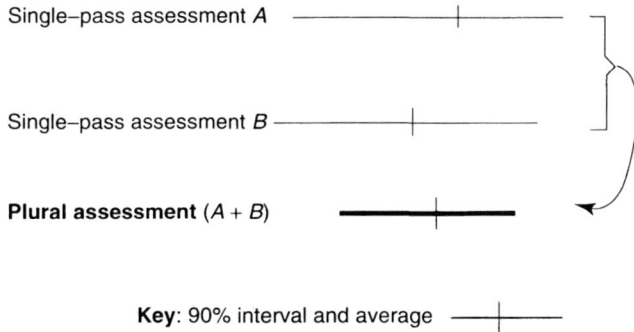

FIGURE 8.1 Plural evaluations usually reduce uncertainty.

initial coarse model may have 10 to 20 inputs (e.g., option evaluations that imply the output.) Each such *input* will initially be elicited from someone's direct judgment, but it can also be derived as the *output* of a subsidiary *feeder* model and/or other method. This is **multitier plural evaluation**.[13]

8.9.5 Combining Single-Pass Evaluations

If single-pass evaluations all point to the same choice, you can be fairly confident in adopting the choice. However, for typically conflicting results, the relative confidence in the single-pass evaluations needs to be taken into account, usually informally. The judger can then reconcile the evaluations by reconsidering the single-pass evaluations in an attempt to bring them into line (Brown and Lindley, 1986).

A less effective combination method, but easier to implement, is to pool plural assessments by averaging them so as to reflect the judger's relative confidence in each. The pooled average estimate will be closer to the single-pass estimate in which s/he has most confidence (see Figure 8.1). Locating the net option evaluation informally between the conflicting individual evaluations, but closest to the one in which you have most confidence, is usually good enough.

8.10 INTEGRATING ANALYSIS INTO THE PERSONAL DECISION PROCESS

The most challenging task of the decision process is to integrate models into D's actual deciding process. Sig Anderson, of DuPont, one of the pioneers of applying

---

[13]Not to be confused with "top-down" modeling, which develops hierarchically but with only one model retained for analysis.

decision analysis, has called this stage "user engineering" and argues persuasively that it should account for 60% of any applied decision analytic effort (personal communication, 1969). It is unfortunately rare for analysts to reserve this much effort for *after* a fully developed and quantified model has been produced. This lack accounts for many failure stories. I make models here as formally simple as possible, for this reason and so that the analyst's effort is not preoccupied with modeling issues that are not substantively related to D's problem.

8.10.1 Head vs. Heart

The decision analysis is not complete until D's intuition or "gut feeling" about the choice and his/her appreciation of all formal analyses are in sync. It will usually take this convergence of "head" and "heart" for D to be prepared to act. It is possible for D, with an aider's help, to digest the formal analysis with enough comfort for his/her intuition to fall into line so that no further integration is needed. However, in my experience it is unusual for D to let his/her intuition be overruled that easily. The action has to "feel right." Remember the old saying: "A man convinced against his will is of the same opinion still."

8.10.2 Sensitivity Analysis

The integration process can be mechanized by *sensitivity analysis*. This consists of systematically changing critical inputs to formal analyses (e.g., of uncertainty, preference, and structure in a DA model) over feasible ranges. Their decision implications are calculated (normally by computer) and compared with the contrasting approach. The most straightforward application of this idea is to determine what, if any, set of formal inputs would reverse the implied choice. For example, if no plausible shift in a particular input (say, a particular probability assessment[14] or value trade-off) would change the choice, there is little to be gained by refining or gathering more information on that input (see Chapter 10). Considering simultaneous changes in several inputs can indicate the most promising directions for gathering new information, but this would require the participation of an experienced aider or consultant.

8.10.3 Consistency with All D's Knowledge

D's final choice of option should ideally take into account everything s/he knows, explicitly and implicitly. An often-useful step to make sure you haven't

---

[14]What Ward Edwards (1954) has called the "flat optimum" phenomenon is the common observation that moderate changes in probability have little effect on the utility of choices based on them (i.e., the choice is insensitive to probabilities regardless of how other inputs may change, usually a difficult condition to meet).

overlooked anything important is a somewhat perverse "thought experiment."[15] Imagine that you learn that someone whose judgment you trust advises *against* the conclusion you are coming to, but you haven't been told on what grounds. You can try then to think what those grounds might be. This exercise may uncover considerations, lurking at the back of your mind, which had previously escaped your attention.

8.11 OTHER STRATEGY ISSUES

8.11.1 Effort on Knowledge vs. Analysis?

This book concerns itself almost exclusively with helping D decide in the light of *knowledge s/he already has*. It does not address directly what will often be a more pressing issue: whether to focus D's attention on getting more knowledge about the issue or on thinking harder about existing knowledge. This choice itself calls for analysis, but normally it is brief and informal. D asks which activity *could* change his/her choice more, and with what benefit; and how much progress in each direction can actually be done. The subtle logic of the value of information is discussed briefly in Chapter 10.

Example. In a joint U.S.–Russian study to compare quantitative and verbal decision analysis methods, I was seeking a decision issue of shared concern on which to test both methods in practice (Brown et al., 1997). We looked hard at a hot issue in the 1990s: What should the international community do about suspected contamination of Arctic waters from Russian nuclear waste? We abandoned that case study when it became clear that there was no perplexing choice to be made before more had been learned about threat. That information was several years off. There were still decisions to be made—on what research to do—but they were fairly obvious, so not a good case for our comparative study. (Instead, we agreed to try out DA methods on another Russian and an American decision, both having to do with fossil fuel transportation.) ♦

In practice, the various steps of an aiding strategy interact. Selecting what decision issue to analyze (Section 8.3) should take into account what can most effectively be analyzed.

8.11.2 How Much Analysis to Do?

How extensive the analysis, if any, should be depends on a judgment (usually informal) about whether the extra analytic burden is justified by the value of any improved analysis. That judgment in turn is driven by the "cost" of making a mistake with and without the added analysis (Watson and Brown, 1978).

---

[15]Suggested by psychologist Marvin Cohen.

D's Expertise Beware of doing more analysis than D can comfortably absorb into his/her decision process or than D or the aider can apply effectively. Otherwise, preoccupation with getting the technical mechanics right may distract you from "keeping your eye on the ball" (i.e., thinking thoroughly about all the relevant considerations). Analogously, an actor can focus on playing a part realistically only if he has got the words mastered "rotten perfect," as they say. Rely only on those analytic tools that you can get down rotten perfect.

Decision Situation Features of a decision situation that favor significant analytic effort include:

- Perplexing choice
- High stakes (i.e., cost of a mistake)
- Lack of urgency
- Multiple sources of input
- Controversy
- Need for after-the-fact justification
- Recurrence of the problem

I once began to codify my consulting experience on this issue and to develop general guidelines for the aider by mapping specific analytic variants onto decision situations, characterized by the features listed above. However, it proved too cumbersome a task to justify the enormous effort it would take to do fruitfully (Brown and Ulvila, 1976).

The potential of DA or any other decision tool may not be realized: for example, because it is too burdensome or too difficult to do right. The tool may introduce mismeasurement and psychological resistance. Moreover, there may be structural errors in the model (sometimes the result of assumptions simplified deliberately to make the tool easier to use). Essential parts of the thinking may fail to be modeled at all.

8.11.3 Appraising the Quality of a Decision Tool

Determining how successful a decision tool is or promises to be requires passing two basic tests (not necessarily in order):

Internal Checks With internal checking, you look only at what is within the analysis being validated. Is it logically coherent (e.g., options mutually exclusive, consistent scaling)? Does it meet scientific tests? Is the argument plausible? Does it take into account the technical state of the art? Is there plausible correspondence between the model and the choice to be aided?[16] Does the model *appear to be* a logical equivalent for the choice? Does it conform to current behavioral theory? Basically, these are the checks that the technical reviewer of a paper, study, or proposal normally

---

[16]Or is that nonequivalence properly treated, as in a bounding model?

performs, or is in a position to perform. *Internal* checks are often the only type of validation that is done, and this motivates the aider to attend only to developing a theoretically sound tool that will pass this test.

External (Reality) Checks Reality checking is concerned with assuring that the model, as quantified, matches the real world, in the light of *empirical* observation and testing. This step is critical, for the model to be useful, but it is often neglected. With reality checking, you observe, as best you can, the tool's real-world performance. Does it appear to work in practice? Is it consistent with other ways of looking at the same problem? Do the findings conform to common sense, or are they plausible to D himself and to well-informed others? If the model diverges from conventional wisdom, or from others' attempts at the same problem, or from historical precedent, is it clear why?

Example. Weather forecasters commonly forecast rain with a probability derived *solely* from a scientific model (e.g., "The probability of rain today is 70%"). A simple reality check is to look outside and see if it actually is raining—and it often is, even when the announced probability is well below 100%. (Check for yourself sometime.) Forecasters could perform the same reality check and adjust their forecasts in such a case to 100%, and/or they could use the observation as an indicator of the reliability of the forecasting tool (model). I suspect they are remiss and do neither. ♦

Satisfying the internal checks is relatively straightforward to learn, to assure, and to confirm. However, satisfying the reality checks is vital to tool usefulness and is exceedingly difficult to assure.[17] Without reality checks, DA is in danger of being reduced to an intellectual game, disconnected from life.[18]

This failure is unfortunately only too common, for technical and motivational reasons (Brown, in press). The temptation for technicians or teachers is to do what they can do demonstrably well and get professional credit for (i.e., internal checking) rather than reality checking (e.g., by trial and error), which is also important. A pedagogical surrogate is for students, singly or in groups, to address live choices, their own or those of others, and determine, as best as they and the instructor can, whether the decider was really helped, after the fact. (See the term project in Chapter 12.)

8.11.5 A Musical Analogy Revisited

Making a good decision is a bit like making appealing music. There are different ways to do so, and the best way depends on the time and skill of D and/or the aider. As an individual, you may be able to hum a decent tune; that is like our intuitive

---

[17]Researchers are seeking a more objective way of reality checking, which does not depend entirely on the user's subjective appraisal. This technique involves hindsight monitoring, measuring the quality of resulting decisions empirically, but it still falls well short of usable methodology (Brown, 1994).
[18]I tried unsuccessfully to interest Yeltsin's environmental advisor, Yablokov, in using DA. He was very familiar with Russian DA efforts, but dismissed them as "dyetskiye igry"—children's games.

day-to-day deciding. To sound better, you can learn a musical instrument. A violin could eventually bring you great pleasure, but it may take years before you improve on humming. So it is with decision modeling. There is always a hierarchy of ever more ambitious models, which *if done right* could result in significant improvements. Until you are really proficient, ambitious models risk major blunders, and you would do better to stick with intuition or use the tools cautiously with the help of a professional decision aider.

The minimal decision analysis tools presented here are like the mouth organ, because too many of us don't have the time (or talent) to get past a screechy violin. In a few hours you can master basic mouth organ technique and can concentrate quite soon on sounding quite good. I hope these decision tools are simple enough that you can learn the mechanics and then focus on the strategy of using them, which is where the real challenge lies.

The music analogy falls short in an important respect. There is enough commonality among people's musical requirements that a given performance can satisfy a large number of people without having to pay much attention to individual differences in the audience. (A Beatles performance appealed to most of us.) I believe this homogeneity is very uncommon in decision aiding in general and in the decision analysis case in particular. Each situation has enough distinct features, by way of decider, problem, and setting, that the tool must be customized.

In the past, I and others have ignored that rule at our peril. As noted earlier, I once attempted to develop a general-purpose computerized tool that would specify for EPA the safety measures to be taken in various toxicity tests. It was never used because each case presented quite different features we had not anticipated. Most attempts I know of to produce anything like universal decision-aiding procedures, especially as software, have disappointed. (To be sure, some of that disappointment is due simply to technical immaturity of the state of the art. The passage of time will surely cure that.)

ASSIGNMENTS

Prepare for Discussion After Reading

Rationality and Emotion

1. "Personal decision analysis provides a way to reduce the role of emotions in choice and thus make it more rational." Discuss.

Prepare for Later Discussion or Submission

2. Mary is considering spending $1000 to store the umbilical blood of her newborn, and then $200 per year for the 1/1000 to 1/200,000 chance event that the baby may need it in a life-threatening situation. How would you help her to decide?

APPENDIX 8A

INFLUENCE SKETCHES

An influence sketch helps identify contributors and settings that may have a significant effect on the utility of options. The evaluation of options may involve considering numerous possibilities intervening between commitment to an option and its ultimate utility to the decider. An influence sketch represents these graphically. Essentially, influence sketches draw attention to critical developments, events, and subsequent choices which may influence evaluation of the target choice and the interconnection between them. In particular, they show what influences what, within the overall influence of target choice on objectives (see Figure 8A.1*a*).

More ambitious *influence diagrams* have been developed and used as computational frameworks to evaluate options, much as decision trees do, but more compactly (Oliver and Smith, 1990). For the purpose of this book, the role of influence sketches is purely to organize thinking on considerations important to comparing options, preparatory to specifying a much simpler quantitative model to be solved. Although the logic of the sketch (what influences what) needs to be sound, the definitions can be looser than in influence diagrams, provided that any that are used in a *quantitative* model are *then* quite rigorously specified.

8A.1 Diagrammatic Conventions

The basic ordering principle is: Choices, possibilities, and criteria are linked by arrows, according to what possibilities causally influence what other possibilities and in what sequence. There are no arrows leading into an initial choice box, just as there are no arrows leading out of the final utility oval (see Figure 8A.1*b*).

Choices and Possibilities A rectangle is D's immediate choice. Rectangles with rounded corners are D's options subsequent to the target choice. Ovals are uncertain possibilities. Ovals with double outlines are criteria (usually also uncertain). Circles are *setting* possibilities that are not themselves affected by options, but influence their impact on other possibilities. Possibilities are in lowercase letters; D's choices are in capitals.

Criteria can influence each other (e.g., "wealth" can influence "quality of life"), although it may be convenient, if possible, to define criteria so as not to affect preference for each other, so the problem of redundancy is avoided (e.g., as "wealth" and "noneconomic quality of life"). Each shape or *box* (rectangle, circle, or oval) represents an *issue*, not its resolution (e.g., choices, not options within a choice; the set of possibilities, not any specific possibility). The box corresponds to a question, not an answer: this is underscored by a question mark in the box. (Possible answers can be noted in parentheses in the box.)

Influences Arrows show causal influence and sequence. The direction of arrows is from cause to effect, which is usually easiest to assess (e.g., the bottom arrow from

(a) Basic function: to show influence of options on utility

(b) Function of detail: to show key influencing factors

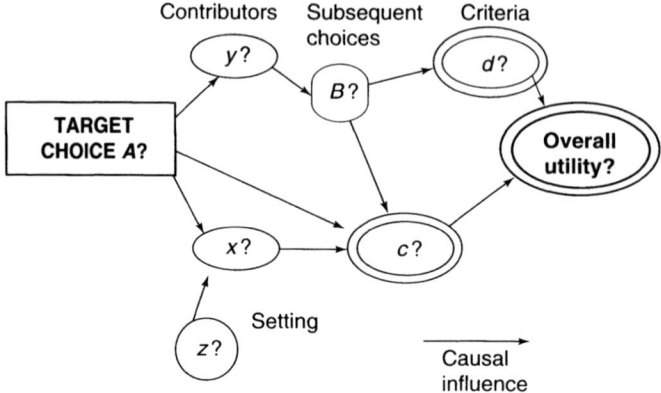

FIGURE 8A.1 Essence of influence sketches.

the target choice box in Figure 8A.1b says: "Whether D takes option A or not[19] influences whether or not x happens"). The figure also says:

- "Whether x happens is also influenced by whether setting possibility z occurs."
- "After D learns about contributor y, he decides on B."

Basically, boxes and arrows are ordered according to "What happens or is learnt next?" Choices may be represented as sequential or parallel, depending on whether or not, respectively, the choice is made after the preceding choice is made or the possibility is learned.[20] A rounded box immediately after the target choice box (without an intervening oval) may correspond to an *implementing choice* (i.e., the specific variant of the target option selected).

Tex Example. Figure 8A.2 shows an influence sketch representing evaluation of Tex's career choice. It says, for example: "Quality of life is partly determined by the weather, and that in turn is influenced by whether Tex emigrates in pursuit of whichever career

---

[19]For convenience of exposition, issues are treated as binary.
[20]The timing of a possibility being realized and of D learning of it needs careful distinguishing when constructing a precise choice model, such as a *decision tree*.

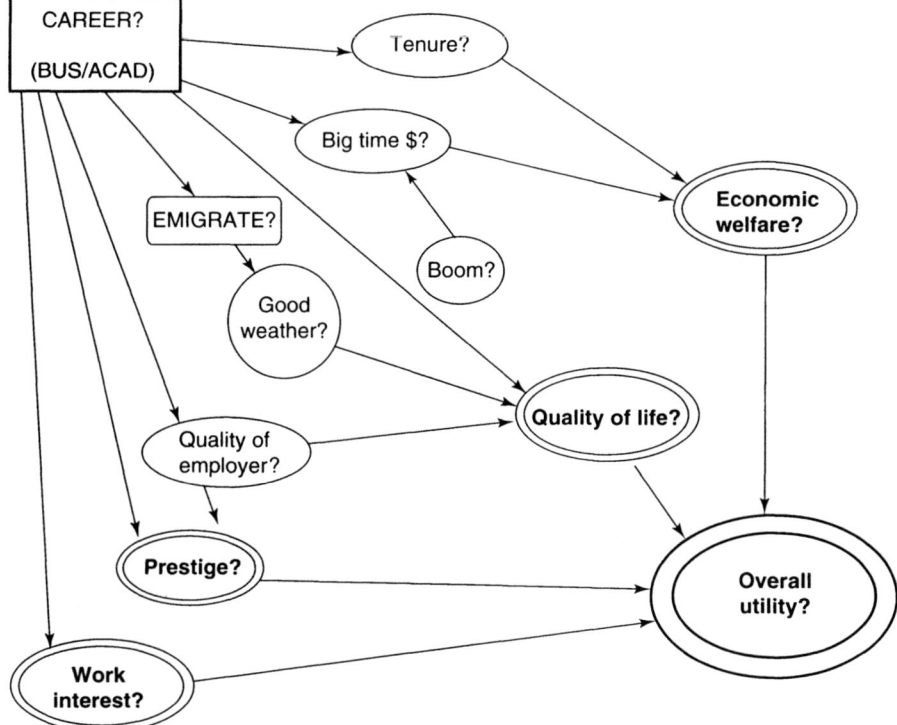

FIGURE 8A.2 Influence sketch for Tex's career choice.

direction he chooses" and "Whether Tex gets tenure depends on whether he goes into academia (no chance, presumably, otherwise)."

Note that there is an arrow that goes directly from the target choice to the quality of life criterion. This means that career affects quality of life in certain ways regardless of weather or employer [e.g., Tex might value the facilities of academia (e.g., library, athletics) whatever the specific scenario]. A "facilities" box could have been put into the sketch explicitly, but the direct arrow implicitly lumps facilities in with any other contributors. ♦

8A.2 Role of Influence Sketches

Influence sketches are an important graphical tool to visualize the phenomena to be modeled, or alternatively, to bear in mind as elements when making an *informal* assessment. Since they are only jogs to the imagination, they do not need to meet the same tests of precision and unambiguity of quantified *influence diagrams*.

It is purely a matter of analytic choice how much detail goes into an influence sketch. *Contributor* ovals can be inserted at will if they help clarify what is going on in an influence link without cluttering the sketch. (e.g., an oval for "autonomy at work?" in the Tex example could be interpolated between "CAREER?" and "Work interest?" at the left of Figure 8A.2). The direct arrow from CAREER? to Work interest? would remain if work interest were also influenced by criterion scores of the career choice other than autonomy.

ASSIGNMENT

Prepare for Discussion After Reading

1. Develop an influence sketch of a binary career choice that you are to make in the near future. Include about three contributors or subsequent choices and about three criteria. Clarify briefly, as needed, what you mean by all box labels. Indicate, without discussion, what option you would favor if you had to choose now.

Chapter 9

Aiding the Professional Decider

The core decision skills presented so far are not specific to any particular decision mode. Developing these skills has been done primarily in the context of private and civic decisions, to which students can most immediately relate. However, the greatest payoff for many of you for having mastered this material will come in the form of enhanced professional decision skills when you are in a job (or on the job market). The private examples will have served primarily as a prelude to applying decision skills to the more complex analysis of major professional choices.

In this chapter we discuss issues of professional decisions that distinguish them from private decisions, generally by adding a layer of complexity. The chapter also distinguishes professional decisions made by an *institution executive*, such as a company manager, from those by a *sole practitioner* in private practice, such as a doctor or accountant.

9.1 DISTINCTIVE FEATURES OF PROFESSIONAL DECISION AIDING

9.1.1 Private vs. Professional Decisions

What mainly distinguishes professional from private decisions is that they are on a much larger scale and involve more than one *interested party*. Private decisions do not often have stakes high enough to justify the effort and expertise of extensive quantitative modeling. Moreover, the private decider usually has no one else to satisfy (although others' interests may contribute to D's welfare), whereas the professional may have many *constituents* (i.e., interested parties on whose behalf s/he is expected to act).

Rational Choice and Judgment: Decision Analysis for the Decider, by Rex Brown
Copyright © 2005 John Wiley & Sons, Inc.

Among professional decisions those of *sole practitioners* have much in common with those of managers and other *institutional executives*. In fact, the distinction blurs when large companies and individuals offer the same services to an institutional market. The client may be an individual, organization, or community. For example, an accountant may work for a private taxpayer or for a company. In both cases, at least two parties are involved, with possibly conflicting interests: D and D's employer/client. A really "professional" professional would have only his/her client's interest at heart, but I have not found that always to be the case. A business auditor is supposedly serving (i.e., protecting) the general public, but s/he may have a financial interest in keeping the business s/he is auditing happy (as with Arthur Anderson in the notorious Enron case of 2001). Again, a doctor may take more costly diagnostic tests than the patient really needs, for fear of malpractice suits if she does not.

Example. A respected surgeon I know told me he was against the use of decision analysis for therapeutic choices. If the tool explicitly evaluated whether having surgery served the patient's interests best, he (the surgeon) said candidly that it could cost him money: if it is not clear whether surgery is indicated, he can use his discretion in favor of surgery that profits himself. ♦

9.1.2 Sole Practitioner

The scale of operation that decisions affect is usually much smaller for the *practitioner* than for the *executive*. Thus, the aiding resources for extensive and specialized modeling and assessment techniques are less justified or available to the practitioner. In this respect, the latter's needs will be closer to those of the private decider.

A practitioner may be more inclined to behave ethically toward society because s/he is not distracted by as many other interests and *parties*. For example, if the practitioner happens to be also the aider, only her own interests and those of her client would distract her from feeling responsibility toward the broader society.

Example. In Chapter 2 I discussed my hip replacement decision, where a surgeon's advice to delay surgery was reversed by my own decision analysis. A significant consideration in my decision to have the operation was that it was free to me (the cost was covered by insurance). It dawned on me later that the public-spirited surgeon might originally have taken the $15,000 cost into account (although it was neither his money nor mine). I suppose this cost should have tipped my decision *against* the replacement had I been more socially responsible and seen the cost as a scarce resource that could be used to benefit a more deserving (i.e., more serious) case than mine. ♦

9.1.3 Institution Executive

Most users of this book are probably training to be *institution executives*, whose needs differ from both *sole practitioners* and *private* individuals. The remainder of this chapter is addressed particularly to the actual or potential institution executive. His/her special circumstances have to do largely with whose interests D has to take into account and the nature of the decision aid that D draws upon. For example:

- The primary constituency whose interest D is supposed to serve, the employer, is an *organization*, whose "interests" are less clear than those of an individual. The employing organization itself has higher-order constituencies as well: A corporation has a set of shareholders; a government agency has society and possibly legislators. Within one organization, D may also have a hierarchy of bosses.
- Within or without the organization, D may have decision aid supplied by a specialist *aider*. How the aid is provided has to fit into an organizational structure, often with a *middleman* intervening between D and aider.
- The decisions D has to make have high stakes, calling for aid on a large scale.

An organization can be thought of as an actor performing **outside** acts (such as going bankrupt), but we are directly concerned with the **inside** acts that some individual executive performs, which may *produce* an *outside* act. (**Organizational decision analysis** analyzes *outside* organizational acts as if the organization were the decider, but our concern is with *personal* DA of *inside* acts.)

9.2 FACTORS AFFECTING CHOICE OF AIDING TOOL

9.2.1 Scale of Analytic Effort

As noted, a major difference in decision aiding between professional (especially institutional) and private decisions is that the stakes (i.e., cost of a subrational decision) are higher. The private D will rarely have decisions where the cost of an error is more than, say, $100k; the professional's errors can cost in the billions of dollars. [It has been argued that the Department of Energy has wasted some $5B over 20 years in deciding where to put nuclear waste (Keeney, 1987).]

Decision analyst Ron Howard has suggested that 2% of the financial stakes of a choice should be devoted to analyzing what that choice should be. On this basis, a personal decision where the difference between best and worst criterion scores is $1000 would merit decision analysis effort only to a value of $20—less than an hour of D's time. That would be barely enough to do a simple plus–minus tally or to reflect informally along the lines of Chapter 3, although having worked through the more time-consuming tools presented here should certainly enhance the quality of D's informal reflection.

9.2.2 Level of Expertise

With no more than the skills you acquire in this course, you can certainly expect to make sounder *informal* professional decisions, drawing on qualitative structuring approaches such as *influence sketches* (see Appendix 8A). However, more advanced decision-aiding skills than you may pick up here are essential to make explicit use of quantitative models. Professional decision analysis draws on the same skills as private decision analysis but calls for additional expertise. This expertise may be available through your own further training, including learning "on the job" or by engaging specialized help from within or outside the organization. On the other hand, you should be well able, as staff for senior deciders, to specify, oversee, and interpret the work of specialist analysts.

9.2.3 Division of Labor Among Inputs

In an institution, the judgments called for in implementing DA may come from different sources (e.g., technical vs. value judgments). For example, in corporate decisions, the human resources manager might assess the impact of an option on "worker morale," and the company president might evaluate the importance of worker morale. Even in personal decisions there may be this kind of division of labor. In the baby delivery decision (see the Prolog), D provided her own importance judgments, but the obstetrician assessed the medical outcome of her options.

This variety of judgment sources makes it particularly important that there be precise interface between sources and model input, especially where parties to a decision must communicate with or persuade each other. In ICE analysis (see Chapter 6), for example, defining scales is especially important in institutional settings. In particular, the same *anchor points* for a rating scale must be used both in determining importance weights and in assessing criterion scores.

In business, it is not uncommon for D (e.g., company president) to combine all the necessary expertise and judgment in his/her own head, having perhaps dealt with comparable decisions for many years. In government, by contrast, decision authority is often diffusely shared among several people who are typically inexperienced enough in the subject matter of the decision to require input from still other sources. DA permits a comprehensive analysis to be broken down into separable inputs, from different sources, which can be put back together soundly.

However, D will always want to judge the "big picture" directly; for example, through a *coarse* DA model, whose inputs correspond to separable informant judgments or to the output of *feeder* models (see Chapter 10).

9.2.4 Computation

In general, the models and procedures presented here are structurally simple enough that nothing more than a calculator is needed to run the numbers. However, if the computations are complex or repetitive (e.g., in *sensitivity analysis*), the operation can usefully be computerized. Even here, the computerization can be customized using simple general-purpose languages (such as Microsoft's Excel spreadsheet program).[1]

---

[1] As was done by one of the decision analysts in the regulatory case study in Appendix 9A.

There are many decision analysis software packages on the market, promoted vigorously by their vendors (or decision analysts associated with them). Until recently, these tended to be cumbersome and rigid to use, but the state of the art has been evolving rapidly. A periodically updated survey of more than two dozen packages has been available at *http://www.lionhrtpub.com/orms/ORMS-archive.html*. It indicates the scope of the software and how to obtain it, but without much user guidance. In any case it is largely oriented toward more complex studies.

Some popular programs available at the time of writing, which have been evolving over a number of years, are:

- HIVIEW for importance-weighted criterion score analysis ("additive multiattribute utility"): offered by LSE Enterprise, London (Barclay, 1986)
- DATA (Decision Analysis by Tree Age): general purpose software, including sensitivity analysis, offered by Tree Age Inc. (*http://www.treeage.com*)
- Decision programming language (DPL): similar to, but somewhat more complex than, DATA, offered by Applied Decision Analysis, Menlo Park, California (*http://www.adainc.com/software*)
- SUPERTREE: offered by SmartOrg, Inc., Menlo Park, California

There are some serious pitfalls for D (or aider) to guard against. However streamlined and technically sophisticated the software, it is usually difficult to use efficiently enough to take it in your stride and to assure that it fits the problem at hand. You risk diverting precious time, effort, and attention from getting the model(s) right. (This is essentially the same argument as that for keeping math to the bare minimum.) A related pitfall is to force-fit the analysis to the software ("To the man with a hammer, everything is a nail"). Above all, beware of proceeding to "programming" before all critical modeling problems have been resolved (e.g., scale definition; see Chapter 5).

9.3 INSTITUTION AS INTERESTED PARTY

Unlike *private* and most *practitioner* decisions, *executive* decisions usually have at least one *organization* as a *constituency* to be served—D's employer and possibly a hierarchy of departments in between. This introduces complications in decision aiding not shared with private Ds, who only have to satisfy themselves. (Professional Ds also have themselves to satisfy, but supposedly in a subsidiary role.[2]) A government executive has an additional nonindividual to serve—whomever is being governed, society, or some community within it.

---

[2] A related issue that we do not address here is whether the institution itself can be treated as a decider, or in Graham Allison's (1971) terms, a "rational unitary actor." For our purposes, only the executive is the decider, although she may cause the institution to take "outside action" (e.g., buying equipment).

Example. A senior regulator at the NRC (Nuclear Regulatory Commission) was responsible for shutting down reactors that he judged presented an unacceptable risk of accident. His constituencies included:

- The U.S. Congress (representing the safety concerns of U.S. society), which had legislated that more than a 1/1,000,000 yearly probability of a fatality within 50 miles of a reactor was unacceptable.
- The local communities at risk, which, paradoxically, tended to put a higher value on the economic benefit of local nuclear industry than on avoiding accident risk[3] [see Brown and Ulvila (1988)].
- The agency, NRC, which had a long-term interest in maintaining a strong regulatory regime, but not one so onerous as to put the nuclear industry and therefore itself out of business.
- D himself, who has a shorter-term interest in avoiding the bureaucratic "hullabaloo" of an accident (even if it has negligible health effects).

As a result, we presented D with alternative standards of acceptable risk implied to use in decision analysis. The standards differed by a factor of 100, implying quite different regulatory decisions. (It was D's responsibility to resolve which standard would dominate.) ♦

9.3.1 The "Utility" of a Nonhuman Constituency

What, if anything, does it mean for D to serve his/her employer's or country's "interests"? Does the employer or country have a *utility* that D may seek to advance, that can usefully be characterized? Where the primary goal is measurable, such as in a business making money, the meaning of *utility* can be made fairly clear (e.g., share price, net earnings).

However, virtually any organization or community can also be considered to have other "interests" to be advanced[4] (i.e., there is some other sense in which some prospects can be considered "desirable" to them). We take this for granted in such familiar statements as: "England is better off under prime minister Blair than under Thatcher," "How can we help Bosnia?", or "What's best for General Motors is best for the country." It is also implied by statements we make about institutional "rationality."

---

[3]Unlike the state governments in which the community and reactor were located, which possibly saw a cost-free opportunity for political grandstanding.
[4]We can treat almost any entity that takes action as purposive (i.e., having "interests" that it pursues). When we say "Our cat seems less happy since we got a dog," or "do what's best for the cat," or "foxes are cunning," we are imputing some kind of utility to the animal. We have diagnostic evidence for the rationality of animals: chimps fish bugs out of a hole with a stick; a dog knows to scratch on the door to be let in, whereas its "stupid" brother doesn't and is consistently left out miserable in the rain; a cat is observed to open doors by jumping on the handle. We don't need to impute conscious cognitive processes: The "rationality" of ants may be programmed genetically. Human organizations may act more foolishly than an ant colony.

For example, "Microsoft is one smart company," "Russia's economic policy is misguided," or "Netscape has been making a lot of costly blunders."

To be sure, we might have trouble producing an uncontroversial interpretation of utility for an organization. However, even personal human utility is surrounded by definitional controversy, and that hasn't stopped us from developing "utility-maximizing" tools. Decision theorist Amos Tversky once said to me: "You don't have to wait for the foundations to be completed before you start work on the roof." My object in this book is to help you keep out some of the "rain" right away, relying on someone else to firm up the foundations later in a way that will keep more rain out eventually. Remember: "The Best is the enemy of the Good."

In imputing differing degrees of rationality to nonhuman entities, I am not saying anything about the process whereby rationality is achieved: whether by reflection, intuition, instinct, or relying on good consultants.

9.3.2 Who Represents Society's Interest?

Society, more specifically a nation's public, is a major (supposedly, the sole) constituency of a national government decider (and similarly in local government). But who provides the necessary value judgments (i.e., of social preference)? In theory, the government could determine social values by edict, and we commonly elicit them from senior government executives such as an office head. The values could also be legislated, but that appears to be politically infeasible.

Example. I was charged by an arm of the U.S. Congress to evaluate whether it should require the executive branch (e.g., the President) to justify any action that involved more than $100 million with some logical rationale (such as decision analysis). I sought the advice of a congressman (who also happened to be an expert in decision analysis) on where that value judgments should come from. Who better, I suggested, than Congress, as the elected representatives of the people, to express their tastes by passing legislation specifying key value trade-offs, such as the value of a human life? He patiently explained that it would be political suicide for any congressperson to support any particular value trade-off, whether $20M or $200k per life. Instead, he said that he could envisage Congress having the National Academy of Sciences produce trade-offs, which Congress could assent to with every show of vote-getting reluctance. ♦

Society's evaluation of utility can also be inferred from its "revealed preference."[5] Congress does pass laws that imply value trade-offs.

Regulatory Example. U.S. government regulation puts a higher monetary value on a life lost through a nuclear accident ($20M according to NRC) than a life lost on the

---

[5]Nobelist A. K. Sen (1985) argues that "Rationality or irrationality as an attribute of the social group implies the imputation to that group of an organic existence apart from that of its components." However, in discussion he concurred with my suggestion that if any group, however "inorganic," acts according to some consistent "revealed preference," it could be treated as "rational" or "subrational."

job ($100k according to the Occupational Safety and Health Administration). This would seem to suggest that government "values" freedom of choice. ♦

9.3.3 Form of Trade-off: Monetary Equivalent

Once the source of social trade-off has been identified, its form has to be specified. Of the alternatives discussed in Chapter 6, we have often found it useful to convert all option effects into monetary equivalents. If an assessment of the net cost–benefit ratio (or other evaluation) of an environmental regulation is required, as in the Clean Air Act case (see Chapter 2), a common measure of costs and benefits is needed in terms of which the difference (net benefit) can be expressed. The measure needs to correspond closely with overall social utility and, if possible, be interpreted readily by the observer. These two requirements may, however, come into conflict.

GDP (gross domestic product) is commonly used by economists, journalists, and others as an indicator of societal progress, and its very familiarity is a strong point in its favor. GDP is a measure of market and other "traded" transactions in which money changes hands. In general, it is probably true that a country whose GDP is going up is doing better economically. However, an increase in GDP may not always signal economic improvement. If goods that previously changed hands "for free" are now paid for in money, GDP will be inflated without a corresponding improvement in social welfare. (A rise in prostitution, for instance, will appear to increase social welfare—if the transactions are recorded.) In evaluating environmental policy, any increase in a traded activity—whether good or bad—will inflate GDP. An increase in pollution will show up as a good thing if it spawns a pollution mitigation industry. A possible remedy might be to ignore any *nonbeneficial* increases in GDP [i.e., increases that do not benefit society (e.g., from economic transactions due to increased pollution)].

The search for an alternative measure, more closely tied to real welfare, runs into the other problem: difficult interpretation. A measure that I and others have toyed with is "equivalent government dollars." That is, any improvement in social circumstances (e.g., reduced pollution) is equated to how much government is (or should be) prepared to spend—if it had to—to achieve the improvement. There are technical problems with this definition, too.[6]

"Equivalent government dollars" (such as GDP) may not be anything that is *actually* affected by the option being evaluated. For example, there may be no actual government savings or costs as a result of the Clean Air Act.[7] This use of a measure that is *not* really affected by the option could be useful if it avoids confusion between real effect (e.g., an option really saves money, or whatever) and an evaluated equivalent. Economists have proposed a gross progress indicator (GPI) that attempts to put an

---

[6]To be an "equivalent substitution," a benefit should correspond to an *increase* (savings) in government dollars, rather than a decrease (i.e., an expense). That concept is difficult to communicate. But this distinction may largely be a nitpick, which can be overlooked, if the option being evaluated has a small value (+ or −) relative to the total government budget.

[7]It is an "unfunded mandate."

explicit value on such things as the state of the environment. Nevertheless, GDP appears to be the prevalent measure used in public discourse, and that in itself is a powerful reason to use it.

9.4 MULTIPLE INVOLVED PARTIES

Executive decisions, especially in government, are particularly subject to involvement of various deciders, constituencies, and other interest groups. Thus, a single choice may call for multiple decision tools or multiple inputs for the same tool, corresponding to different active and interested parties. A government decision may also involve the participation of more than one institution (e.g., executive, legislative, and judicial branches).

9.4.1 Decider vs. Nominal Constituency

A difficult issue in the quest for "better" decisions is "Better for whom?" Deciders will often have a private agenda that conflicts with the interests of the constituencies they are supposed to serve. One avenue for the aider to pursue is to propose to D a "parametric" DA model to which D can input any preference judgments (self-serving or not) keeping the resulting, possibly embarrassing, analysis confidential.

Legislative Example. The U.S. Senate Committee on the Judiciary was deciding whether to recommend a $100M/yr community anticrime bill that would support activities like Neighborhood Watch. Our DA indicated that society's interest would be best served by funding the activity (taking into account the impact on crime and the use of scarce funds). However, as a politician, the committee chairman wanted to be reelected, and the politically influential Association of Chiefs of Police was known to oppose the bill (since it would divert funding away from the criminal justice system, of which they were a part). As aider, I addressed this dilemma by giving the committee a computer model, which allowed them to put in whatever value judgments they chose (e.g., on the relative importance of "electoral security" and crime reduction). I was not privy to the values they decided to put in, but I learned later that they had opposed the bill and that it was defeated. ♦

Reluctance to acknowledge suspect values or preferences is especially strong in controversial decisions in which the DA could be made public.

Example. A congressional agency had me look at the case for legislation that would require the administration to support with systematic analysis any decision involving more than $100M. An ex-EPA administrator (William Ruckelshaus) told me he would "fight it till his dying day. Congress gets to meddle enough already." He was not arguing against systematic (rational) analysis for the *administration* decider (like himself), but against putting this analysis into the hands of adversaries who could put it to political advantage. ♦

Example. A presidential aide directed me not to share my analysis of a strategic export control decision with any senators, who might leak it to interested U.S. companies, where it could be used as a weapon against administration policy. (He seemed to have little problem with the Russians—against whom it was directed—getting it!) ♦

Example. A decision analysis for the state of Louisiana favored the safety measure of "seeding" an impending hurricane (Howard et al., 1972). The governor decided against it, apparently favoring his professional interests over the public good. Although he accepted that seeding would reduce total damage, it seems that he was afraid he would be held responsible for any resulting community damage. (He would not be blamed if he took no action and the greater damage were attributed to "an act of god.") ♦

9.4.2 Distributed Decision Making

It is not uncommon for institutional *outside* decisions (such as setting the price of a company product) to be the result of the participation of several individuals rather than of a sole D. For example, a decision may be modified or approved through a chain of command. The decision can be analyzed from the perspective of any D within it. One particularly successful form of DA is the ***decision conference***,[8] where the top-level decision-making group in an organization is closeted together for several days, with a DA facilitation team iteratively organizing their deliberations within an interactive DA computer framework (Phillips and Phillips, 1993).

9.4.3 DA as Advocacy

There are often situations within and between organizations where one party proposes a position and another "disposes" of it. Subordinates try to sell superiors on buying fancy equipment; government officials try to persuade Congress members to pass legislation; a seller tries to convince a buyer to buy. Often, it is the proposers who commission DA as a tool, not as decision aid, but as advocacy; the disposers are the real deciders. However, in such a relationship, the disposer (decider) may turn the tables, so to speak, and adapt the proposer's DA to evaluate what is proposed—and indeed actively require the proposer to couch the proposal in DA terms, so that it can be second-guessed.

In environmental regulation, the stakes are high, and ill-considered decisions can lead to the misuse of natural resources or the dominance of special interests. Regulatory agencies, where the state is the ultimate decision maker, have to balance arguments from industrial applicants (who tend to think primarily in terms of commercial opportunities), from environmental groups (for whom the preservation of nature is a

---

[8] Introduced by Cam Peterson in the 1970s.

priority), and from other public interests (such as tax revenues), not to speak of bureaucratic and political considerations.

D, the regulator, can *require* the party regulated to make its case in DA terms, so that D can more effectively evaluate and second-guess it. In Appendix 9A we discuss such a situation, where an oil company's *informal* proposal to build a controversial causeway through an arctic waterway to transport oil was translated into a DA model that the regulator could adapt to fit his/her own judgments.

9.4.4 When Decision Aid Is Not Needed

Organization theorist Jim March has observed that an organization often acts more "foolishly" than the least rational executive within it (March and Shapira, 1982).

Military Example. In the context of a submarine time-of-fire decision situation (Brown, 1982), a DA tool was under consideration, motivated by a "top brass" consensus that submarine commanders wait too long to fire their torpedoes. The conclusion of our DA was that a decision aid was *not* needed. Instead, it suggested a change in the Navy reward system for submariners in peacetime exercises, which currently favors targeting accuracy (and hardly penalizes being detected and destroyed!). In this "motivational field," it is only rational for the commander to wait until he knows just where the enemy target is, even if in a real war this could get him killed. ♦

9.5 DECISION-AIDING ORGANIZATIONAL ARRANGEMENTS

Organization designers have to determine how DA is to be provided to Ds within the organization.

9.5.1 The Aider

When a decider in a professional organization wants to use DA explicitly to improve, or to better communicate, some decision, s/he will usually call on the assistance of a decision aider who has skills substantially beyond the scope of this book. Some impediments to usefulness have to do with the orientation of the aider, which may conflict with D's interests.

"Decision analysis and other quantitative aid have great potential to improve the quality and defensibility of many decisions. However, they have not yet always proven useful, and sometimes have even misled the decider. A tool may be logically impeccable, yet have fatal flaws—such as addressing the wrong question, disregarding key knowledge or using unsound input. According to one experienced practitioner, this is often because aider's priorities are not well-aligned with those of the decider. The aider may favor analytic technique over usefulness, tractable over realistic assumptions, well-documented over relevant knowledge.... The root cause appears to be that the aider is subject to pressures that go beyond—and may conflict with—serving the decider. They include educational mind-set, professional standing, mental comfort and even material gain" (Brown, in press).

However technically competent an aider may be, s/he may adopt an analytic strategy at odds with D's interests. This obliges D (e.g., you) to be more intrusive in designing and implementing an analytic strategy than you would otherwise be.

9.5.2 The Middleman

Decision-aiding practice often involves a *middleman* operating between D and aider. The middleman acts on D's behalf to engage and manage a specialized aider and is often seen as the aider's "client" (rather than decider being the client). The middleman may be an individual or group, usually consisting of technical support staff, reporting either to D or to a higher authority in the organization.

Although middlemen certainly have value as convenient buying agents for decision-aiding services, I believe they are almost always a hindrance—sometimes fatal—to the usefulness to D of DA (or any other decision aid) if they intervene between D and the aider in the aiding process itself. This is because the middlemen transmit their priorities and understanding of D's aiding needs to aider (Brown, in press), whereas the decider must have active control of the aiding process if s/he expects to benefit significantly from it.

9.5.3 Fitting Decision Aid to Institution

A serious obstacle in the way of successful implementation of decision analysis is failure to assure that what is offered—and how—takes due account of organizational context. The appropriate decision aid—if any—to be used, and the form it takes in any given case depends on the kind of decision to be made: how high the stakes, how clear the options, how perplexing the comparative evaluation, and so on. The form of aid also depends on the resources available to the analysis: the skills and training of deciders and aiders, sources of knowledge, as well as more obvious limitations on time, money, and equipment.

Certain features of an organizational setting put a premium on different properties of a tool. These, in turn, favor different aiding strategies—including using no aid at all.[9] No hard-and-fast generalizations are possible, since the total determinants of an appropriate decision-aiding strategy (including the characteristics of any given decision problem) are immensely complex. Discussing a few impressionistic cases may, however, illuminate the issues involved.

Businesses (as contrasted with government agencies) commonly vest clear decision authority in managers who can make their decisions as they please and who have demonstrated competence in making them without much input or control from others. The managers are not therefore generally under too much pressure to enhance their decision-making performance. Pressure to perform, especially financially, makes them conscious of DA cost. All of this can reduce demand for DA. On the other hand,

---

[9]For a general approach to matching taxonomies of aids and problem situations, see Brown and Ulvila (1976).

perplexing, high-stakes decisions are also under more pressure to be rational, than in government.[10]

In government, in contrast, it is common for decision authority to be diffusely shared among several people who are typically inexperienced enough in the subject matter of the decision (especially political appointees) to require input from still other sources. This argues for a decision tool, such as DA, that can serve as a comprehensive vehicle for communication. If the issue is also controversial, such that the decision comes under severe public scrutiny, the pressure may be irresistible to make the analysis open to inspection, especially if the motives of the government deciders are challenged.

It is not uncommon for Congress members to urge that major executive branch decisions be supported by something like reviewable decision analysis. Executive branch officials, by the same token, resist it on the grounds that it gives Congress unwonted power to intervene in executive branch affairs (Porter, 1987). The acceptability of a tool depends on who has to be impressed for it to be adopted.

9.6 OTHER EXECUTIVE ISSUES

To make better *current* decisions is the most straightforward purpose for decision aiding, but by no means the only one.

9.6.1 Prospective Decisions

Organizations often establish *decision rules* to determine what should be done if some contingency occurs. This may be because there will not be time for human judgment to make an appropriate choice (e.g., emergency response to alert of an incoming enemy torpedo). Or the sheer volume of choices may make it prohibitively costly or slow or politically suspect to rely on D's discretion (e.g., government screening thousands of potentially toxic substances). In such cases, *prospective* DA may be used.

A common request from deciders is for decision rules for recurring or future decisions. If the intent is for rules to generate decisions that are binding to the decider, I am generally skeptical of their usefulness. One can rarely predict the circumstances of a choice D is not yet facing sufficiently well to determine firmly what should be done. However, stable administrative procedures are often called for, for example, to limit D's controversial or arbitrary discretion. If these procedures are guidelines rather than hard rules, the risks of serious unforeseen error can be tolerable, especially if guidelines are subjected to DA logic.

9.6.2 Decision "Aid" as Advocacy

In my experience as a consultant, "decision aid" clients are often looking not so much for help in making up their *own* minds as for an authoritative and persuasive argument for someone *else* to make a choice our client wants him to take (see

---

[10]For a fuller discussion, see Ulvila and Brown (1982).

Section 9.4.3). In effect, the client's interest is in a marketing aid. In practice, considerable moral fiber (or financial security) may be required for an aider to resist client pressure to come to a particular conclusion.

In theory, this advocacy consideration should not affect the analysis the aider does—at least, if you see your consulting task as helping the decider (who is not your client) to make the best decision in *his/her own* interests. For example, a parent helping a child make a responsible choice; or a doctor helping a patient with a therapeutic choice; or a public interest research group making a disinterested recommendation or health care insurance. Even in these cases, the aider would do well to be conscious of possible conflicts of interest.

ASSIGNMENTS

Prepare for Discussion After Reading

1. Describe distinctive problems or opportunities you know of, in an organizational or institutional context that you are familiar with, where decision aid might be used.

Prepare for Later Discussion or Submission

Reactor Backfit Case

2. In late 1985, the head of the east coast (Area III) office of the NRC had to make a major decision about reactor PBII, about whose safety he was concerned. In particular, he was considering requiring the owning company to install an expensive venting system to better contain radioactive emission in the event of a severe accident. (Lack of containment had been a major cause of the 1979 Chernobyl disaster.)

   Read Brown and Ulvila (1988, "Does a reactor need a safety backfit"). Hand in no more than two pages of notes on the following questions as a basis for class discussion. Pay attention to the interface between model and reality. Document your answers with specific references to the text, especially tables. Assume initially that you accept all technical and value judgments embodied in the text. If anything is not clear, say so, but make a plausible guess.

   (a) The article refers to two different monetary evaluations of risk in terms of societal value trade-offs: one is based on harm to health (e.g., $1M/prompt fatality), the other on exposure to radioactive emissions ($1k/person-rem). Which of these conflicting value judgments are most favorable to the interests of the industrial reactor business (as opposed to those of, say, the environmentally sensitive public)? Which of these two trade-offs better reflects *your* values?

   (b) According to the analysis, is the vented containment option expected to be worth its cost? Clarify what you mean by "worth its cost"?

   (c) What, if any, are the strictly economic benefits (rather than the effect on health or safety) attributable to the vented containment option (compared with no safety backfit)?

(d) The far right bar in Figure 4a in the paper—net benefit of the ADHR option—is mainly above $0, but the mean estimate (crosshatch) is shown as negative. How could that be?

(e) Why might the regulator consider deferring his decision on backfitting?

(f) If you were the regulator and used only the 1-in-10,000 core-melt test of acceptable risk and $1k/rem trade-off (and accepted all the other numbers in the paper), would you close the reactor down now, leave it as is, require one or two backfits, or wait before making a decision?

(g) As a *responsible citizen*, would you take issue with this conclusion?

APPENDIX 9A

ENVIRONMENTAL REGULATION CASE STUDY: DECISION AID FOR THE MANAGEMENT OF ARCTIC RESOURCES

This appendix presents a decision analytic tool developed in 1997 to support recurrent regulatory decisions on environmentally hazardous project. It is illustrated in the context of a real but past problem, involving all the parties who had originally participated four years earlier. The case shows how DA tools could be used by regulatory agencies and applicants for permits, had the tools been available at the time (Larichev et al., 1995; Brown et al., 1997; Flanders et al., 1998). It is not so much a case study of DA in use, as of developing a re-usable DA tool in a live current context.

9A.1 Regulatory Problem

9A.1.1 Permitting Procedure The CoE (Corps of Engineers) is the governmental body that has the primary responsibility for evaluating construction permit applications, using the guidelines of the Clean Water Act. A staff within a CoE District Regulatory Branch would typically make a recommendation to accept the application or not, based on available evidence, through the branch chief, to the district engineer. The district engineer would confer with various other federal and state agencies, such as the EPA (Environmental Protection Agency) before making a decision, subject to central CoE approval.

9A.1.2 Interest in a Decision Aid At the urging of an industry group—AOGA (the Alaskan Oil and Gas Association)—the federal ARC (Arctic Research Commission) engaged us (DSC, Inc.) to develop a "scientific" procedure for making such regulatory decisions. The procedure was intended to make the regulatory process more predictable, reviewable, and defensible, particularly in the context of the ongoing controversy about oil drilling in the Alaskan National Wildlife Refuge.

Generally, until then, "scientific" had meant "cost–benefit" analyses, which, when applied to regulatory decisions, had tended to favor industry. This was because in practice, cost–benefit analysis paid more attention to regulatory costs, which could readily be measured, than to environmental benefits, which normally could not. It may not have been clear to AOGA at the outset that we intended to give full weight to *all* considerations, however intangible. The declared intent of our analysis was to develop tools that could readily be adapted for future decisions. An efficient set of tools should help make the regulator's decision process sounder, smoother, more defensible, and less wasteful of national resources. In the past, U.S. arctic resource decisions seemed to have been made in a rather unstructured and nonreplicable way, often swayed by volatile political considerations.

9A.1.3 Testing a Reusable Aid We decided to test the feasibility of a preliminary reusable DA tool on what we thought was a "dead" issue, to avoid attracting unwelcome attention before we had something that could stand up to disputatious scrutiny. (We discovered that the embers of that political fire had by no means died out!)

9A.2 The Niakuk Permitting Case

We settled on a recent difficult choice CoE had faced, where the U.S. government had to decide whether to permit BP (British Petroleum) to build a causeway to its Niakuk oil field on an island in the Arctic Ocean.

9A.2.1 Application Setting In the late 1980s, BP sought permission to develop an oil field on the artificial island of Niakuk, 1.25 miles off the arctic Beaufort Sea shore, with a gravel causeway to pipe the oil ashore. BP could, alternatively, use other means of transporting the oil, such as slant drilling. (Slant drilling means directional drilling from the shore, which does not affect the sea directly.) CoE had to decide whether to permit BP to develop the oil field, and how.

The causeway (CW) presented several environmental hazards, including disruption of fish habitat and degradation of water quality. Slant drilling (SD) involved less environmental risk but was more expensive and might make the development of the oil field less profitable. BP also argued that a significant source of domestic oil could be lost to the United States, with implications for its energy independence, a national policy objective, if the oil was not developed at all (thus, this criterion favored either option, in contrast with the "do nothing" option).

9A.2.2 Historical Sequence Directly following BP's application, four years before the our team worked on this problem, the CoE had given a conditional permit to develop the Niakuk oil field but did not allow for construction of the proposed causeway. The main argument for this decision was that the proposal did not comply with the Clean Water Act, which says that permission cannot be given if a fish population would be adversely affected (without defining precisely what constituted an adverse effect). Causeways were believed to affect the habitat of arctic cisco fish by changing coastal current patterns.

According to existing regulatory procedures, the perceived overall social value of the causeway could *not* be traded off with the negative environmental impact, although one regulation required taking account of "the public interest." The Alaska District also issued a general directive favoring alternative means of accessing offshore oil (including slant drilling) over causeways. This directive raised the case from a single decision to a precedent guiding future permitting decisions.

A Republican administration subsequently put pressure on CoE headquarters in Washington to rescind these decisions, pending additional data. CoE acquiesced. A Democratic-controlled congressional committee in turn challenged the reversal, claiming improper industry influence on the administration. BP finally dropped the causeway proposal in favor of slant drilling. In the event, the exploitation of the oil field proved quite profitable, since it turned out that slant drilling allowed greater recovery of oil.

9A.2.3 Active Parties   A decision like this typically involves several parties, which may have very different perspectives on the question being considered. The criteria scores and the importance given to them will vary according to who is proposing them. BP was presumably concerned primarily with profitability. The state and local authorities were particularly interested in the potential revenues (through royalties). The local population was interested in the effect on employment and the local economy. The general public and environmental organizations were moved to protect this natural space. At a national level, there was also motivation to limit the dependence on foreign countries for the provision of oil. The goals of the various parties being sometimes very different, their preferred options were also likely to differ. For example, an environmental group would be likely to prefer no oil exploitation in the region, unlike BP.

9A.2.4 Helping the Parties   Our study team developed an analysis of the Niakuk proposal to be treated "as if" BP had submitted it to justify their application (of which we had a copy). We had in mind a future regulatory regime where the format of the application was to be specified by CoE, to assure that all considerations that they wished to take into account when making their permitting decisions would be addressed in a form they could use. It turned out that BP's written application did not address all the relevant issues (but did address some irrelevant issues). The analysis was intended to reflect faithfully whatever knowledge and thinking had been available to BP at the time (without attempting to improve on them). The next step would be for CoE (and other interested agencies) to second-guess BP's application, including the decision analysis. They would substitute CoE's own judgment if they took issue with BP, and decide accordingly.

As it happens, we had access to almost every significant player in the original permitting process, and all were willing and able to recapture the thinking and responses that they had at the time.

9A.3 Aid Description

To increase usefulness of any resulting regulatory procedure to all concerned, we framed the analysis as far as possible to fit the traditional categories and definitions of impacts with which regulator and regulatee were familiar.

9A.3.1 Criteria The criteria on which the options were to be scored were associated with the main parties affected. The general public is, for example, concerned primarily by environmental questions: fish populations, animal populations, aquatic sites (wetlands), other fauna (endangered species), water quality, and wilderness. The impacts of the various options were evaluated on all the criteria. Options were evaluated based both on acceptable thresholds for each impact and on value trade-offs among criteria. This means that some scores could fail to meet a threshold and thus lead to an option being ruled out. (However, not all parties considered this an absolute prohibition, in view of the regulatory requirement that the decision be "in the public interest.")

9A.3.2 Qualitative Format The application format proposed included both a qualitative and a quantitative form. Table 9A.1 shows a structured, but qualitative, DA representation of the application format, illustrated by inputs that we *imputed* to BP. The table shows that some outcomes are better for the SD option and others better for CW. The fifth column summarizes the definition of a "very high" impact, in terms that should be comprehensible to the parties involved. This definition is very important, as the various people involved in the decision must have a common understanding of it.

The data take into account not only the importance of the various criteria, but also whether a criterion impact is identified as unacceptable according to some law or regulation. For example, the top row says that the impact of CW on fish populations is "very high" (col. 3), which is unacceptable because "high" (col. 5) would already be unacceptable. According to row 5, both CW and SD are considered unacceptable on water quality. On the face of it, therefore, since neither option is acceptable, the project should be abandoned. However, recall that regulation also requires that the determination be "in the public interest." D has, in any case, some discretion in legalistically interpreting "unacceptability" to allow an option that, on other trade-off grounds, appears desirable.

9A.3.3 Quantitative Format The vehicle for the quantitative analysis was the "sum-of-boxes" format for ICE (importance-weighted criteria evaluation) suggested in Chapter 6. Figure 9A.1 shows how the quantification of the various impacts and importance weights can be done in graphic form. Numbers do not appear on the figure, but the width and height of the rectangle are quantitatively meaningful. The judgments that are represented (e.g., impact and importance) are the same as for Table 9A.1, but presented in a quantitative and more precise format.

The level of an impact is represented by the width of a box. Negative impact goes toward the left, positive impacts go toward the right. For example, the impact of CW on fish population (top row) is big relative to the impact of the same option on other fauna (fourth row), and both these impacts are negative.

The height of a box represents the importance of a criterion. For example, in the graphic we can see that the criterion "animal population" is given more importance than the criterion "employment." The area of a box is thus the product of the impact of an option on a criterion and the importance of that criterion. The most meaningful components are the ones that combine big impact with big importance on the relevant criteria.

TABLE 9A.1 Qualitative DA Format for Niakuk Permit Application (Hypothetical Data)[a]

Party Affected	Type of Outcome	Causeway Impact	Slant Drilling Impact	Definition of Very High Impact	Unacceptable[b]	Importance
General public (environmental concerns)	Fish populations	*Very high*	Extremely low	10 years to restore	High	++
	Animal populations	*Low*	*Low*	10 years to restore	Low	+++
	Aquatic sites (wetlands)	Medium	Medium	Comparable to the Everglades	High	++
	Other fauna (endangered species)	Very low	Very low	Probability of extinction up 5%	—	+++
	Water quality	*Low*	*High*	Two spills over project life	Low	++
	Wilderness/ecology	Very high	Medium	Comparable to Deadhorse case	—	+
National interest	**Oil independence**	**Very low**	**Very low**	5% less oil imports	—	+++
State and local	**Revenue (royalties)**	**High**	**Medium**	$1B over life of field	—	++
	Fisheries	Medium	Very low	One major species out one year	—	++
Local population	Subsistence (waterfowl)	Very low	Very low	One major species out one year	—	+
	Employment	**Very low**	**Very low**	200 more permanent jobs	—	+
Industry	Economy	Very low	Very low	20% improvement	—	++
	Niakuk profitability	**Medium**	***Very low***	$1B earnings (cumulative)	Very low	+++
	Other BP profitability	**High**	Low	$1B earnings (cumulative)	—	+++
	Other firms' profitability	Medium	Extremely low	$1B earnings (cumulative)	—	+++

[a] An impact in italics is unacceptable. Rows in bold are for positive impacts.
[b] The level of impact defined to be unacceptable. If no level of unacceptability is defined, "—" appears instead.

174 AIDING THE PROFESSIONAL DECIDER

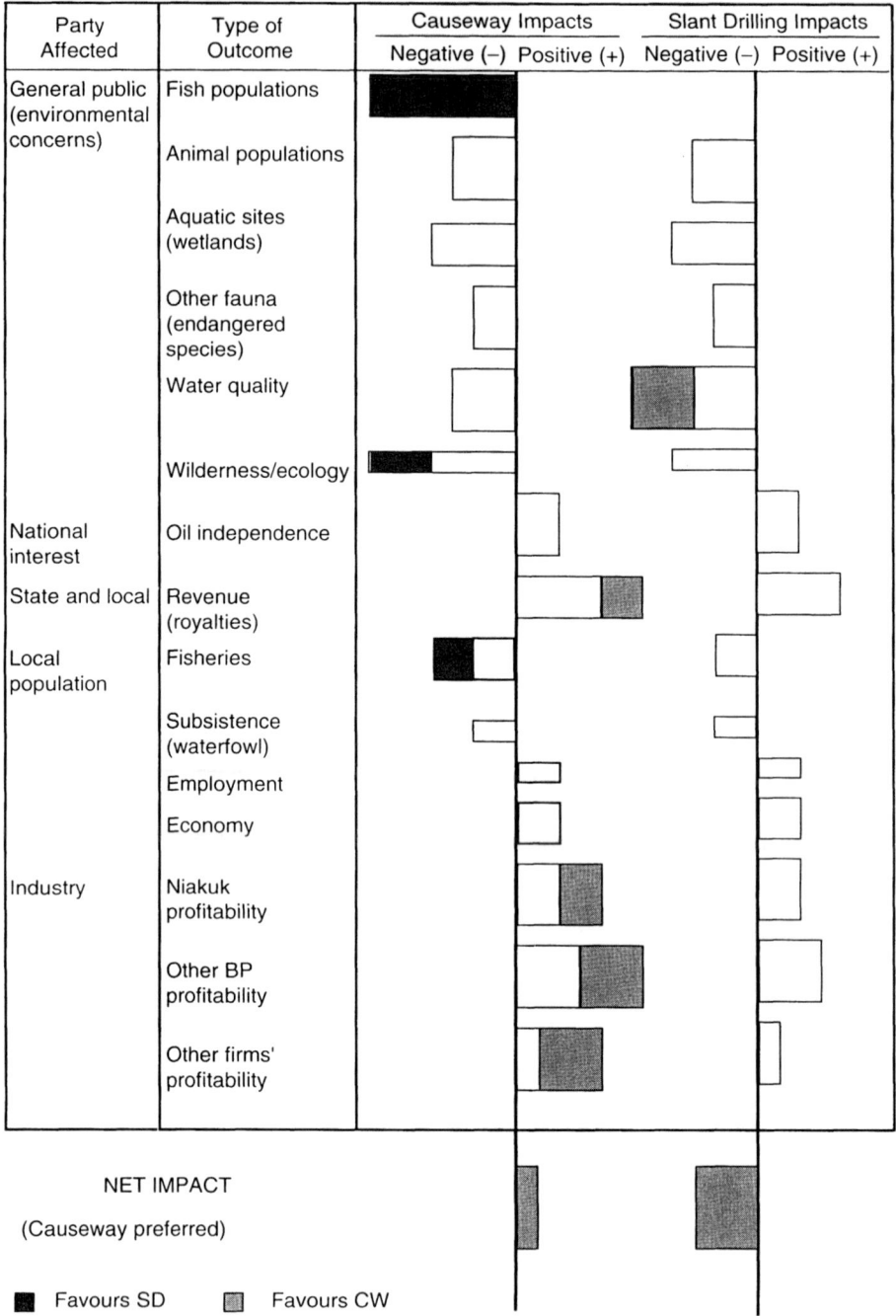

FIGURE 9A.1 Quantitative format for Niakuk permit application (hypothetical data).

For example, the negative effect of the CW option on "fish populations" (Figure 9A.1, first row) is large and important, and is shown as a tall wide box to the left of the center line. Summing negative and positive box areas in the CW column shows a small net positive area at the bottom, indicating that the CW option appears slightly better than DN (do nothing).

The SD column of boxes is interpreted comparably. SD impact on "wilderness/ecology" (sixth row) is large, but the criterion is less important, and so is shown as a wide but low box whose area is much less than in the preceding CW case. Accordingly, CW's net negative effect is seen to be much less on wilderness than on fish. Summing the SD boxes shows SD to be substantially worse than DN.

Comparing the two bottom boxes shows CW to be greatly preferred to SD. The sources of the superiority of CW over SD on each criterion are indicated by shading the difference between the boxes. If it favors SD, the shading is black; if it favors CW, it is gray. The CW box for impact on fish population is entirely black because SD is shown as having no impact there at all (no box in SD column). On the other hand, both CW and SD impact "water quality" (fifth row) negatively, SD more than CW. The difference between the two water quality boxes is shaded gray and shows how much that criterion contributes to CW's superiority.

The implication of the whole analysis is that CW is better than nothing, but SD is worse. Remember, however, that the judgments on which this is based are attributed (as accurately as we could) to the applicant, BP, who wants CW to look best. The regulator can substitute his own input judgments, which may point to a different conclusion.

Initially, we had tested whether simply presenting the impacts to the decider and letting him factor in importance as he pleased could be a useful, perhaps sole, product of the analysis. He and his staff indicated, however, that they would like more guidance than that, so we pressed on with the ICE.

9A.3.4 Dealing with Uncertainty Neither of the formats above deals explicitly with uncertainty. Impact and importance weight are evaluated without reference to the degree of certainty about them. This omission may not be crucial in comparing CW and SD if the impact of both options is equally uncertain. (One way of dealing with uncertainty is to discount the value of uncertain impacts by a *risk penalty*, thus giving conservative estimates.)

We might nevertheless have to make the treatment of uncertainty explicit so that the decision is readily reviewable, for example, with *sensitivity analysis* (see Chapter 8). Uncertainty could also be dealt with by using different shades or colors for the boxes corresponding to the level of certainty of the estimates. When working with numbers, an *uncertainty range* for the various impacts can be displayed.

9A.4 Application to the Niakuk case

9A.4.1 BP's Permit Application The quantities used above were those imputed to the applicant (as realistically as we could manage). BP was not, however, asked to participate actively in this exercise (though we had several discussions and briefings with all AOGA members). Our reconstruction was based on our team's reading of BP's original application, with informed guesses where the application was silent. The analysis above concludes that CW is to be preferred, based on the inputs used (treated as if proposed by applicant). We can see, for example, that the high impact and importance attached to the criteria related to industry profitability[11] had a large part in deriving a preference for the causeway option. (Of course, our model may not be how BP would actually have completed the analysis according to our format.)

9A.4.2 CoE's Version of BP's Quantitative Analysis

The regulators may not agree with BP's assessments, and therefore favor a different option. A comparable set of judgments was extracted for CoE, from the same people who made the original qualitative determinations and regulatory ruling. They were asked to use their recollection of the knowledge and judgments they had at the time.

Although we are not at liberty to disclose numbers, this CoE analysis was reasonably close to the one above attributed to BP in many ways, but put much lower weights on the criteria under "industry" (which lowered the heights of the related boxes). Some additional criteria also appeared in their analysis. The conclusion derived from their analysis in fact confirmed the decision they had made at the time, which was to permit the development of the Niakuk oil field but on condition that an alternative to a causeway (i.e., SD) be used to transport the oil.

This CoE analysis was also presented to a series of other regulatory groups that had been involved (such as federal and state agencies and the head of the regulatory branch at CoE headquarters in Washington). Almost all commented (perhaps out of politeness) on the usefulness of such an analysis for making their contribution to the permit decision. The various groups and individuals often offered predictably different assessments of impacts and weights and even different criteria.

9A.4.3 Aftermath of Pilot Exercise

The senior BP executive involved in the initial application reacted negatively—and strongly—to the proposed analysis and procedure, although he had proposed the exercise in the first place. Possibly he was uncomfortable having to give a systematic and transparent explanation of a decision and how it was reached, especially on the importance of criteria, such as BP's economic motivations. In any case, the industry group, AOGA, of which BP was a leading member, withdrew its support for our effort and ARC declined to renew our consulting contract.

Following this research on the Niakuk problem, the CoE invited us to look at a *current* decision that it had to make. It had to decide whether or not to permit the same company (BP) to construct a dock at the Badami oil-field with a buried pipeline. We helped them to construct and supply complete input to a "sum-of-boxes" aid, based on the same principles as the one for Niakuk. In view of the permitting process extending beyond the end of our research project and the drying up of funding, we were not able to observe how our analysis affected their actual permitting decision.

---

[11] Profit was scaled with $1 billion ($1B) as 100, and no profit as 0. This *could* be a *plausible range*, but that would be an unusual coincidence, since these round numbers were chosen for convenience. The "independence of foreign oil" criterion, on the contrary, was scaled with 0 to 100 corresponding to a *plausible* 0 to 5% reduction in oil imports. If the company anchors were unrealistically far apart, the importance weight would need to be greater than the "intuitive" weight (see 6.3.4).

9A.4.4 Presentation to CoE Headquarters We later met with the head of CoE's regulatory branch in Washington, DC, to discuss our efforts. He suggested that some desirable uniformity among CoE's local regulatory decisions might be achieved by promulgating our kind of standard application format, along with guidance on the importance weights, although some adaptation to special circumstances would no doubt be needed. We do not know whether this exercise has had any effect on CoE's regulatory procedures.

ASSIGNMENTS

Prepare for Discussion After Reading

1. According to Figure 9A.1: Which is/are the most important criterion(a)? Why?
2. (a) Which criterion(a) have the greatest effect on the comparison between the causeway and slant drilling options? Why?
   (b) What would the analysis recommend if the only options were slant drilling and doing nothing?
3. Can you tell which option would be preferred if no weight were given to industry profitability (as many argued should be the case)?
4. The following criticism has been received on this analysis. The beneficial net effects on "other BP/industry profitability" in the last two rows of Figure 9A.1 are due to a precedent effect [i.e., permitting BP to drill on Niakuk (under either option) improves the prospects for other firms in similar situations]. Shouldn't there be a balancing precedent effect for environmental concerns that favors "permit nothing"? What do you think?
5. If regulatory permission for comparable future projects is decided on the basis of applications in the form of Table 9A.1 and Figure 9A.1, whose interests do you think (regulator, industry, public) could potentially benefit or be harmed? In what way?

Prepare for Later Discussion or Submission

6. How would Figure 9A.1 look if it were displaying *only* impacts and not addressing importance at all? Answer in words.
7. What criterion scales are implicit in Table 9A.1? What can you say about the type of base, interpretation of anchor points, and/or units?
8. What are the relative advantages, in terms of effective decision aiding, of including *importance* in presentation to decider/user, or not?
9. Give examples of other public policy decisions that could be helped with tools such as those used in this case study.

Chapter 10

Assessing and Inferring Probabilities

We have been using personal probability as a numerical measure of D's uncertainty (in Chapter 7 and elsewhere), without paying too much attention to where it comes from. In the present chapter we propose guidance on how to make those probabilities realistic and useful.

A person may take different roles in an assessment, including possibly several roles by the same person. There is the *decider* D, the *aider* (who incorporates the probability into an analysis), the **informant** (who is the source of knowledge to be tapped, e.g., an expert) and the *elicitor* (who turns informant's knowledge into an assessment). The *assessor* is both informant and elicitor. In any case, Ds must adopt the probabilities as their own, in order to rely on them in a decision.

10.1 PERSONAL PROBABILITY

Ideally, the knowledge on which assessors' probabilities are based would include all the knowledge they have, or have access to, and would be analyzed perfectly.[1] In practice, that ideal judgment is unachievable and often unnecessary. Moderate errors in assessing criterion scores do not typically lead to costly mistakes. Errors in eliciting goals (preferences) or in specifying options (the other two elements of the GOO process) are usually much more serious (see Chapters 8 and 11). Nevertheless, getting sound probabilities can be important.

---

[1] Exactly how "perfectly" would be carried out is not quite clear, at least to me, but my working hypothesis is that it exists.

Rational Choice and Judgment: Decision Analysis for the Decider, by Rex Brown
Copyright © 2005 John Wiley & Sons, Inc.

Example. If D is deciding whether to undergo surgery and uses a 10% chance of crippling side effects, where she should have used 1%, she might misguidedly choose not to undertake surgery. In this case, the assessment error was large—a factor of 10—but such large errors are quite common if assessment is flawed. ♦

10.1.1 Meaning of Probability

People generally understand intuitively the meaning of probability well enough for most purposes, especially when referring to binary (two-valued) possibilities (e.g., whether you will pass this course) or multiple possibilities (e.g., what your grade will be). It is fairly clear what you mean if you say "my probability of rain (today) is 60%."[2] If the possibility is an uncertain quantity that can take any value on a continuous scale, the corresponding statement might be "my probability of more than 1 inch of rain is 60%."[3] In any case, probability as used here is a strictly personal expression of an informant's belief.

There are a number of other interpretations of the word "probability" not addressed here.[4] Weather forecasters will often say "*The* chance of rain is 60%," which suggests that there is some objective *impersonal* probability of rain. I prefer to think that they are simply asserting that qualified forecasters in possession of the same meteorological data would give the same personal probability as they do. However, this is a controversial position in some risk assessment circles.

10.1.2 Sensitivity vs. Assessment

Instead of making a quantitative probabilistic assessment to handle uncertainty, sensitivity analysis can be performed. That is, a model of choice can be run with different possible values, within the plausible range of the distribution, to see what difference that makes to the option preferred. If it is small, the uncertainty can probably be ignored. Only if it is significant is it necessary to go to the trouble of assessing a better probability.

10.1.3 Assumptions vs. Assessments

In everyday parlance, an "assumption" is sometimes what the speaker really thinks (as in "I assume that Republicans will win the presidency"). To make this interpretation clear, let us call it a **realistic** assumption. However, an assumption can also be a

---

[2]Equivalently "I assess a 60% chance of rain" or "I give odds of 3 to 2 that it will rain."
[3]A more precise definition would be "*A's personal probability P(F) for possibility F* is such that *A would be equally surprised* by *F* being true and a *random* selection of balls marked *F* from a set with proportion $P(F)$ so marked." You should be indifferent between getting some prize either if *F* is true or if you draw an "*F*" ball (see Schlaifer, 1978).
[4]When traditional risk assessors assess the "probability" of a nuclear accident, they usually interpret it as a "frequency," but I find that when applied to a unique event, this is, at best, confusing (Brown, 2002).

supposition, not necessarily related to informant's **actual**—as opposed to **hypothetical**—belief. The assumption may be made as a convenient step toward a more complex assessment (e.g., "assume that a block slides down a slope without friction" or "assume that D has perfect information"). Let us call this an **arbitrary** assumption. A useful cue: If the speaker says "I assume that...," it is a realistic assumption; if the speaker says "Assume that...," it is an arbitrary assumption.

Cop-out Evaluations   With any elicitation of possibility (or preference or option), we are often tempted to make a special type of arbitrary assumption, what I call the "cop-out judgment." For example, if we see no definitive grounds to support one position or another, we say 50%. Using cop-out judgments in a model may save the informant some hard thinking, but lead to unsound conclusions. You would be well advised to avoid cop-outs on almost any possibility, even where you *think* you are "completely ignorant."

Health Example. In the twin baby delivery decision in the Prolog, Karen's choice about whether to have a double caesarian hinged on her probability that the doctor would be able to "turn" the fetus that was pointed the wrong way. When asked, the doctor said "It's very difficult to predict; I'd have to say 50:50." I hadn't met the doctor, but my experience with professionals in this kind of situation has been that they tend to "play it safe" and err on the pessimistic side (possibly related to avoiding malpractice suits). This suggested that his best judgment (certainly fallible, but that's all we had) was *more than* a 0.5 chance of turning Sam. Luckily, that perception was enough to confirm even more strongly the DA indication that Karen should try natural delivery first—which she did. ♦

Hypothetical Example. Suppose that an all-powerful wizard forces you to vote for one of two possibilities, say, whether there is life on Mars; or whether there will be civil war in Russia within 20 years. The wizard will turn you into a toad if you're wrong and get you a Nobel prize if you're right. Wouldn't you scratch your head to come up with something other than 50:50 if you had *any* inkling whatsoever? (Based on what little I know, I would personally go firmly for no life on Mars and cautiously for no Russian civil war.) ♦

Informants can be motivated to produce "honest" probabilities by applying "scoring rules" that reward them according to their assessment record.

Example. For some time, weather forecasters have been giving probabilities of rain, etc. In the beginning it was found that they were overly cautious, erring toward 50:50. It rained about 80% of the time that they said 60%, and 20% of the time that they said 40%. In an experiment by NOAA (National Oceanographic and Air Administration), a group of forecasters was scored with a "Brier" scoring rule (Brown et al., 1974) and the winning forecaster each week was recognized. The forecasts improved quickly and dramatically (Murphy and Winkler, 1992). ♦

10.2 DIRECT ASSESSMENT OF DISCRETE POSSIBILITIES

10.2.1 Simple Interrogation

The most straightforward, if not necessarily the most reliable, way to assess one's probabilities of discrete possibilities (which can take on one of only a few values) is to elicit them directly from an informant. It is often sufficient simply to ask an informant directly for the required probability, especially for a binary (yes/no) possibility that is neither rare nor virtually certain. The wording of the question requires care. Often-useful phrasing includes: What would you say the chances are that this candidate will be elected? What odds would you give? Do you consider it more likely than not? Would you sooner bet that he does or doesn't get elected?

A serious danger arises when, because of a complex model structure, the same possibility needs assessing many times but in different circumstances. Due to fatigue or boredom, the informant may be tempted to repeat the same probability for each pair, especially when separated in time by other assessments. In fact, it is usually the *different* impact of options on that probability that distinguishes them. That consideration, then, gets disregarded completely.

This danger can be avoided if the informant is asked what *difference* the option makes to probability—which may be all that matters. If the model-builder is skilled and aware of this danger, she can either reformulate the model or simplify it. However, that does not always happen (especially when the informant is someone other than the modeler). This is another reason to go for simple rather than complex models.

It is often more effective for the *elicitor* not to ask the *informant* directly for a probability but to engage him/her in free-form conversation, on the basis of which the elicitor *infers* the informant's probability. This is a common practice in industrial market research, where the best way to get an answer may differ from one respondent to another, due to heterogeneity of units. (Other indirect methods are discussed below.)

10.2.2 Rare Possibilities

Probabilities within a normal range, say 10 to 90%, are not usually much of a problem to assess, and errors do not usually distort choice much. This is not true for rare events, where direct assessment is difficult. The informant may have difficulty distinguishing 0.01 from 0.00001 probability, and the difference may be critical to choice.

Example. A thorough and competent risk assessment of a nuclear accident might be a socially acceptable probability of 1 in 10 million. An inexperienced assessor, however, might assess it as 1 in 1000, which, by regulation, would call for instant emergency shutdown of the reactor. (For this reason, reactor accident probabilities usually are established by elaborate indirect procedures—see below.) ♦

In cases of rare possibilities, the best elicitation may be for the assessor to have an informant judgmentally equate the probability of the rare event to an event the informant may be more familiar with (say, getting a royal flush if the informant is a card player), or for which there is statistical evidence (say, being struck by lightning, or winning the state lottery).

10.2.3 Human Actions

There is a special challenge when the possibility to be assessed is a human action, since, for example, a human being can react to the decision situation. A preliminary clue to what people are likely to do may be what we suppose it is rational for them to do, in terms of what we think they want. Then we have to allow for the prospect of subrational action. I may think a rational wife would be most unlikely to splurge on an expensive mink coat that she will rarely wear. I am, nevertheless, not too surprised if mine comes home with one!

Example. My company was once asked to predict how many days it would take for NATO to respond to an impending (but unknown to NATO) Soviet attack, as ambiguous intelligence was evolving (Brown et al., 1977). We first predicted that a rational NATO would respond in seven days, then added a further delay of another seven days (with a wide uncertainty range), due to institutional and political dithering. ♦

10.2.4 Decider's Own Subsequent Actions

The aftermath of D's current choice commonly includes D's taking some subsequent action after learning something new. Analysts used to analyze that aftermath as if they could predict with certainty D's subsequent action, given any new knowledge *modeled in the analysis*. We then realized that unless everything that D might learn to change the action had been modeled, D could not be sure of his/her action. Therefore, the subsequent action was an uncertain possibility and had to be modeled as such (Brown, 1978). However, assessing that possibility would certainly take *some* account of what D's rational action might then be.[5]

Hypothetical Business Example. In our "ore broker" example illustrated in Figure 4A.1, we assumed that if the broker bought the ore and waited for government approval to resell it, and the sale *was* approved, the broker would *certainly* resell it, for a profit of $300k. During the wait, however, he *might* learn of something unmodeled (i.e., other than the government approval) to change his action—for example, learning that the buyer had gone bankrupt and would not pay. Considering such unmodeled possibilities informally would not only leave the broker uncertain about his conditional profit, but might also make him assess a *lower* average profit and possibly change his decision to buy.[6] ♦

---

[5]An alternative is to treat the existing model as a *nonequivalent* substitute for the real problem (see Appendix 7A) and adjust informally.
[6]The consideration *could have* been included in the analysis, but the point is that it wasn't, and usually isn't.

Personal Case. A young woman I know was apprehensive that the fetus she was carrying might have Down's syndrome. She was considering having amniocentesis, a procedure that she understood would diagnose the disease reliably. If the results were bad, she intended, based on her projection of the prospects, to abort. The health risks (all she cared about) from the procedure itself, however, still appeared appreciable, but lower than that of delivering a sick child. This appraisal indicated to her that she *should* have the procedure. However, in the event of the procedure showing bad results, she might *not* after all abort, for one reason or another, despite her present determination. This possibility tipped the scales in favor of *not* having the procedure done (i.e., uncertainty about her subsequent action changed her decision). ♦

10.3 DIRECT ASSESSMENT OF UNCERTAIN QUANTITIES

Where the possibility to be assessed is not discrete but continuous or quasi-continuous, the assessment logic is similar, but with special features.

10.3.1 Form of Assessment

There are standard probability distributions available (e.g., "normal") for special cases, such as random sampling, but these cases are uncommon except in certain structured decisions (e.g., quality control). In less structured decisions, more common in real life, the assessor can draw a continuous curve freehand (see Figure 7.5), but this is difficult and generally calls for more information than is strictly needed to make a choice.

10.3.2 Simple Bars

Simpler alternatives to drawing curves are available. For example, as introduced in Chapter 7, a bar can be drawn on the relevant scale that covers the middle part of the distribution (e.g., 90%), with a hatch to mark a central value (see Figure 7.5). However, even the hatched bar is sometimes too precise. Upper and lower limits, without a hatch, may be all that reliably can and need be assessed. For example, many informants balk at assessing an average or any other single central estimate. If an average is needed for subsequent analysis the analyst can often simply take the midpoint as an approximate substitute (adjusted if there is any clear reason not to do so, say, for obvious asymmetry), without consulting further with the informant.

This approach has been used with some success in getting scientific experts to assess arguments in a physical model (e.g., of groundwater travel time in a radioactive release model). The scientists were resistant, even to the point of hostility, to being pressed for more than the 90% range. This was partly from psychological and social discomfort at being tied to a particular number—however hedged it may be by a plausible range—and partly from the burden of time and effort, given that each busy scientist may be called upon to assess scores of probabilities.

10.3.3 Betting on Intervals

A continuous distribution can be assessed by dividing the scale graphically into, say, four equiprobable subranges. To do this, the elicitor initially arbitrarily picks a "middling" value. He gets the informant to say on which semirange s/he would place a bet, and moves the dividing line until the informant can't say where s/he would bet (i.e., is indifferent). This is the median. Then the elicitor repeats the procedure on each half of those halves until the informant would be indifferent betting on any of the four segments defined. Each is then a quartile (25% probability).

10.4 INDIRECT ASSESSMENT OF DISCRETE POSSIBILITIES

In addition to trying to capture directly the informant's uncertainty about possibilities, there are a number of important indirect modes of assessment. Probabilities can be assessed by inferring them from other probabilities that are easier (or more reliable) to assess, using basic rules of probability. The modeling process, here as elsewhere, typically parallels a "commonsense" line of intelligent reasoning about uncertainty (see Chapter 3), but uses well-known findings of probability theory.

All probabilities depend on, or are *conditioned* on, some body of knowledge, including **background** knowledge that is not specified (symbolized as **&**). Normally, this knowledge is whatever the informant knows when the probability is assessed. If nothing is indicated to the contrary, we assume a probability to be conditioned on that background knowledge.[7] If the probability is also conditioned on a specified possibility, it is a *conditional* probability, given whatever the **conditioning possibility** is.[8]

10.4.1 Relation Between Probabilities

Indirect assessment exploits related possibilities. For example, if the assessor knows that possibility A is true, this knowledge may affect his/her assessment of possibility B. Possibilities A and B then *covary*.

Suppose I believe that my tall readers tend to be fat. If I know you are tall, my probability that you are fat goes up, meaning that *in my judgment* height and fatness *covary* among my readers. Figure 10.1 gives a diagrammatic representation of my covarying uncertainties about your dimensions. The area within each shape (box, circle, oval) corresponds to the probability of the possibilities that shape represents. It may be easier to visualize if the assessor thinks of the areas as corresponding to percentages of my total readership, from which you have been picked at random.

From Figure 10.1, for example, my judgment about you is that:

- My probability of your being a reader at all is the area of the big square box, 100%.

---

[7] That probability $P(x|\&)$ is often referred to, misleadingly I believe, as the **unconditional** probability of a possibility.
[8] Symbolically, conditional probability $P(F|G)$ = probability F is true given that G is true.

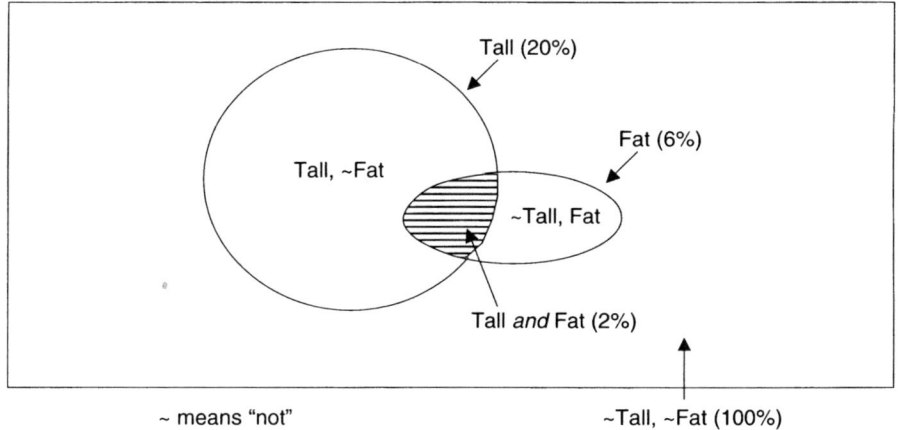

FIGURE 10.1 My covarying probabilities of reader being tall and fat.

- My *unconditional* probability of your being tall is the big circle as a percentage of the box, say 20%. Comparably, my unconditional probability that you are fat is the area of the smaller oval, say 6%.
- My *joint* probability of your being fat *and* tall—or the percentage of tall, fat people among my readers—is the hatched overlap as a fraction of the whole *box* (say, 2%).

From these probability judgments we can infer others; for example:

- My probability that you are fat if you are tall is the hatched overlap between circle and oval as a fraction of the circle, which is 10% (2/20)—more than the 6% I would assess if I didn't know that you were tall.
- My probability of your being neither tall *nor* fat is the area of the big box *outside* the labeled regions, as a fraction of the whole box [i.e., 76% = (100 − 20 − 4)].

This diagram reflects a central result of probability theory: **the probability of both A and B equals the probability of A times the probability of B conditional on A.**[9]

For example, suppose that Tex assesses an 80% probability of tenure if he publishes in major journals and a 40% probability that he does indeed publish. Then his probability of both publishing and getting tenure should be $0.8 \times 0.4 = 0.32$. From this simple rule, a great body of mathematical statistics has been developed, which in turn has generated many useful inference procedures. However, most of what we are interested in here can be shown and exercised through the simple graphic device of *flipping probabilities*.

---

[9]That is, the probability of a possibility in one set and also another possibility in another set is the probability of the first times the probability of the other if the first occurs. $P(A,B) = P(A) \times P(B|A)$.

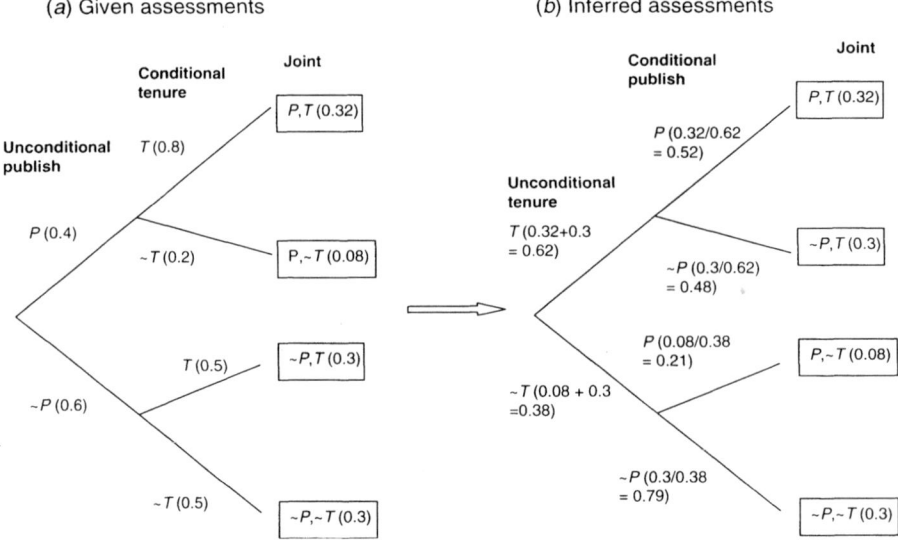

FIGURE 10.2 Flipping probability trees (Tex case).

10.4.2 Flipping Probabilities

The left side of Figure 10.2 represents in tree form a set of "unconditional" and conditional probabilities of two covarying uncertain possibilities, from which, on the right side, another set of unconditional and conditional probabilities can be inferred. This is flipping probabilities. (The inference could equally well be made in the other direction, from right to left, depending on which assessments you start with and which you want to end up with.)

For concreteness, let us interpret T as "Tex gets tenure" and P as "Tex publishes in major journals." Thus his unconditional probability of publishing (P), shown on the leftmost possibility fork of part (a), is 40%, and the complementary unconditional probability of *not* publishing is therefore 60% (100 − 40).

The graphic convention of a ***probability tree*** is that all probabilities are taken to be conditioned by possibilities on the ***tree path*** to the left. Thus, the upper branch of the topmost fork of Figure 10.2a says that *if* Tex publishes (P), the probability that he gets tenure (T) is 0.8. As another example, the bottom branch of part A says that if Tex does *not* publish (~P),[10] the probability that he does *not* get tenure (~T) is 0.5; and similarly for the other two paths of this tree.

The numbers in boxes to the right of these branches are ***joint*** probabilities. For example, the probability that Tex both publishes (P) *and* gets tenure (T) is 0.32, calculated as the product of the unconditional probability of P (0.4) and the probability of T conditional on P (0.8). These words may sound confusing, but looking at the figure should make it clearer. Basically, you get joint probabilities on the right by multiplying probabilities along the tree paths that lead to them from the left.

---

[10]In logic, the symbol "~" represents "not" or "it is not the case that."

The implied probabilities, conditioned in the other direction, in Figure 10.2b on the right are calculated in reverse. The four joint possibilities and their probabilities are unchanged [e.g., P, T (0.32)], but the corresponding paths give the reverse conditioning. The unconditional probability of tenure (T) is 0.62, the sum of the two corresponding joint probabilities; that is, P, T (0.32) and $\sim P, T$ (0.3). The remaining conditional probabilities, of P and $\sim P$ on T and $\sim T$, are a little trickier to think through. The conditional probability of P given T is equal to the joint probability of P and T (0.32), divided by the unconditional probability of T (0.62), which is 0.52. This logical connectivity permits a number of useful, practical inferences.

10.4.3 Conditioned Assessment: "It All Depends"

A particularly useful procedure for reasoning about uncertain events corresponds to a common intuitive inferential process: "It all depends" (see Chapter 3 for an informal version). As an application of the example above, suppose that Tex wants to assess the probability that he will get tenure but finds it easier to assess the probability of publishing and of the probability of getting tenure if he does or doesn't publish. Using the same input numbers as above, if he is logically consistent, he will infer a 62% probability of getting tenure.

A comparable procedure can concretize any argument that would be expressed informally in terms of "it all depends." For example, the chances that the incumbent president gets reelected can be thought to "depend on" whether there is a major downturn in the economy. The informal argument can be sharpened by quantitative conditioned assessment. For assessment conditioned on multiple uncertainties, probability trees would have more than two tiers of forks. The logic is a simple extension of the single-uncertainty conditioning dealt with so far.

Example. An uncertainty of interest to those of us who live in the Washington, DC area is whether terrorists will detonate a nuclear bomb here within the next 10 years. Figure 10.3 shows my assessment conditioned on whether terrorists acquire a nuclear bomb they know how to use, and on whether they can smuggle it undetected into Washington, DC. With the unconditional and conditional probabilities shown, multiplying out along the pathways through the tree gives a 10% probability of a terrorist nuclear explosion in the DC area within 10 years. If you disagree with this conclusion, to be consistent you must disagree with at least one of my input assessments. ◆

10.4.4 Assessment Updating

A quite different inference procedure is based on the same probability relationships. D's reasoning task now is to revise his uncertainty about a target possibility in the light of some new evidence that is indicative, to some degree, of the target possibility.[11] The target assessment is **enriched** by incorporating new knowledge. The degree to which the evidence is indicative of a possibility is its ***diagnosticity***.

---

[11]This is familiar to statisticians as prior–posterior analysis (the transition of uncertainty from prior to posterior on the receipt of diagnostic evidence) or Bayesian updating.

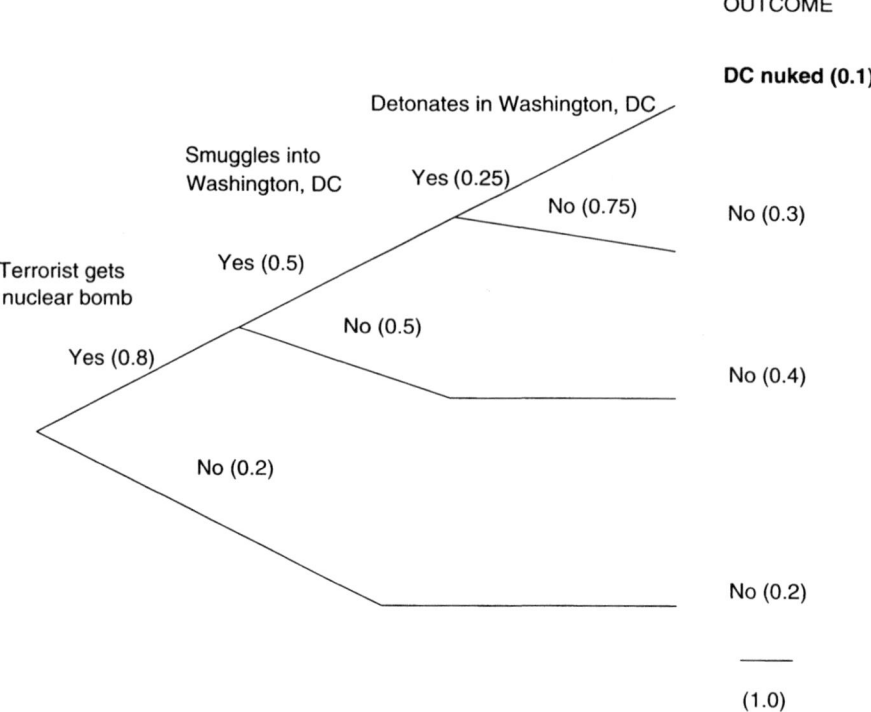

FIGURE 10.3 Assessment conditioned on several uncertainties (terrorist nukes Washington, DC).

To fit this case, let us reinterpret the symbols P and T in the example above, but leave the tree and numbers the same. P now represents Tex's becoming president of the company he works for, to which he gives a 40% chance. Then T (evidence) represents the possibility that the department he heads becomes the top profit center in the company. In the past, the president has always previously headed the top profit center, and Tex judges that if he is destined to become president, his probability of T would be 80%. Otherwise, his probability of T would be 50%. These assessments coincide with the numbers in Figure 10.2a.

Now, suppose that Tex actually becomes the head of the top profit center (possibility T). How should Tex update his prediction of becoming president in the light of this development, T? Given that he *did* get the top profit center, Figure 10.2b tells him that his updated (conditional) probability of becoming president (P) has risen to 0.52.

Note that Tex is interested in a different part of Figure 10.2. When he was doing conditioned assessment, his target was the unconditional probability of T (tenure, then), not the conditional probability of P (publish). In the latest example, this time of *assessment updating*, his target is the conditional probability of P given T. (Since T has occurred, he does not now need to know what the (unconditional) probability is that T would occur (62%), nor the conditional probability of P (21%) had T *not* occurred.

10.5 INDIRECT ASSESSMENT OF UNCERTAIN QUANTITIES

10.5.1 Substituting Discrete Possibilities

Since the distribution of a UQ can be substituted by a discrete three-possibility distribution (see Section 7.4.4), the indirect assessment methods for discrete possibilities described above (Section 10.4) can be adapted straightforwardly.

10.5.2 Decomposed Quantity Assessment

Decomposed quantity assessment is a useful technique, specific to UQ assessment. In general, statistical theory tells us how to infer uncertainty about a target quantity from uncertainty about other quantities, in terms of which it can be expressed. For example, uncertainty about sales of widgets can be decomposed into uncertainties about the number of customers and about purchases per customer. Alternatively, total sales can be decomposed into domestic plus foreign sales. Whether any decomposition is worth doing depends on whether the components are easier, or more reliable, to assess than the target quantity.

If the target quantity is a sum (or difference), or product of other quantities, there are simple formulas of propagation, and some corresponding graphic devices (Brown, 1969). In particular:

- **The average of a sum of UQs is the sum of the averages.**
- **The average of a product of UQs is the product of averages if the variables do not covary.**

According to standard statistics:

- **The plausible range (e.g., 90%) of a sum is approximately the root of the sum of squares of component plausible ranges.** The range can be expressed as the difference between the upper and lower ends of the range.

For example, if your prediction of domestic sales of widgets is $20M ± $3M and of foreign sales is $15M ± $4M, your average assessment of total sales will be $20M + $15M = $35M. Your plausible range is approximately +/− the root of ($3^2 + 4^2 = 25$), which is 5. Your target uncertainty is thus $35M ± $5M, or $30M to $40M.

This formulation can be expressed diagrammatically by a right-angle triangle, exploiting Pythagoras theorem. Figure 10.4 shows how the average and plausible range of the net benefit of clean air legislation is approximated from the average and plausible range of benefit and cost (which is a negative benefit).[12]

---

[12]This is drawn from a real clean air evaluation, where the costs and benefits and their associated uncertainties were themselves derived from complex decomposition models, based on major scientific and economic studies.

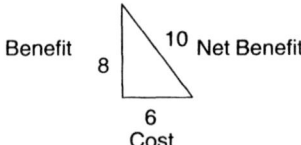

FIGURE 10.4 Propagation of uncertainty (net benefit of Clean Air Act).

The formula[13] for plausible range of a product is the same as for a sum, but the target and components are each expressed as percentages of the average. For example, if D assesses the number of widget customers as 2M ± 20%, and widgets per customer as 15 ± 15%, his average for total widgets sold will be 2M × 15 = 30M. D's plausible range is approximated as +/− the root of ($0.2^2 + 0.15^2 = 0.0625$), which is 0.25. D's target uncertainty is thus assessed as 30M ± 25%, or $22.5M to $37.5M.[14]

10.6 GENERAL ASSESSMENT ISSUES

10.6.1 Anything Else

When breaking down a broad possibility (e.g., business failure for Tex) into narrower components or instances (e.g., bankruptcy and unemployment), it is always

---

[13] Approximate, if components covary.
[14] Both sum and product decompositions are subject to approximation error if the components are judged to *covary*. If any *covariation* is positive (i.e., if D knew one component was high, it would raise his assessment of the other), this covariation should increase D's target uncertainty (Brown, 1969). For instance, if D were to learn that there are 2.4M widget customers (the upper end of D's range), this would lead D to raise his/her average of sales per customer. Thus, D has positive covariation between assessments. D's plausible range for total sales would increase from $22.5M to $37.5M, say, to $21M to $39M. (See Brown and Pratt, 1996.)

prudent to allow for possibilities that nobody has yet thought of—referred to earlier as "anything else."

Example. Market demand for new commercial products has been historically about double what had been predicted 10 years earlier on the basis of all *identified* applications. A 1985 U.S. government study predicted steadily *declining* demand for space on commercial satellites, simply because *known* prospects were fewer the further ahead one looked. A realistic forecast would have had to take "unknown unknowns" into account and would certainly be less pessimistic. (Commercial space demand has, in fact, greatly increased since 1985.) ♦

My better-than-nothing approach to making an assessment like this is by analogy. My experience with forecasting demand for technologically new products is that demand 10 years out is, on average, around twice the demand for applications of the product that anyone had thought of at the time (with a large uncertainty range). I applied this rule to the satellite space problem and it turned out I had still underestimated by a factor of 2 (but the forecast was much closer than treating "anything else" as zero).

Sometimes the situation is so novel that analogy seems hopeless. I usually try to reformulate D's choice to minimize the importance of the issue—but *some* allowance is always better than none.

Example. Regulation on radioactive emissions from a nuclear repository over 10,000 years requires that the probability of release from human intrusion be assessed. Risk analysis technicians identified only one documentable intrusion scenario, mining for minerals, which they carefully assessed at a probability of 0.1%. However, they reported this 0.1% as the probability of *any* human intrusion, any other intrusion scenarios being treated as impossible. I argued that it would be more reasonable to judge it "quite likely" that humans would do *something or other* to disturb the site over 10,000 years. They dismissed this position as "unscientific."

I proposed to them (unsuccessfully) the following imaginary analogy. About 10,000 years ago an Indian tribe was deciding whether to permit its ancestors' bones to be buried 20 feet underground in a bone repository. Tribal regulation required them to assess the probability of human disturbance over the next 10,000 years. Their PRA (probabilistic risk assessment) high priest could think of only one intrusion scenario: an enemy tribe desecrating the site, with a probability of 0.1%. Accordingly, the high priest reported a 0.1% probability of *any* human intrusion. The site came to be called Manhattan. It is true that we have the benefit of hindsight, but still. . . .

My proposal for handling human intrusion was this: Rather than trying to assess the absolute probability of human intrusion, address instead how the repository candidates *differed* in susceptibility to human intrusion. (One of the sites appeared less accessible to any intrusion than were the other sites, giving it an edge in this respect.) ♦

My usual analytic strategy in a case like this (and many others) is to study the informal reasoning that D would *have to use* if the evaluation were obligatory, and search for a formal counterpart (as here).

10.6.2 Canvassing Others' Opinions

I put particular store in the opinion of reliable informants, in situations fraught with emotion for me, and I think that this is true for most of us. ("Sis, do you think she really loves me?") In public policy decision making, where the appearance of "impersonality" is important, it is common to formally structure the elicitation of a number of "expert opinions" on controversial uncertainties, which has the appeal of a replicable and therefore somewhat objective procedure.[15]

10.6.3 Analogy

Analogy can also be valuable. Ask yourself: What has happened in comparable situations? (If I am wondering whether opening a new restaurant will be a success, I might bear in mind that most have failed within two years.) A key consideration is always to ask whether the target possibility is different from the analog, and how (e.g., Because I have more money reserves or experience than do the general run of new restaurateurs, my average time to failure might be longer, say, four years).

10.6.4 Plural Assessment

We looked at the general case of plural evaluation in Chapter 8. As elsewhere, it is a powerful approach to factual assessment. In Section 10.5.2, two decomposition formulations of total widget sales gave rise to two different target assessments. This discrepancy is typically the case when evaluations are made using different approaches, each of which may be subject to different errors. These single-pass evaluations can usefully be combined by an assessor, so as to take account of his/her relative confidence in the two (or more) approaches (see Section 8.9).

In Chapters 6 and 7 we presented various ways of modeling a complete choice, such that the output indicates a preferred option directly. Each of the resulting models calls for inputs that can themselves be supplied in any of a number of ways. One is direct judgment; another is to construct *feeder* models that produce, as output, the inputs required for the *core* model.

10.6.5 When Assessing Uncertainty Really Matters

A certain equivalent, even one that allows for risk aversion, may not be an adequate substitute for a UQ if extreme possible values could have major outcomes, such as

---

[15]In the Delphi group assessment method, the participants are anonymous, to avoid contamination or the undue influence of power imbalance among them, and their assessments are pooled mechanically (Zadeh, 1965).

reversing D's subsequent action, or even disaster. For example, if D judges a business investment to have an acceptable average return but a real possibility of leading to bankruptcy, failure to model the uncertain return could lead to an unacceptable risk. (In theory, substituting a certain equivalent could handle that, but it would usually be more trouble to determine it than to model the uncertainty.)

Example. In the DA of a government decision on permitting an oil company to drill on an arctic island, various uncertain environmental impacts were substituted by certain equivalents (see Appendix 9A). For example, the impact of the "causeway" option on "aquatic sites" was noted to be "medium" (Table 9A.1). According to environmental regulation, the impact on "aquatic sites" is allowed to be "high," so the impact here would appear to be acceptable. However, if there appeared to be a good *chance* that the impact could be worse (greater) than "medium," and therefore unacceptable, D would want to be alerted to that possibility—for example, by some probabilistic assessment. We did *not* model this uncertainty explicitly because of time and cost constraints on our analysis. We relied (perhaps optimistically) on our qualitative certain equivalent (and later, quantitative) being an acceptable approximation. ♦

10.7 VALUE OF MORE INFORMATION

D usually has the option of getting more information, before settling on a probability assessment for decision purposes. The question is: Will the additional information be worth the cost, trouble, or delay? There are analytic methods for addressing this issue rigorously, but they would take us well beyond the scope of this book (see Schlaifer, 1978). An informal sense of the value of getting more information might be obtained as follows. First appraise the amount that perfect information, provided by a *clairvoyant* who would remove all uncertainty, might be worth. How big a mistake, by hindsight, might D make through lack of accurate knowledge?

Say that Tex plans on going into business, based on comparative prospects as he now sees them. But it is possible that his future in academia would have been better, and he would have chosen academia *had he but known* what would *actually* happen. How much would that ignorance cost him? How likely is that hindsight mistake? Put simplistically, the value of *perfect* information is the probability of making a mistake times the cost of the mistake. This formulation, as I have stated it, is not precise enough to calculate a dollar figure.[16] But if, informally, Tex thinks it is not very likely that he is making a mistake going into business, and even if it is, it won't be a great loss, he would not put much store in getting perfect information about job prospects.

In any case, the best information that Tex can realistically get is far short of *clairvoyance*, and so worth much less. He might consider paying for vocational testing, but that testing will not get him anywhere close to certainty about relative career prospects. So it will only be worth a small fraction of perfect information, which itself, he thinks, isn't worth all that much. It doesn't look like it would be worth

---

[16]For a quantitative evaluation of the value of perfect and imperfect information, see Schlaifer (1978).

paying, say, $2000 for testing. He could, of course, size the situation up differently. Tex might think he could easily be making a big mistake going into business, even though it looks best now on what he knows, and that the testing would go a long way to resolving his uncertainty. Then the $2000 might look like a good investment.

All too vague to be useful? Perhaps, but at least Tex is focusing on the right issues to make up his mind (which he might not do otherwise). One alternative for deciding whether to invest in more information is to try to construct a realistic quantitative model, which would produce a precise answer (Clemen, 1996). However, the value of information is quite challenging to determine formally with any confidence, and I do not have space to get into that here.

Example. General Mills marketing staff constructed a value-of-information model. It indicated that test marketing a potential new product was *not* worth the cost. This conclusion was based on the aider's position that the opposite errors of launching a product that ended up losing money, and of failing to launch a winner, were neither likely enough nor costly enough to justify the expense of a test market, which would still not predict product success with any certainty. Top management backed its contrary intuition that test marketing *was* worth doing and went ahead. In my judgment, their decision could have been sound, because the value of a test market also includes valuable knowledge (e.g., how to market the product if they do launch it), which the formal analysis did not include. ◆

ASSIGNMENTS

Prepare for Discussion After Reading

Classroom Exercises

1. Consider all students in your class in respect of gender and height, specifically whether or not they are taller than 5 feet 7 inches.
   (a) Suppose that the instructor secretly selects a student at random. What probability do you assess that the student is a tall male?
   (b) Then the instructor informs the class that the student selected *is* "tall." What is your probability that s/he is a female?
   (c) Repeat this exercise for the population of all students in your university, using judgment only, no statistics. (Assess percentages only, not numbers.)

2. Think about your probability of intelligent life elsewhere in the universe.
   (a) Suppose the instructor gives you a choice between two gambles with a prize if you win: *A*, you win if there is "life"; or *B*, you win if the instructor flips a coin and gets "heads." The instructor will ask for a show of hands for which student would take which gamble.
   (b) The instructor offers a similar choice, where option *B* is: you win if the instructor gets 10 heads in a row.

Direct Assessment of Discrete Events

3. Be prepared to discuss the following. Before the next class (i.e., before the event happens), assess informally (without seeking any new evidence) and write down your probability for the following events, which will become known by the time of class.
   (a) It rains on the day of the class.
   (b) The lead story on that day in the local newspaper has something to do with politics or government.
   (c) All students registered for this course turn up for class.
   (d) Assignment for the next week will have more than 200 (or other plausible number of) words.

   If you wanted to make a better assessment, in each case, what readily accessible information would you gather?

Direct Assessment of Uncertain Quantities

4. Be prepared to assess, in the form of an average and 90% uncertainty range, your probability distribution for the following quantities:
   (a) The percentage of foreign citizens at your university (or other population if you are not at school).
   (b) The life expectancy (average age at death) of U.S. residents.
   (c) The percentage of U.S. lawmakers who *would have* lied and denied improprieties with Miss Lewinsky under oath if they found themselves in President Clinton's predicament [without benefit of hindsight of what befell him (i.e., that he was suspected, found out, and impeached)].

Prepare for Later Discussion or Submission

Joint Probability

5. According to Figure 10.1, what is my probability that you are tall if you are fat?
6. In the flu diagnosis example in Section 3.4.1, replace the doctor's qualitative assessments with any plausible probabilities.
   (a) What is the doctor's implied *unconditional* assessment that Sean has flu?
   (b) If the doctor knew only that Sean has the flu, with what probability should she assess that he has had a flu shot?

Decomposed Assessment

7. In course X, J estimates (most likely) that in the next term 12 students will be enrolled, with a 90% uncertainty range of 10 to 14; in course Y, J's corresponding assessments are 15, 10 to 20; in course Z, 20, 16 to 24. What should J estimate

the total number of students in all three courses to be, with a 90% uncertainty range?

8. How many students do you judge are registered in the same university program as you (e.g., public policy, psychology)?
   (a) Give your "best estimate" and a 90% uncertainty range (+/−).
   (b) What other program in your university, etc. do you consider closest to yours in orientation? Give your best estimate and a 90% range (+/−) for the number of students in that program.
   (c) What is your best estimate and 90% range for the total students in the two programs together?

9. Tex projects his income from salary next year to be $60k ± $15k, and from investments to be $20k ± $20k (average and 90% range), i.e., $0–$40k. What should he project his combined income to be?

Assessment Updating

10. In mid business career, Tex assesses a 20% chance of "success." Then he is named "businessman of the year" in his city. He judges that if he were *not* going to be a success, the probability of getting this award would be 10%, and if he *were* going to be a success, that conditional probability would be 30%. To be consistent, what should Tex's probability of success be after the award?

11. In the run-up to the Iraq invasion in spring 2003, Saddam Hussein, the Iraqi leader, refused to allow UN inspectors to search for WMD (weapons of mass destruction), whose discovery could provide grounds for the invasion. I, like many others, took this refusal as compelling evidence that Iraq *did* have WMD. Our conviction was reinforced by reports by Iraqi dissidents that they had seen the WMD.
    (a) If (as later appeared) Iraq did *not* have WMD, where (if at all) did our thinking go wrong?
    (b) My first assessment that Iraq had WMD (based in part on dissident reports):

    $$P(\text{WMD}) = 0.9$$

    My diagnostic assessments, at that time, probability of R (evidence of Saddam's refusal) given WMD and given ~WMD (no WMD):

    $$P(R|\text{WMD}) = 0.8$$
    $$P(R|\sim\text{WMD}) = 0.1$$

    What should my updated assessment, $P(\text{WMD}|R)$, be?

12. Carl Rowan, a noted black columnist, has said that when he encounters a group of young black men on the street, he prudently crosses to the other side. Is he a racist?

13. Moshe is reevaluating his strong, but not absolute, conviction that there is a just god, in the light of the experience of the holocaust. He thinks it unlikely that a just god would permit that to happen.
    (a) Should he therefore think it unlikely that there is a just god?
    (b) What if he thought it impossible that a just god would permit it?

Conditioned Assessment

14. In the "nuclear bomb on Washington" example in Section 10.4.3 (Figure 10.3):
    (a) Substitute your own probabilities on the tree, and calculate the implied unconditional bomb attack probability.
    (b) How would the tree change if you considered the possibility that a terrorist acquires a bomb but detonates it in DC *other than* by smuggling it into the United States (e.g., on a plane or missile)?

15. Joe is trying to predict how many votes candidate X will win in the next U.S. presidential election.
    (a) Joe intuitively assesses that X will get 20 million votes $+/-$ 5 million (90%). Draw a bell curve consistent with this assessment.
    (b) Construct graphically, on the same figure, a judgmentally equivalent three-possibility distribution for number of votes. Note the resulting values and probabilities and calculate the resulting average estimate.
    (c) Now, Joe assesses a 20% chance of a stock market crash. With a crash, Joe's assessment of X's number of votes is 14 million $\pm$ 3 million; without a crash, 25 million $\pm$ 8 million. Make a three-possibility substitute for each conditional distribution. What is now Joe's best estimate of X's vote?

Advanced extensions of same question
    (d) Construct graphically two-possibility substitute distributions for both conditional assessments in part (c) using plausible judgments to pick representative values for two halves (i.e., 50% of distribution in each segment) of each distribution.
    (e) From these assessments, derive a four-possibility distribution that Joe might now unconditionally assess (as a judgmental equivalent) for X's votes.
    (f) What is Joe's best estimate of X's vote based on the judgments in part (e)?
    (g) Joe estimates (average) that 12 million women will vote for X, ± 2.4 million, and 10 million men, ± 3.2 million. Calculate an average and plausible range for X's total vote.

(h) Joe has about equal confidence in his five single-pass assessments of the number of votes for X [from parts (a), (b), (c), (f), and (g)]. Make an *intuitive* guess at what you think might be Joe's best estimate, based on all five approaches.

Plural Evaluation

16. Consider the house or apartment that you or your family live in. If it were put on the market tomorrow, what price do you think it would fetch? How did you figure it out? Think of as many alternative ways of making an estimate of the price as you can come up with. Order them in terms of how much confidence you would have in the results.

17. Analyzing past performance and economic trends, Tex projects his investment income next year at $20k ± $20k (average, 90% range). His stockbroker, however, projects $40k, but based on the broker's past forecasting record, Tex always scales back broker's projections by 20%, reducing this projection to $32k. Tex's new projection is $32k ± $20k (based on the broker's input alone). Taking into account both estimates, what would be a reasonable average projection (with a 90% range) by Tex of his investment income next year?

Chapter 11

Eliciting Preferences

In this chapter we offer some guidance on how best to elicit the preference inputs called for in the models of Chapters 4 to 7. It covers holistic consequences, identification of criteria, and the value trade-offs among them. These observations apply to both private and professional deciders within institutions. As usual, the examples here are largely private,[1] but the extrapolation is less natural than with factual assessments.

11.1 IMPORTANCE OF PREFERENCE ELICITATION

Being clear on goals is critical to sound decisions. If you don't know where you would like to get to, how can you tell the best way to get there? Otherwise, an analysis may not cover all that is important, let alone indicate *how* important it is. The analysis can be worse than useless if D acts on the unsound results that may ensue. Fortunately, D will usually trust his/her informal judgment enough to be skeptical of DA output that is way off and override it.

Example. An acquaintance was considering where to retire to. I did a single-pass DA, based on everything she said was important to her, and came up with South Florida. She rejected it out of hand, explaining that she didn't want to be that close to a tiresome relative. She had not thought to mention that when I had elicited what she said was a complete list of her criteria. I adjusted the analysis with the additional

---

[1] However, as discussed in Chapter 9, institutional interests (as contrasted with the interests of professionals within institutions) have no counterpart in private life.

Rational Choice and Judgment: Decision Analysis for the Decider, by Rex Brown
Copyright © 2005 John Wiley & Sons, Inc.

criterion and settled on *North* Florida. It had a slightly worse climate, but was farther from her relative—which was fine by her. This was another example where *plural evaluation* of the most basic kind, comparing DA output with D's intuition, saved the day. ♦

11.2 MEANING OF PREFERENCE

Utility is the ultimate measure of *welfare*, the term I use for happiness or whatever governs personal preference. Psychologists are only just beginning to get a handle on what we mean by happiness, let alone how we measure it, and even less on how we engineer it (Kahneman, 2000). No one has come up with a "joy-meter" that tracks D's lifetime happiness in a form that permits comparison with another life path (D's or someone else's). Like uncertainty assessment (chapter 10), eliciting D's preferences is determining what is in D's head.

However, unlike uncertainty, there is no objective reality (such as observable outcomes) to which to anchor preference judgment. One can observe what economists call "revealed preference"[2]: inferring what people value from what they do. Town dwellers often claim to prefer to live in the country, but we observe constant migration from country to towns. I have been heard vaunting the superiority of the quality of life in England over the United States for the past 40 years ago, yet I am still here! People vote with their feet. However, revealed preference only gives one *clue*, among others, to real preference, since people act inconsistently and *subrationally*.

11.3 HOLISTIC UTILITY OF PROSPECTS

Prospects, including option consequences, can be evaluated holistically or disaggregated into criteria (see Chapter 6). Pure uncertainty models (as in Chapter 7) call for a single utility number attached to each possible prospect, i.e., holistic preference. The default elicitation strategy is, here as elsewhere, intuition. That is, locate "by eye" where, on whatever scale is specified where the option consequence lies. This generally involves appreciation of a complex set of ill-defined consequences, which is quite a stretch of the imagination. (However, as we shall see, multicriteria alternatives have problems at least as great.)

11.3.1 Thought Experiments

The essence of preference elicitation is assessing how satisfied D *will be* with option consequences. D may be able to evaluate preference for *past* circumstances quite reliably. ("I was much happier when I lived in Venezuela than now" or "Our shareholders were better off before I sold Time-Warner to AOL.") This experience may, however, help D anticipate satisfaction in comparable alternative future cases.

---

[2]See 9.3.2 for an adaptation of this idea to professional choices.

I generally favor preference elicitations that have D visualize detailed prospects that illustrate a broader consequence, and decide *intuitively* how much s/he would like to experience it. If s/he were in situation A (possibly the one s/he is already in) and had the chance to be in situation B, would s/he feel good about the move? This is likely to be more realistic, and thus be more useful, than producing an abstract number (e.g., an importance weight) or intellectually deducing what s/he *ought* to prefer from basic principles.

Thought experiments are easiest if the visualized scenario is within D's range of experience, especially if s/he has actually been there, or somewhere comparable. D, contemplating a second marriage, can ask herself, "Was I happier single or married to my first husband, and is there anything about my current choice that alters that comparison?" The effect of completely novel situations on D's welfare, however, may be far more difficult to anticipate. I certainly find it extraordinarily difficult to project my own welfare in uncharted waters. Unlike for factual uncertainties, there is usually little research we can do to sharpen our judgment.

Example. My mother was dreading the prospect of moving from the flat she had lived in for 35 years and into a strange retirement home. However, when circumstances made it unavoidable, she was delighted to find her life transformed dramatically for the better. ♦

11.3.2 Generalizing from Imagined Aftermaths

I like to *imagine* one or more very specific and detailed illustrations of the life I might lead following each specified option consequence, or indeed of the option itself directly (which is an alternative method to explicitly modeling specified outcomes). I examine by introspection how eagerly I look forward to each such aftermath and then generalize to the whole range of possible aftermaths to that consequence[3]. I believe that replicating concrete aftermaths gives the best fixes on D's real values[4]. For example, imagine the most plausible story of what your future would be if you married Jane or Lulu, or, if Democrat A or Republican B becomes president of the United States. Imagine yourself, say, five years out. Looking back, then, under which scenario do you think you would have least regrets?

Example. D is deciding whether to have an extramarital romance. How does she compare three possible prospects: "status quo (null option)", and the consequences "caught in affair", and "not caught in affair" (to each of which she will attach a probability)? The comparison involves dwelling on such things as guilt, physical fulfillment, and marital upset. If D has no experience of the second or third options,

---

[3] A more advanced method for generalizing aftermaths is "step-through stimulation" (Brown and Ulvila, 1978).
[4] A comparable argument applies to holistic scale *anchors*. Visualizing and evaluating an outcome is easier if it is a real situation. Would you sooner be Bill Gates or Napoleon, bearing in mind salient features of their lives? The more richly textured the scenario, the better.

comparing them to the status quo may be so problematic and unstable (e.g., dependent on her momentary mood) as to make her preferred choice indeterminate. If she does have experience of both, and the analogy is close, it should be much easier. (E.g., she remembers saying to herself, "I'll never go through this again"). ♦

11.4 DISAGGREGATING UTILITY INTO CRITERIA

Where there is only one criterion and it is a natural metric (such as money), there may be little problem evaluating option criterion scores. Otherwise (e.g., where there are multiple conflicting or intangible criteria), this evaluation can be extraordinarily difficult.

11.4.1 Identifying All Criteria

The most important (and common) source of unsound choice is failure to identify all relevant criteria. Criteria can be identified initially by informally discussing why D tends to like one option more than another. Catching criteria overlooked this way is usually successful after feeding back to D the results of a plausible pilot model, which may produce a choice that D finds patent nonsense.

After doing the best one can to identify all usefully distinguishable criteria (as with uncertain possibilities), there is nearly always some irreducible "anything else." It is useful to single out as a separate criterion anything major in "anything else."

11.4.2 Criteria as Factual Predictors of Utility

It can be argued that ultimately D has only one welfare criterion, which is utility (however difficult it might be to measure or even define). Anything else that might look like a criterion is no more than a predictor of, or *contributor* to, utility. However, it is usually useful to distinguish criteria *as if* D cared for them in their own right, and indeed, D may feel that he does care for them in their own right.

D may think that, say, brains and beauty are criteria in choosing a potential spouse. However, logically, they are of interest only to the extent that they influence D's welfare broadly enough defined. With this perspective, all decision analysis is factual assessment (i.e., a prediction of utility). "If I prefer Jane's combination of brains and beauty to Lulu's, it is because I predict it will lead to a happier life (other things being equal)."[5] Value judgments are then really exercises in descriptive psychology. "What will make this person most happy?"

What is distinctive about what we *call* criteria is that D feels a direct sense of preference among them, expressed, for example, as a "value trade-off." Thus, "I wouldn't engage in political sleaze if you paid me a million dollars." This kind of directly perceived trade-off, though, however accurately measured, could involve an error in factual assessment. If I examined my soul and past experiences more carefully, I might

---

[5]Thus an ICE model is in effect a linear regression of utility on the various "criteria."

conclude that in fact a million dollars would more than compensate for any distaste for sleaze I might feel. The distinction between "criteria" and "*contributors*" is still useful, because perceived "value trade-off" among criteria avoids the cognitive burden of making an explicit prediction.[6] Nevertheless, D can ask herself perfectly reasonably "Would I be happier with Woody Allen or Woody Harrelson?" and then explore the question of why. Is it Woody Allen because he has more brains (as D thinks) and handsomeness matters less?

The perspective of criteria as instruments of welfare allows D to go beyond introspection in eliciting values. D can treat it as a technical task rather than a preference elicitation. The only irreducibly subjective consideration is whether D prefers one comprehensively described situation to another, in which case D, by definition, will judge it to have higher utility.

Example. My friend Geoff died a sad and lonely old bachelor. In his youth he decided not to get married. He once told me that that was the decision in his life that he most regretted, because it denied him the prospect (uncertain, at the time, to be sure) of children. When he made his young decision, he may have thought of parenthood as a low-importance criterion. A thorough *factual* assessment would have thrown light on the probable contribution of parenthood to welfare, and to his in particular.[7] ♦

Example. In Chapter 4 we saw a case where it appeared rational for a youth to choose to become a drug dealer, given his particular antisocial and short-term preferences. Colleagues have argued that he was making a *factual* error in evaluating his criteria. If he thought harder (possibly with our help) or had better knowledge, they contend he would have realized that pursuing his stated goals was not the best way to a happy life, and that therefore, he will (probably) be glad in the long run if he doesn't deal drugs.[8] ♦

11.4.3 Evaluating "Anything Else"

It is usually very difficult to handle an "anything else" criterion within the ICE procedure treating *criterion score* and *importance weight* the usual way. I favor the alternative of disregarding the issue until choice time and then ask D "Could taking any other criteria into account affect the choice?". If it could affect the choice, elicit

---

[6]Time discounting in financial analysis is a special case of trade-off standing in for prediction. When we talk of a 5% discount rate (for purposes, say, of calculating the *present equivalent* of a future cash flow), we may think of it as the preference judgment that we are indifferent between $1 today and $1.05 in a year's time. If we dig deeper (which we may prefer not to bother with), we are predicting something like "$1 could be turned into $1.05 in a year's time."
[7]I read a study appearing to show that middle-aged married men are more contented than their unmarried counterparts.
[8]They may be right, but they don't have to be. I charged them with seeking to "reduce cognitive dissonance," a widespread psychological trait, like the man who said "What's good for GM is good for America" (Festinger, 1957).

it as an adjustment component of utility (without attempting to disentangle score and weight as in ICE). The form might be "I judge that taking into account any criteria other than those listed would add to (or subtract from) about 10% of the option utility already derived."

11.5 ELICITING ADDITIVE CRITERION COMPONENTS

11.5.1 Plus–Minus Tally Models

When constructing a plus–minus tally model (see Chapter 4), how do you assure that the relative number of pluses and minuses you assign as components of options to overall utility realistically reflects what you know about option outcomes and criterion importance (which are not distinguished in plus–minus tally)? One way is to probe for inconsistencies.

Example. In our Jane and Lulu date example, D is choosing which to ask out. He gives each of them pluses and minuses on brains and beauty according to the following table. It compares each to the average lady of his acquaintance (i.e., *standard fixed base*).

	Jane	Lulu
Brains	+	–
Beauty	–	++
Cooking	+	0
Humor	+	–
Pleasantness	–	–
Accommodating	0	+++
Net	+	++

This analysis suggests that both are above-average dates, but Lulu is one plus ahead and so would be favored. However, some thought experiments may help to check out the realism of this analysis:

- Would D really prefer Jane to some specific person he can think of who is average on all six criteria (since she nets one plus)?
- Is Lulu's advantage over Jane on beauty really just as important as her advantage on being accommodating (three pluses for both criteria)?
- Would D really be indifferent between Lulu and a woman who differed from her only in being average on brains and humor (an improvement at 0 vs. – –), and average on beauty (which is worse at 0 vs. ++)?

Any incoherence that the questions above uncover could mean that the original or thought experiment evaluations, or both, are at fault. ♦

Such checks can be made sharper if the evaluations are made more precise than plus–minus tallying with quantitative utility partitioning (e.g., on a scale from 0 to ± 10). That increase in precision would be a natural progression for the analysis. However, the mental exercise is essentially the same and its success depends on how good the decider's imagination is. Can he really put himself in the hypothetical situation and know what he would choose? As noted earlier, it is always prudent to allow for possible criteria other than those specified. Eliciting how much they contribute to option utility is tricky, since there is going to be little in the judger's head to go on.

11.6 ELICITING ICE IMPORTANCE WEIGHTS

With ICE, the key preference judgment, after identifying the criteria, is in assigning importance weights to each of these criteria. A useful practice is to identify the most important criterion (appropriately interpreted), define its weight as, say, 10, and then assign lesser weights to the other criteria. In principle, the relative importance that D attaches to conflicting criteria can be handled in different ways, depending on how the criteria interact with each other (Keeney and Raiffa, 1993). I have only addressed the simple (and not always realistic) ICE case, where utility of outcomes is the *sum* of criteria utility components. Departures of this approximation from realism can be handled by judgmental adjustments to total utility.

11.6.1 Comparing Scale Ranges and Units

The basic task in assigning importance weights is to compare the utility of going from 0 to 100 on the criterion scales. Important questions to be asked are: "If you were starting at 0 on two criteria, would you sooner go to 100 on one than the other? By how much?" or alternatively, "Would you sooner improve by one unit (on the 0 to 100 scale) on one criterion than on the other? How many units on one criterion trade off against one unit on the other?" To be usable, the weights need to reflect the relative importance of criterion units on the specific scale used [e.g., "I would trade two units of sweetness against one unit of tartness" (on the scale used) implies that the importance weight to be used for tartness is twice that for sweetness]. (The absolute values of the weights are not critical, just the relation between them.)

Consistency of Scale Ranges With ICE, the first requirement of the comparison task is to assure that the *same* scale is used for weighting a criterion and interpolating its score. The danger of disconnect is greatest when a different judger provides each input. Often, a content expert will judge criterion score and the decider will determine importance. If scenarios are described precisely to correspond to scale anchor points, the answers to questions above will tell you which criterion has the greater importance weight. For example, if D is comparing candidates for a job, it would be best to identify specific other individuals with the required favorable and unfavorable criterion

11.6.2 Dangers of Miseliciting importance

There are a number of serious potential pitfalls in eliciting weights.

Cop-out Weights As with factual assessments, "cop-out" values may be assumed arbitrarily for preference judgments, especially since preference judgments, unlike factual possibilities, are usually difficult to substantiate or refute. (*De gustibus non disputandum.* Tastes are not to be disputed.)

A common and major error in assigning importance weights in an ICE model is to differentiate too little between criteria (i.e., to give all criteria almost equal importance weights). In fact, there is a tendency to make their weights differ by no more than a factor of 2. The most important is treated as only twice as important as the least important. In actuality, that small range among importance weights is quite rare: factors of 20 or more are more common. It is largely a question of how criteria are grouped. Underdifferentiation can be checked by regrouping. Suppose that 10 criteria are specified, with, say, three of them major and seven minor. The same seven minor criteria can be grouped into a single criterion. If that new criterion is weighted against the three major criteria, and its weight is less than the sum of the seven original weights, the elicitations are inconsistent and need to be changed.

In Tex's case, we distinguished five criteria, with the following importance weights imputed to him (see Figure 6.3b): peak income, 0.2; final wealth, 0.1; quality of life, 0.3; work interest, 0.2; prestige, 0.2. The weights are not very different. We could have specified several "quality of life" criteria instead of lumping them together as here. Chances are that Tex would have assigned individual weights that implied more weight to "quality of life" as a whole. Possibly: entertainment, 0.1; social life, 0.2; physical environment, 0.1; creature comforts, 0.05; freedom from stress, 0.15; other quality of life, 0.1; with a total quality of life weight of 0.7, more than twice that obtained earlier.[9] If "other quality of life" had been broken out further, I predict the effect would have been even stronger. In any case, the numbers used here were hypothetical, introduced in Chapter 6 purely to illustrate modeling method.

This bias can be exploited by an unscrupulous decision "aider" to make one criterion appear more important than it should, by splitting it into several criteria.

Intuitive Importance Weights Having D elicit her own importance weights for ICE intuitively, rather than having someone else elicit them more systematically is a tempting but dangerous practice. As demonstrated in the Lulu–Jane exercise in Section 6.3.4, any change in the scale changes the interpretation of the weight. I surmise that intuitive weights will work reasonably well if the range of the scale corresponds to what D considers a *plausible* range, but I know of no empirical evidence.

---

[9]Part of the problem could be the coarseness of measurement (nearest 0.05), but that can be remedied easily by finer measurement (say, the nearest 0.01).

11.6.3 Caution in Splitting Holistic Elicitation into Criteria

Any *judgment-intensive* model can be made more *structure-intensive* by disaggregating elements within it. Put another way, elicitation can always be replaced or augmented by disaggregation. In particular, any *holistic* evaluation of an option or outcome can be split into criteria as part of a multicriteria model or criteria-plus-uncertainty model (see Chapter 7). However, it is not always wise to disaggregate, even when there are significantly conflicting criteria. Splitting into criteria may not produce an *enhanced substitute* for unaided judgment.[10] Although disaggregation usefully focuses D's attention on specific sources of utility (i.e., distinguishable criteria), multicriteria models are prone to miss much that a competent unaided judgment should—and does—take into account. For example, it may be the case that:

- Criteria are not exhaustive.
- Surrogate metrics are used that do not entirely reflect how one criterion compares with another.
- Criteria do not really combine in a simple function as expressed (e.g., additive or multiplicative).

11.6.4 Reviewing Rationale for Inputs

When reviewing the analysis of a choice with other people (friendly or not) or for oneself, it is often helpful to note briefly the *rationale* (argument) for any given set of preference inputs (or factual inputs, for that matter). This rationale helps other judgers to check whether they agree and helps the original judger to reconsider inputs.

For example, in the ICE analysis in Figure 6.3, Tex's "economic criteria" are split into "peak income" and "final wealth." A rationale footnote might say: "Any difference between other economic criteria (e.g., average income) I expect will not change the choice of career, and so need not be included as a separate criterion." The importance weight for "peak income" is given as 0.2 and for "final wealth" as 0.1. The rationale might be: "Don't care too much about how much I leave for my heirs. Peak income also seems to capture pretty well what I accumulate and consume over my lifetime, which is at least as important. But it might bias career choice toward business, because income is more variable than in academia." Peak income scores (factual judgments) are 80 for business and 40 for academia. The rationale might be: "Might need to adjust the 80 down, because business income is more variable, which is a minus."

11.6.5 Plausible Implied Judgments

Informants often balk at producing input judgments, especially value judgments, for reasons of privacy or reluctance to commit themselves. However, they may

---

[10] I suspect that much of the popularity of multicriteria models among decision analysts is that some analysts (e.g., with an engineering rather than behavioral or decider background) are more comfortable with challenges of model structure than of judgment elicitation.

more readily confirm a judgment that is *presented* to them. They may not want to take the initiative to volunteer, say, "I would give up $100k of company earnings if I could double our size." On the other hand, if a statement like this is *presented* to informants for comment, they may not blink an eye at responding something like "More than $100k, probably twice as much."

Example. During a project to evaluate a U.S. "oil diplomacy" initiative, I needed to elicit preference trade-offs (a utility curve) for the Saudi oil supply from the National Security Council staff. I had great difficulty getting answers to questions like "How much would you spend from the federal budget to increase oil supply by 50% (at current prices)?" But when I said "According to the preference curve I have drawn for you, if you had to, you would support spending $2 billion from the federal budget to increase Saudi oil supply from 6 million barrels a day to 9 million," the informant would answer "sounds a bit high to me" without discomfort. ♦

There is a similar but lesser phenomenon with factual judgments. I will say: "My guess is that you would be amazed if the impact of the proposed agreement were to increase Saudi oil supply by more than 1 million barrels a day." The informant might say: "No, not at all—in fact probably a good deal more." The danger of such prompting is "leading the witness," what psychologists call "anchoring" judgments, which can distort elicitation. One solution is to *infer* the prompt from other judgments that the informants themselves make. "If I understand what you just told me, you would not tilt U.S. policy this much toward the Arab cause if it cost 10 points in Jewish political support."

ASSIGNMENTS

Prepare for Discussion After Reading
Revealed Preference

1. Public statistics indicate that the suicide rate in Sweden is the highest in the Western world. Does this indicate that Swedes are, on average, the least happy?

Prepare for Later Discussion or Submission
Holistic Evaluation

2. Consider whether you were happier last year than the preceding year.
   (a) Suppose that a wizard could guarantee that *next* year would be as "good" for you as either last year or the preceding year. Which would you choose? Say why, if you can.
   (b) Take the worst and the best for you of the last five years as having utility of 0 and 100 (i.e., bad/good anchors). Where on that scale would you put each

of the last two years? (It is OK if *one* of them is 0 or 100, but if *both* are, pick a different range of years, so that one of them is *not* 0 or 100.)

Identifying Criteria

3. Work in pairs. Student A makes as complete a list as s/he can of criteria that s/he would use in choosing a flat to rent, and constructs an ICE rule. (Define the criteria broadly enough that there are not more than about 6 criteria.) Student B attempts to identify two flats that contradict this ICE rule. That is, A should prefer one flat according to the ICE rule, but in fact prefers the other flat.

    (For example, A's choice could be affected by some additional criterion that s/he initially missed (e.g., it is next to a sewage farm!).

Importance Weights

4. Compare intuitively or informally two plausible options for your next vacation. Now do an ICE on the same options, where there are just two criteria: economic and noneconomic considerations. Is the preferred option the same? If not, why?

Chapter 12

Applied Term Project

This book is intended to enhance your skill at making professional and personal decisions by integrating quantitative representations (models) of your judgment into your real thinking through the application of DA tools. In this chapter I have you exercise this ability on a single live issue, with tasks being assigned to fit the progressive introduction of material throughout a course based on this book.

Each student participates in one project, singly or in a group. Normally, in courses intended primarily to develop private decision skills, I encourage each student to work individually on a personal decision of his/her choosing. In courses intended to develop professional decision skills, I recommend group projects dealing with civic issues (see the sample report in Appendix 12A) unless class members happen to have a suitable project arising from their current work experience.

Administrative suggestions below, including assignments and student evaluation (Section 12.8) are, of course, at the instructor's discretion.

12.1 OVERVIEW

12.1.1 Choosing an Appropriate Decision

My intent is to have you exercise skills under problem circumstances as similar as possible to problems on which you eventually want to use them. Most important is that the issue has to be *real to you* (not hypothetical).

Rational Choice and Judgment: Decision Analysis for the Decider, by Rex Brown
Copyright © 2005 John Wiley & Sons, Inc.

Private-Oriented Course Project choice is straightforward in courses aimed at improving private decisions, since students' everyday experience provides representative problems to work on. If you are working on your own individual project, I recommend a personal choice that you are currently considering (e.g., whether to propose marriage), to which you can make a firm (but confidential) commitment by the time the project is due. If you are working in a group, I recommend a topical public policy controversy (e.g., social welfare legislation), although there is no real commitment involved and therefore less motivation for students to take the project seriously.

Professionally Oriented Course The choice of project is less straightforward where the targeted students are professionals in training (e.g., MBAs or MPPs). If you are training for a career that you are not yet (or not currently) involved in, you are unlikely to have a live issue available on which you can form a real opinion. Then, I favor a topical public policy issue that *someone else* (e.g., in government) will make professionally but that as citizens you can take positions on. Such civic decisions have useful analogies to your own future professional decisions, and the whole class can readily participate in their discussion.

Civic policy cases have the advantage of being of interest to both private individuals and professionals, although with a different perspective. On the other hand, personal issues have the built-in discipline of committing a person, to some extent at least, to a significant choice that s/he really has. This motivates you to make the choice responsibly rather than taking the lazy route of simply adopting model output as is.

If you are already an *active* professional (e.g., a manager studying part-time), you can work individually on a live professional choice for which you are responsible (or at least, where you are close to whoever is responsible, for whom you can serve as a consultant).

12.1.2 Use of Tools

The issue you choose has to fit into the course schedule (i.e., it can use only the techniques already covered by that time). If the course is structured on this book, students may, say, be called upon to model their chosen problem after Chapter 6, where only tools for analyzing multiple criteria will have been covered in any detail. Therefore, multiple criteria would have to be a significant feature of the decision problem (as is the case in most public policy).

On the other hand, problems where uncertainty about one criterion dominates (as in most business cases and in safety regulation) can only be modeled after uncertainty models—introduced in Chapter 7—have been covered. Stages A and B of the project schedule (see Section 12.1.4) can be assigned earlier, since no *formal* modeling is involved until stage C.

Making the soundest decision you can may draw on thought and experience that go well beyond this book. If it is an important decision, you have no obligation (now or in the future) to limit yourself to what you have learned here. DA may not even have the lead role in your thinking. However, if you are making the best decision you can and don't use anything in this book, you or I will have gone seriously astray!

12.1.3 Project Development

You will develop the project technically, much as you would if it were a real effort to aid a decision (e.g., in the sequencing of tasks), with two significant exceptions. One difference is that you must limit yourself to using factual *knowledge you already have*. Acquiring new knowledge before deciding might be the sensible thing to do if you were really facing the problem in the real world, but for learning DA it would not be the best use of your time here. Thus, you should not devote effort to researching the problem, which would distract you from exercising course skills. If you are completely unfamiliar with the issue, talking to, at most, one outside person familiar with the issue, or reading some brief press discussion, should provide enough background. The emphasis should be on using what you (or someone you are advising) already have in your head.[1]

The other difference from real problem solving is that you are allotted a fair amount of time in the course to work on the project (say, five assignments of four hours each). This may be more time than you would normally want to spend on a private choice (although you will speed up with practice). However, you are developing skills that can be transferred later to professional decisions that may call for much *more* effort (sometimes several person-years). The scale of analysis done in this project may be appropriate for a preliminary analysis by a professional decider before involving a decision analysis specialist for more intensive study.

12.1.4 Project Stages and Assignments

The development of the project unfolds over the course of the term and breaks down into the following distinct stages:

A. Set up the project and specify the choice to be aided and whose choice it is. Form teams (group projects only).
B. Evaluate the choice informally.
C. Evaluate the choice formally—qualitatively (based on Chapter 3).
D. Evaluate the choice formally—quantitatively (based on Chapters 4 to 7).
E. Make the actual choice, with any commitment to act, integrating model(s) developed in stages C and/or D into the decider's decision process.
F. Submit the final report, including a comparison with the stage B report ("before" and "after"), what if any action has or will be taken, and a postmortem on the project.

---

[1] You may, in fact, incidentally develop more knowledge about the issue than you started with, as you work on the project. This will result in improved choice that is *not* due to our tools—except to the extent that tools alert you to what new knowledge is needed.

Each of these stages has one or more assignments, covered in one or more class sessions, and is timed to draw on material covered so far. Assignments are identified as:

- **WA**: written assignment, to be submitted by the next class period (usually with a suggested length), or
- **OA**: oral assignment that students prepare by the next class period.

12.2 STAGE A: SET THE STAGE

(At the outset of the course, or as early as possible thereafter)

A1. Preliminaries

Read Section 12.1. You will only need to read the other sections of this chapter as the course unfolds. Clarify with the instructor your project mode (e.g., working individually on a personal project or in a group on a civic project).

A2. Set Up for the Group Civic Project

You will be evaluating a public policy issue from a citizen's perspective. Imagine you have been asked to advise a citizen, say on how s/he should vote in a referendum, or a legislator on how s/he should vote on a bill in Congress. Think broadly about issues you might address that involve an interesting choice with at least two clearly distinguished options (*OA*). Form three- to four-person groups. Submit a statement (one per group) of who is in the student group, with an asterisk designating a student to be contacted (*WA*).

A3. Identify the Problem

Identify a significant dilemma to be analyzed, at least partially using tools of this course. Specify what problem or opportunity is to be addressed and when firm action is to be taken (if there is some deadline), and by whom. *Tentatively* identify and define a few promising options. You can change the issue and/or options in assignment A4 if your initial pick does not prove promising. You are only required to evaluate two options, since comparing more options would not exercise any additional course material. You must envisage having to make a definite, but possibly reversible, commitment to one of two courses of action.

(*Personal choice only*) The issue should be one of real concern and perplexity to you, on which you would value help: i.e., the best thing to do should not be at all clear to you now. The issue should be your own choice and fairly pressing. It should ideally be a choice you will commit to after the course, so that it is a live issue throughout the course. However, it should make sense to make up your mind on, at least provisionally, by the end of the course. If you prefer, discuss the issue privately and confidentially with the instructor. (The instructor will undertake not to disclose anything about your individual projects to students or others without your permission.)

If you don't have any key personal choice, you can substitute someone else's decision. You may advise a friend or relative on what he/she ought to do, to advance his/his own interests, but you would need to involve him/her actively. The test of success then would be how, if at all, you help him/her with the decision s/he actually takes (or will take).

A4. Define the Options

(For the class following A3) Carefully define two promising and well-defined options (exclusive, but not necessarily exhaustive) that you will evaluate. Make clear what implementing each option would entail, but only to the extent needed to clarify what the options are[2]. (*WA: Use no more than three lines for each option.*)

12.3 STAGE B: EVALUATE THE CHOICE INFORMALLY

(Before Chapter 3 is assigned)

B1. Write a Preliminary Report

Evaluate the two options *informally*, as you would in the *absence of any formal tools*, and give your current preference, however tentative. Try not to draw on anything you have learned in the course so far (see below). Make your report thorough enough to make your case as convincing (but balanced) as possible, so that it covers all the issues you might normally take into account. (You might cast a civic choice as an opinion piece for a newspaper.)

Some Suggestions Take account of any lines of reasoning that might sway you in the real world. This might include your intuition, your own and other people's past experience with similar problems, conventional wisdom, and whatever else other people whom you trust think. What do you think opponents of your position, and/or experts in the field, say? How do you interpret the difference between you and them (e.g., in terms of your and their values, beliefs, etc.)? As noted above, don't do any new research on the problem, just rely on what you already know.

You should pay *no attention*, for the time being, to how you might turn your reasoning into a quantitative model. Thus, do not include or refer to any formal techniques we may have covered in the course (or that you have learned elsewhere). This stage will be treated as the "before" of a "before-and-after" appraisal of the course

---

[2]See Hammond et al. (1999, Chap. 4) on generating options. Timed, preferably, before much, if any, technical material has been introduced.

experience. Your informal reasoning about the choice is not limited in *any way* to what you might eventually model explicitly.

Your written hand-ins here (and later) can include group minority views, in whatever form you like. (*WA: Use up to two pages.*)

KEEP A COPY OF THIS REPORT (without changes) to attach to your final report as an appendix for comparison and reference.

B2. Report Orally

Group Projects Prepare an oral presentation to the class of about 5 to 10 minutes. Divide the writing and talking between members of your group as you please. Bear in mind that there will be one or two more written/oral reports later in the course, and by the end we would like everyone in the group to have participated in some oral presentation. Identify who, if anyone, has a minority opinion.

Individual Projects 1- to 2-minute presentations.

12.4 STAGE C: STRUCTURE REASONING QUALITATIVELY

(*Following Chapter 3*)

C1. Pros and Cons

Briefly, list all significant pros and cons of options (possibly reiterating parts of assignment B1).

Optional If feasible, identify balancing pairs of pros and cons such that they roughly cancel each other out in your judgment, and then eliminate them. See if the remaining pros and cons can be evaluated judgmentally more readily than before the others were eliminated (*WA*).

C2. Criteria

List about six main *criteria* on which to compare options (e.g., wealth), define them, and note subcriteria *if needed for clarity* (e.g., average income, final assets). The list may be a grouping or adaptation of pros and cons identified above (*WA*).

C3. Going Through the GOO

Submit a "G-O-O" table as in Figure 3.1, covering all the criteria you listed for C2 and noting which option appears favored under each criterion. Don't be concerned if the table appears to be inconsistent with any previous evaluation; your perception of the problem may have evolved. (This allowance for inconsistency and evolution in your thinking also applies to future assignments.) (*WA*)

12.5 STAGE D: MODEL REASONING QUANTITATIVELY

D1. Plus–Minus Tally

(*Following Chapter 4*)   Construct a "plus–minus tally" table like the second example in Section 4.1. If one of the options is "stay as is" (null option), some or all of its cells can be left blank (meaning that only the *impact* of that option on the criterion, not the absolute score of the criterion, is assessed). (*WA*)

D2. Scales

(*Following Chapter 5*)   Specify *scales* for each criterion, including the interpretation of any *good/bad anchor points* (*WA*).

D3. Create a Multicriteria Model

(*Following Chapter 6*)   Construct an *ICE* model in the form of a table. Include tentative *scores* and *importance weights* (noting any minority opinions). Briefly note the reasoning behind your scores and importance weights. Calculate the implied choice.

This exercise should demonstrate and provide only an *internal check* on technical feasibility and basic soundness of the ICE tool. Note any significant differences in considerations addressed between this ICE analysis and your informal B1 evaluation, and whether the same option is favored. (*WA, or oral briefing for group projects.*)

D4. Create the Uncertainty Model (*Optional*)

(*Following Chapter 7. NOTE: Chapter 7 on uncertainty modeling may be assigned too late in the course for this assignment to be doable at the time.*)   Reanalyze project choice with an uncertainty model, if feasible. Reconcile, if you can, any discrepancy with your multicriteria model analysis. Which type of model better fits the nature of your problem? Which seems most critical in this case: uncertainty or conflicting criteria? Which findings do you have most confidence in, if they differ? (*WA*)

12.6 STAGE E: INTEGRATE MODEL(S) INTO THE DECISION PROCESS

(*Possibly for the last day of class*)

E1. Make a Choice

Use model(s) and any other reasoning you can come up with to make your decision. That is, say which option you feel comfortable with acting on—that you accept as realistic and appropriate and are prepared to commit to. Contrary to many students' initial inclination, this stage in the project deserves at least as much effort as any other stage.

Your decision does not have to coincide with any particular model's output (and often won't), but hopefully, it benefits from some of your modeling. Draw on material from this course, but only to the extent that it helps you decide. In particular, review the results of any modeling you have done, plus–minus tally, ICE, and so on. Comparing and reconciling them may be helpful, particularly if they do not coincide (e.g., adjusting or reconciling inputs in plausible ways so that the outputs do coincide). However, although they are alternative approaches to the same judgment, they are not independent and may tap into substantially the same knowledge while still not exhausting all your useful and available information. (*No special assignment*)

E2. Oral Report

Prepare to present and discuss your decision. State your present views on the choice to be made and what your modeling showed. Make a balanced case for your final position to the rest of the class, much as if they were an audience to be enlightened. Be prepared to respond to questions and comments from other students and to reconsider your position if you become persuaded. Compare with the original stage B informal choice.

Group Projects Issues of general interest should be allotted enough time (say, 20 minutes) to entertain more substantial and probing comments and counterarguments from the rest of the class. The presentation may conclude with a vote on whether others agree with your choice. Note any minority findings.

Individual Projects Only a few minutes may be available for each student.

12.7 STAGE F: WRITE THE FINAL REPORT

(*WA: About 10 pages, including figures. Submitted one week after the last class.*)

F1. Main Report

The object of your report will be to demonstrate your ability to apply analytic tools covered in this course to a real problem. (The technical mastery of the tools is tested elsewhere in the course.) See the sample student report in Appendix 12A.

Sections

- Task statement, including the decision context, who is to decide, on what (two options), by when (*no more than two paragraphs*)
- Summarize initial informal appraisal (stage B), including the preliminary choice (*half a page*)
- Formal analysis (stages C and D), including the analytic strategy and a summary of steps and results (*no more than one page*)

- Conclusions (stage E), including the final decision, the relation to project analyses, other considerations, and the decision process (*four to eight pages*)
- **ACTION** (if there is action for students to take): specifically, what you (or whoever) is going to do (or have done), and when (*one paragraph*)

Where appropriate, the report can incorporate briefly material submitted in earlier assignments, with a reference to the assignment stage. These can be abbreviated or updated.

F2. Postscript

Evaluate what, if any, value the formal analysis appeared to have for your own decision process. Make any generalizations from this experience, such as role and dangers of DA, but only as illustrated in the context of *this project* (no free-floating generalizations). Explain how and to what extent the modeling has contributed, in total, to making up your mind (and/or communicating it to others). If your only concern had been to make a sound choice efficiently, how prominently would the formal modeling have figured in your total effort? As it is, how much of what you now conclude about the choice is due to the modeling exercise and how much to the informal thinking you did initially (or have done during the project)?

If there was a change in preferred option, or how strongly it is preferred, or if any considerations that appeared in your informal evaluation appear to be missing in the formal evaluation, discuss why. You may have acquired more *knowledge* during the project. Since *using* available knowledge, not developing more knowledge, was the course objective, you will not get credit for the latter.

Suggest follow-up decision-aiding activity that would be appropriate if you had the time. What is the highest-priority information to gather next? What, if any, further formal analysis would be useful, including elaborating your model or adding single-pass analyses?

F3. Appendix

This comprises a copy of the informal evaluation of options (submitted as assignment B1), without changes. This permits before-and-after appraisal of progress in your decision process.

12.8 EVALUATION OF STUDENT EFFORT

This project may represent an important part of your course evaluation. The paper and/or presentation (individual or group) will probably be evaluated primarily on the evidence that you have effectively integrated what you have learned into your decision process. Thus, you will not get credit simply for accepting the output of your model(s) as a guide to action, which may well *not* be the smartest thing to do. Although it is a major part of what you are learning here, modeling is an *aid* to deciding and may not be the dominant activity in making a real choice.

You should feel free to ask the instructor for further clarification of what is called for (but not for feedback or advice on your particular case or its analysis). You can ask the instructor any technical or other questions *not* specific to this case. It is not easy to check that students have made good decisions. Internal checking, by verifying that models are technically sound, is not enough (as discussed earlier). Some reality checking may be done by having the rest of the class challenge the individual or group findings.

12.8.1 Evaluation Criteria

The criteria for evaluating the project include the following (the most important three are indicated by an asterisk):

1. The quality of your initial informal reasoning and its convincing relation to any provisional choice you *then* made based on it
*2. The appropriateness of the model type(s) as implemented, including compatibility with informal reasoning (but not necessarily in a similar form)
3. The ambitiousness of analysis attempted, including the extent to which course material was drawn upon
*4. The technical quality, including sound modeling, avoiding logical errors, and defining inputs unambiguously
5. The quality of input derivation and rationale, including soundness and persuasiveness (e.g., interpretation of critical importance weights)
*6. The apparent soundness of the final decision *process*, based on the model(s) used and alternative perspectives and information given [including the initial informal analysis; how *well informed* the choice was is not relevant (see assignment F2 above)]
7. The student's realistic appreciation of the role that modeling played in this choice, including shift in, or confirmation of, the option preferred initially
8. The presentation, including clarity and conciseness of expression, and organization of material

Overall evaluation may include some aspects not covered above. However, you will not get credit for technical or other generalizations that are not *specific to the case*, or for knowledge that is not related to *course purpose*.

12.8.2 Evaluating Individual Contributions in a Group

Students may not participate equally in a project's performance, and this should be recognized somehow in project evaluation. Otherwise, the evaluation may be unfair, and students may be less motivated to devote effort to the project. However, it is difficult for the instructor to attribute credit to individual group members without being disruptively intrusive. Students may be called upon to self-evaluate their and others' relative components. For example, groups could note their combined impression of the relative contributions of individual members of the group as follows. Each student assesses everyone's contribution, including his/her own, on this scale: above average (for this group), 3 points; average, 2; below average, 1; none, 0. One member of each group submits the total score for each student by name; or, each student submits directly to the instructor (depending on where the anonymity is more important). Although fair grading of individual students is difficult, I think that it must be tried, to assure that everyone is motivated to give the project the high priority it deserves.

APPENDIX 12A
STUDENT PROJECT REPORT: ABOLISH THE DEATH PENALTY?

The following final project report is based on a very good student effort. It illustrates the type of project where a small group of students evaluates a public policy issue as responsible citizens.

Task Statement

Opinions on the question of death penalty vary between individuals. Some states do and others don't permit it. Internationally, some countries do maintain the death penalty, whereas others have abolished it. The death penalty is a perpetually revisited issue at the federal and state levels in the United States. An initiative for a change in the law could occur at any time. Possible legislative options vary in severity: for example, abolition for all but exceptional crimes (e.g., wartime crimes) or maintenance of death penalty but exemption for special groups (e.g., mentally impaired, under 18 at time of crime, defendants receiving inadequate legal representation).

Options Whether the U.S. Congress should abolish the death penalty under any circumstances anywhere in the United States. (Yes, abolish; or no, maintain as is.)

Initial Informal Position

See assignment B1 report below.
   Proponents of the death penalty argue that:

- The death penalty is more cost-effective than other forms of punishment (where convicts have to be housed and fed by the state throughout their lives).
- The death penalty helps reduce crime, and thus crime rates are lower.
- The death penalty encourages personal responsibility.

- The United States must assert its views and should not abolish the death penalty purely to please other nations or simply to conform to practices encouraged by the international community (notably, Europe).

Opponents of the death penalty argue that:

- The penalty is immoral and barbaric.
- The death penalty is contrary to the Universal Declaration of Human Rights (UDHR), which was ratified by the United States.
- The death is irrevocable, and there is the risk of executing innocents.
- The death penalty is unfair, as jury decisions seem largely to be dictated by the race of the defendants and victims.
- A life sentence has the advantage of making convicts think of what they have done to victims and families.

The clincher for us, at this time, was the recent articles and images produced on the occasion of the execution of Timothy McVeigh, the "Oklahoma bomber," which shocked us profoundly. We think that society should not behave like its worst members, which is what it does when it executes criminals. Thus, before engaging in any sort of systematic analysis, based on this informal reasoning, we tend to *favor abolition of the death penalty*, primarily on moral grounds. (But we also had the feeling that it could be difficult for us to communicate our reasoning to others.)

Analysis

Since the analytic assignment was set before Chapter 7, we did not have uncertainty modeling to draw on, so our models are all multicriteria. However, we have tried to take some informal account of uncertainty about criterion scores.

Criteria See Table 12A.1 for descriptions of the death penalty criteria.

"Going Through the GOO" Criteria are marked (A) or (M) to indicate whether they favor abolishing or maintaining the death penalty. Cells in the body of Table 12A.2

TABLE 12A.1 Death Penalty Criteria Descriptions

Criterion	Description
Morality	Morality of U.S. society
Individual responsibility	Degree to which U.S. individuals in the United States take responsibility for their acts
Injustice	Irrevocable miscarriages of justice
Crime	Crime rates in the United States
International law	Conformity to international law by the United States

TABLE 12A.2 Death Penalty GOO

	Option	
Criterion	Maintain DP	Abolish DP
Morality (A)	Produce more barbaric acts	
Individual responsibility (M)	Strong	Weak
Injustice (A)	Risk of irrevocable miscarriage	Less risk
Economic (M)	Will save money	
Crime (M)	More likely to reduce crime	
International law (A)	Conflicts	Conforms
Other considerations (?)	None?	None?

show our evaluation of either relevant aspects of an option or its probable outcomes. A blank cell means that the corresponding option is the base with which the other option is compared (e.g., the first row says we think that maintaining the death penalty produces more barbaric acts than would abolishing it).

Evaluation after GOO. Each option has three criteria favoring it, but the pros for abolishing the death penalty seem weightier. No change in our moderate **preference for abolition.**

Plus–Minus Tally Pluses and minuses are defined as how much better or worse "abolish DP" is than the null option "maintain DP" (Table 12A.3).[3]

Current Group Opinion. The pluses and minuses appear to cancel out. However, we are not really satisfied that this model is an acceptable substitute for our judgment.

TABLE 12A.3 Death Penalty Plus–Minus Tally

	Option
Criterion	Abolish DP–Maintain DP
Morality	– – –
Individual responsibility	+ + +
Injustice	– –
Economic	+
Crime	+ +
International law	–
Overall utility	0

[3]*Author's note:* There is a significant error in Table 12A.3—see "Instructor Comments" below.

Bearing in mind the direct evaluation that we had performed previously, we still tend to favor slightly the abolition of the death penalty.

Importance-Weighted Criteria Evaluation

Scales for ICE (D2). Morality of society is interpreted as the level of morality of American society, due to maintaining or abolishing death penalty with the ends of the scale as specified (Table 12A.4). Other morality values (e.g., adultery, tax frauds) are held constant at current level; and similarly for other criteria.

Uncertainty. We do find uncertainties about criterion scores: How many more/fewer capital crimes would there be if the death penalty were abolished? How much more/less cost? And so on. However, we feel that the trade-offs between values are central to our choice, and in the context of this exercise, none of the uncertainties justify the effort of building a model dealing with it explicitly (e.g., decision tree, including probabilities). So we dealt with uncertainty implicitly, judgmentally assessing an average value, and adjusting it for any risk aversion to come up with a certain equivalent for the uncertain criterion score, as in Table 12A.5.

Weights. In our judgment and on our scales, 1 unit of morality is worth 1.5 units of individual responsibility, 1.5 units of injustice, 6 units of economic, 2 units of crime rates, and 6 units of international law; 1 unit of individual responsibility is worth 1 unit of injustice, etc. (see Table 12A.6).

TABLE 12A.4 Death Penalty Criteria Scales

Criterion	Anchors	Base
Morality	0 = South Africa under Apartheid 100 = Sweden with current level of social care	Fixed
Individual responsibility	0 = no crime ever punished 100 = Taliban law for women in Afghanistan	Fixed
Injustice	0 = 20 innocent people executed yearly 100 = 0 innocent people executed yearly	Fixed
Economic	0 = cost for the state of $2M per killer arrested 100 = cost for the state of $300k per killer arrested	Fixed
Crime	0 = +20% murders in the United States 100 = −20% murder in the United States	Fixed
International law	0 = reputation of China for human rights 100 = reputation of the Hague tribunal	Fixed

TABLE 12A.5 Death Penalty ICE

Criterion	Weight	Maintaining		Abolition	
		Score	Product	Score	Product
Morality	6	35	210	75	450
Ind'l resp.	4	65	260	40	160
Injustice	4	25	100	75	300
Economic	1	70	70	15	15
Crime	3	65	195	40	120
International law	1	30	30	75	75
Total			**865**		**1120**

TABLE 12A.6 Death Penalty Criteria Weights

Criterion	Weight	Normalized Weight
Morality	6	0.32
Ind'l responsibility	4	0.21
Injustice	4	0.21
Economic	1	0.05
Crime	3	0.16
International law	1	0.05

Model Input and Output. With normalization of weights, D overall scores become 45.5 for maintaining and 59.05 for abolition (i.e., the same ratio). This now **strongly favors abolition.**

Source of Score Assessments. Some of our reasoning behind the certain equivalent scores is as follows.

Crime Rates. The effect of maintaining or abolishing the death penalty on crime rates is certainly uncertain. We have come across figures that tend to show that having the death penalty may have only a small effect on crime rates. Overall our feeling is that the death penalty has a limited positive effect on crime rates, but we are uncertain about the exact effect and find it difficult to quantify. We first defined a range in which we were confident the criterion scores will lie. Our conservative estimate (reflecting some risk aversion) is that abolition would increase murders in the United States by 4% (40 on scale).

Economics. The supporters of the death penalty argue that executing culprits is less costly that keeping them in jail. We have sometimes heard a contrary argument, but less often. We have never seen precise numbers on the question, and feel uncertain about the outcomes of the two options on this criterion. We first defined an interval in which we feel the values would be found and used the extremities as anchors for the scale (0 = cost for state of $2M per convicted jailed for life; 100 = cost for state of

$300k for convicted sentenced to death). Within this interval, we assessed the scores of the options in a way that we feel is conservative, again to allow for risk aversion.

Other Criteria. Reasoning is comparable.

Conclusions

Reviewing Analyses The initial informal evaluation (stage B) and "going through the GOO" both slightly favored abolishing the death penalty. The plus–minus tally was a wash. The ICE model clearly favored abolition. This consistent support for abolition coincided with our ending updated intuition (which it was, at least implicitly, based on). However, all four approaches were by no means independent. They were based on the same underlying perceptions and knowledge of team members, looking at them in slightly different ways. Thus, they could be lacking in some important way. So we tried to "think outside the box," by tapping radically different data.

International Comparison The United States still executes convicted murderers, whereas most European countries do not. Based on our general experience, we are inclined to trust the responsible behavior of these European legislatures more than ours. This tends to strengthen a little the case for abolition. The U.S. murder rate is much higher than in comparable countries (who do not have the death penalty). Although that could be due to other international differences (e.g., the availability of guns), it tends to discredit somewhat the argument that the death penalty deters murder. Again, it reinforces the case for abolition.

Examining Conflicting Perspectives. We talked to a few responsible and intelligent people who disagree with our position and favor maintaining the death penalty in order to see if we had overlooked some telling consideration. Their disagreement with us seemed to stem largely from their attaching more importance to reducing crime than to ethical considerations, and also believing that the death penalty deterred crime more than we believed. Politicians appeared to be pandering to bloodthirsty voters. These arguments did not sway us significantly, and we remained strongly in favor of abolition.

Postscript

Refining Inputs

Crime Rates. If we had more time and resources, we could do statistical analysis: for example, comparing the murder rate in U.S. states that do and don't have the death penalty, taking into account what else might differentiate states (e.g., different gun control laws).

Economics. We could do a comparative cost study of states and countries that do and don't have the death penalty, but to do that might take more effort than it is worth.

"Intangible" Issues. Studying what philosophers, political analysts, and others have written about other effects, especially with a moral component, could help clarify our somewhat confused feelings and thoughts as they affect plus–minus tally, importance weights and scores, and the synergy or redundancy between criteria.

Role of DA We feel that our informal reasoning has been greatly enhanced by more formal modeling. We now have, for example, a much better understanding of why we are in favor of the abolition of death penalty (especially our values). We also feel more confident about our choice and can communicate its rationale to others. This rationale facilitates dialogue between opponents and supporters by pinpointing the source of disagreement, and makes it easier to persuade a skeptic. We are aware that parts of the models could be refined further but feel that it would not be productive, and unlikely to reverse our position.

INSTRUCTOR COMMENTS

1. Basically, a very sound and well-balanced study. I was particularly impressed with their plural evaluation and with the honest intent of challenging their own perspectives and testing any possible "tunnel vision."
2. However, there is a clear technical error in the plus–minus tally exercise (Table 12A.3), which is potentially serious. Defining the plus–minus column as "abolish–maintain" means that you are evaluating abolish, but using maintain as the zero option base (for all criteria), which is fine. However, the pluses and minuses in the cells had the *wrong sign* (see Chapter 5). For example, *morality criterion* shows three minuses, indicating that abolish is *worse* on morality than maintain, which is the opposite of the team's view. As it happens in this case, the pluses and minuses cancel out in total, so the mistake has no practical impact—although it could have.
3. Also, the evaluation of 65 as the score for maintaining death penalty option on the crime criterion represents a 6% drop in crime if no action is taken with regard to the death penalty. This relatively large effect requires either explanation or reconsideration.

Epilog

I have tried to present here a "minimal kit of tools" that will be useful on a wide variety of decision issues. They range from minor adaptations of common sense (such as "going through the GOO" and *plus–minus tally*) to quantitative models that elaborate familiar lines of informal reasoning according to decision theory logic (such as importance-weighted criteria evaluation and probability-weighted utility).

State of the Art

Bear in mind that this book is just one person's approach to decision aiding, albeit a person with a good deal of varied decision-aiding experience. Important developments are surely on the way. In particular, I expect expertise and technique to become more specific to application domains (such as business, defense, and energy), as aiders develop comparative advantage in a particular substantive knowledge and client base.

The practice of DA has been dominated by application generalists (like myself) until recently, largely because the limited number of trained decision analysts have found it more rewarding to serve a wide and varied market than a narrow one. However, we generalists no longer have a monopoly on technical prowess and are increasingly at a comparative disadvantage over application specialists who also have technical strength. Application specialists can concentrate on a limited group of client organizations and draw on decision analysis in conjunction with other decision-aiding approaches. However, there have been successful examples of this mode of consulting as far back as the 1970s (see McNamee and Celona, 2001).[1]

The purest form of application-specific DA is where the decision aiders are employed by a single organization, even by a single decider, and aiders are adept at DA but not committed to it over other approaches. This mode may potentially be the most useful. The aiders are then up to speed on the setting and players involved in decisions and are free to use DA where it is most useful. Most important, they are motivated to serve the decider alone (Brown, 1970) to the best of their ability.

Where Do You Go from Here?

This course book is designed to be self-contained, but there are several productive further directions for the eager student to go, depending on your interests. For example:

- Theoretical depth (Watson and Buede, 1987)
- Domain specifics [e.g., business (Clemen, 1996), medicine (Weinstein, 1996)]
- Psychological foundations (Tversky, 1996)
- Software tools (Barclay, 1986)
- Advanced decision analysis methodology (Zeckhauser et al., 1996)

There are appealing alternative and complementary decision-aiding approaches, and I encourage students to broaden their armory of decision tools by exploring them, either in parallel with or after this material.

Professional Resources

If you have reasonably mastered the substance of this book, you should already have skills that you can use productively on your own as a private or professional decider. However, where the stakes are high, as in much executive-level deciding in business and government, you should benefit greatly from the assistance of specialist resources. Foremost among those is the Decision Analysis Society (*http://www.fuqua.duke.edu/faculty/daweb*), which can refer you to others, and its new journal, *Decision Analysis* (*http://www.da.pubs.informs.org*). Leading academic centers of research and teaching include the Fuqua School at Duke University, the Kennedy School of Public Administration at Harvard University, the Department of Engineering-Economic Systems at Stanford University, the Environmental Engineering Policy School, and the Social and Decision Sciences Department at Carnegie-Mellon University.

Professional decision aiders, well grounded in DA theory and experienced in its application, are essential in any explicit use of DA, if only to check on the soundness

---

[1] As early as the 1970s, this mode of consulting was active. Paul Marshall, a star DA student of mine at Harvard Business School, has concentrated since then on serving the steel industry with eclectic tools.

of analysis that you may do on your own. In particular, you will generally be ill advised to use decision aiding software, even fairly primitive, without a consultant at your side.

A Request

There will inevitably be mistakes in this first edition, and I would very much appreciate anyone pointing them out to me at *rbrown@gmu.edu*. [In fact, I will send a free copy of the second edition (if any) to whomever first sends me any comment that I use.]

References

Allison, G. 1971. *The Essence of Decision: Explaining the Cuban Missile Crisis.* Boston: Little, Brown.

Barclay, S. 1986. *A Brief Description of HIVIEW and EQUITY.* London: The London School of Economics and Political Science (University of London).

Baron, J., and Brown, R. V. 1988. Why America can't think straight. Outposts. *The Washington Post*, August 7.

Baron, J., and Brown, R. V. (Eds.). 1991. *Teaching Decision Making to Adolescents.* Mahwah, NJ: Lawrence Erlbaum Associates.

Bell, D. E., Raiffa, H., and Tversky, A. (Eds.). 1988. *Decision Making: Descriptive, Normative, and Prescriptive Interactions.* New York: Cambridge University Press.

Brown, R. V. 1969. *Research and the Credibility of Estimates.* Boston: Harvard University, Graduate School of Business Administration, Division of Research. (Reissued by Richard D. Irwin, Homewood, IL, 1972).

Brown, R. V. 1970. Do managers find decision theory useful? *Harvard Business Review*, May–June, pp. 78–79.

Brown, R. V. 1978. Heresy in decision analysis: modeling subsequent acts without rollback. *Decision Sciences*, 9:543–554.

Brown, R. V. 1982. Prescriptive organization theory in the context of submarine combat systems. In *Proceedings of the 5th MIT/ONR Workshop on C systems.* LIDS-R-1267. Cambridge, MA: Laboratory for Information and Decision Systems, Massachusetts Institute of Technology, December, pp. 149–155.

Brown, R. V. 1987. Decision analytic tools in government. In Karen B. Levitan (ed.), *Government Infostructures.* Westport, CT: Greenwood Press.

Rational Choice and Judgment: Decision Analysis for the Decider, by Rex Brown
Copyright © 2005 John Wiley & Sons, Inc.

Brown, R. V. 1989. Toward a prescriptive science and technology of decision aiding. *Annals of Operations Research, Volume on Choice Under Uncertainty*, 19, 467–483.

Brown, R. V. 1992. The state of the art of decision analysis: a personal perspective. *Interfaces*, 22(6):5–14.

Brown, R. V. 1993. Impersonal probability as an ideal assessment based on accessible evidence: a viable construct? *Journal of Risk and Uncertainty*, 7:215–235.

Brown, R. V. 1994. The role of statistical decision theory in decision aiding: measuring decision effectiveness in the light of outcomes. In *Aspects of Uncertainty: A Tribute to Dennis Lindley*, Freeman P. R., and Smith A. F. M. (Eds.). New York: Wiley.

Brown, R. V. 2002. Environmental regulation: developments in setting requirements and verifying compliance. In *Systems Engineering and Management for Sustainable Development*, Sage, A. P. (Ed.). *Encyclopedia of Life Support Systems (EOLSS)*. EOLSS Publishers, Oxford. http://www.eolss.net.

Brown, R. V. 2004. Naming concepts worth naming. *Decision Analysis*, 1(2).

Brown R. V. In press. Can decision aider priorities hurt decision aid usefulness? *Interfaces*.

Brown, R. V., and Lindley, D. V. 1978. *Reconciling Incoherent Judgments (RIJ): Toward Principles of Personal Rationality*. NTIS AD A059639. McLean, VA: Decisions and Designs, Inc., July.

Brown, R. V., and Lindley, D. V. 1986. Plural analysis: multiple approaches to quantitative research. *Theory and Decision*, 20:133–154.

Brown, R. V. and Pratt, J. W. 1996. Normative validity of graphical aids for designing and using estimation studies. In Zeckhauser, R., Keeney, R. L., Sebenius, J. (eds.). *Wise Choices* Symposium in honor of Howard Raiffa. Wiley.

Brown, R. V., and Ulvila, J. W. 1976. *Selecting Analytic Approaches for Decision Situations: A Matching of Taxonomies*. Technical Report 76-10. McLean, VA: Decisions and Designs, Inc., October.

Brown, R. V., and Ulvila, J. W. 1988. Does a reactor need a safety backfit? Case study on communicating decision and risk analysis information to managers. *Risk Analysis*, 8(2):271–282.

Brown, R. V., and Vari, A. 1992. Towards an agenda for prescriptive decision research: The normative tempered by the descriptive. *Acta Psychologica*, 80, 33–47.

Brown, R. V., Kahr, A. S., and Peterson, C. R. 1974. *Decision Analysis for the Manager*. New York: Holt, Rinehart and Winston.

Brown, R. V., Kelly, C. W., III, Stewart, R. R., and Ulvila, J. W. 1977. A decision-theoretic approach to predicting the timeliness of NATO response to an impending attack (U). *Journal of Defense Research*, Special Issue 77-1 (Crisis Management), May, pp. 126–135.

Brown, R. V., Flanders, N. E., and Larichev, O. I. 1997. Decision science for regulating the Arctic environment. *Arctic Research of the U.S.*, Issue 10, fall/winter, pp. 24–33.

Buede, D. M. 1986. Structuring value attributes. *Interfaces*, 16(2):52–62.

Buede, D. M., and Bresnick, T. A. 1992. Applications of decision analysis to military systems acquisition process. *Interfaces*, 22(6):110–123.

Cantor, S. B. 2004. Clinical applications in the DA literature. *Decision Analysis*, 1(1).

Carlin, F. 2005. Happy hour. *Psychology Today*, February.

Clemen, R. 1996. *Making Hard Decisions*, 2nd ed. Belmont, CA: Duxbury.

Clemen, R. and Kwit, R. 2001. The value of Decision Analysis at Eastman Kodak Company, 1990–1999. *Interfaces,* (Sept–Oct), 31:5, 74–92.

Corner, J. L., and Kirkwood, C. W. 1991. Decision analysis applications in the operations research literature, 1970–1989. *Operations Research,* 39:206–219.

De Bono, E. 1970. *Lateral Thinking.* New York: Harper & Row.

Edwards, W. 1954. The theory of decision making. *Psychological Bulletin,* 51:380–417.

Festinger, L. 1957. *A Theory of Cognitive Dissonance.* Stanford, CA: Stanford University.

Flanders, N. E., Brown, R. V., Andre'eva, Y., et al. 1998. Justifying public decisions in Arctic oil and gas development: American and Russian approaches. *Arctic,* 51(3):262–279.

Fong, G. T., Krantz, D. H., and Nisbett, R. E. 1986. The effects of statistical training on thinking about everyday problems. *Cognitive Psychology,* 18:253–292.

Grayson, C. J. 1973. Management science and business practice. *Harvard Business Review,* July–August.

Hammond, J., Keeney, R. L., and Raiffa, H. 1999. *Smart Choices: A Practical Guide to Making Better Decisions.* Boston: Harvard Business School Press.

Henrion, M. J. S., Breeze, J. S., and Horvits, E. J. 1991. Decision analysis and expert systems. *AI Magazine,* 12(4):64–91.

Hogarth, R. M. (1987). *Judgment and Choice: The Psychology of Decision,* 2nd ed. Chichester, West Sussex, England: Wiley.

Howard, R. A. 1992. Heathens, heretics and cults: the religious spectrum of decision analysis. *Interfaces,* 22(6).

Howard, R. A., and Matheson, J. E. (Eds.). 1983. *Readings on the Principles and Applications of Decision Analysis,* Vol. II. Menlo Park, CA: Strategic Decisions Group.

Howard, R. A., Matheson, J. E., and North, D. W. 1972. The decision to seed hurricanes. *Science,* 176:1191–1202.

Janis, I. L., and Mann, L. 1977. *Decision Making: A Psychological Analysis of Conflict, Choice, and Commitment.* New York: Free Press.

Kahneman, D. 2000. Experienced utility and objective happiness: a moment-based approach. Chapter 37 in *Choices, Values and Frames,* Kahneman, D., and Tversky, A. (Eds.). New York: Cambrige University Press and the Russell Sage Foundation.

Kahneman, D., and Tversky, A. (Eds.). 2000. *Choices, Values and Frames.* New York: Cambridge University Press and the Russell Sage Foundation, pp. 673–692.

Kahneman, D., Slovic, P., and Tversky, A. (Eds.). 1982. *Judgment Under Uncertainty: Heuristics and Biases.* New York: Cambridge University Press, pp. 422–444.

Keefer, D. L., Kirkwood, C. W., and Corner, J. L. 2004. Perspective on decision analysis applications, 1990–2001. *Decision Analysis,* March.

Keeney, R. L. 1987. An analysis of the Portfolio of Sites to Characterize a Nuclear Repository. *Risk Analysis,* 7:195–218.

Keeney, R. L. 1992. *Value Focused Thinking: A Path to Creative Decision Making.* Cambridge, MA: Harvard University Press.

Keeney, R. L., and Raiffa, H. 1993. *Decisions with Multiple Objectives, Preferences and Value Tradeoffs.* New York: Cambridge University Press.

Klein, G. A. 1989. Recognition-primed decisions. *Advances in Man–Machine Systems Research,* 5:47–92.

Laskey, K. B., and Campbell, V. N. 1991. Evaluation of an intermediate level decision analysis course. In *Teaching Decision Making to Adolescents*, Baron, J., and Brown, R. V. (Eds.). Mahwah, NJ: Lawrence Erlbaum Associates.

Lindley, D. V., Tversky, A., and Brown, R. V. 1979. On the reconciliation of probability assessments. *Journal of the Royal Statistical Society, Series A*, 142(2):146–180.

Majone, G., and Quade, E. 1980. *Pitfalls of Analysis*. Chichester, West Sussex, England: Wiley.

March, J. G., and Shapira, Z. 1982. Behavioral decision theory and organizational decision theory. In *Decision Making: An Interdisciplinary Inquiry*, Ungson, G. R., and Braunstein, D. N. (Eds.). London, England: Kent Publishing Co.

McNamee, P., and Celona, J. 2001. *Decision Analysis for the Professional*, 3rd ed. Menlo Park, CA: SmartOrg.

Mendez, W., Brown, R. V., and Bresnick, T. A. 1984. *Laboratory Level-Of-Control Decision Aid* (Advisory Committee Review Draft for EPA Office of Administration). Washington, DC: ICF, Inc., January.

Merkhofer, M. W. 1977. The value of information given decision flexibility. *Management Science*, 23(7):716–727.

Murphy, A. H., and Winkler, R. L. 1992. Diagnostic verification of probability forecasts. *International Journal of Forecasting*, 7:435–455.

Oliver, R. M., and Smith, J. Q. (Eds.). 1990. *Influence Diagrams, Belief Nets and Decision Analysis*. Chichester, West Sussex, England: Wiley.

Peters, B. M. 1990. Making decisions: how to balance reason and intuition. Health. *The Washington Post*, October 23.

Peterson, C. R., and Beach, L. R. 1967. Man as an intuitive statistician. *Psychological Bulletin*, 68:29–46.

Phillips, L. D., and Phillips, M. C. 1993. Facilitated work groups: theory and practice. *Journal of the Operational Research Society*, 44(6):533–549.

Porter, H. 1987. Dr Logic. *Illustrated London News*, October.

Pratt, S., Raiffa, H., and Schlaifer, R. O. 1995. *An Introduction to Statistical Decision Theory*. New York: McGraw-Hill.

Raiffa, H. 1986. *Decision Analysis: Introductory Lectures on Choices Under Uncertainty*, New York: Random House.

Raiffa, H., and Schlaifer, R. O. 1962. *Applied Statistical Decision Theory*. Boston: Harvard University Graduate School of Business Administration, Division of Research.

Savage, L. J. 1954. *The Foundations of Statistics*. New York: Wiley. (Reprinted in 1972 by Dover Publications, New York.)

Schacter, R. D. 1986. Evaluating influence diagrams. *Operations Research*, 34.

Schlaifer, R. 1978. *Analysis of Decision Under Uncertainty*, Melbourne, FL: Robert E. Krieger.

Sen, A. K. 1985. Rationality and uncertainty. *Theory and Decision*, 18:109–127.

Simon, H. 1986. Report of the Research Briefing Panel on Decision Making and Problem Solving. *Research Briefings*. Washington, DC: National Academy of Sciences.

Tversky, A. 1996. Contrasting rational and psychological principles of choice. In *Wise Choices*, Zeckhauser, R., Keeney, R. L., and Sebenius, J. (Eds.). Harvard Business School Press, Boston, MA.

Ulvila, J. W., and Brown, R. V. 1982. Decision analysis comes of age. *Harvard Business Review*, September–October, pp. 130–141.

U.S. Department of Energy, Office of Civilian Radioactive Waste Management. 1986. A Multiattribute Utility Analysis of Sites Nominated for Characterization for the First Radioactive-Waste, Repository: A Decision-Aiding Methodology. Nuclear Waste Policy Act, Section 112, May.

U.S. Nuclear Regulatory Commission. 1982. *Safety Goals for Nuclear Power Plants: A Discussion Paper*. NUREG-0880. Washington, DC: NRC, February.

Von Winterfeldt, D., and Edwards, W. 1988. *Decision Analysis and Behavioral Research*. New York: Cambridge University Press.

Watson, S. R. 1992. The presumptions of prescription. *Acta Psychologia*, 80(1–3):7–31.

Watson, S. R., and Buede, D. M. 1987. *Decision Synthesis: The Principles and Practice of Decision Analysis*. New York: Cambridge University Press.

Watson, S. R., and Brown, R. V. 1978. The valuation of decision analysis. *Journal of the Royal Statistical Society, Series A*, 141:69–78.

Weinstein, M. 1996. Decision analysis in health and medicine: two decades of progress and challenges. In *Wise Choices*, Zeckhauser, R., Keeney, R. L., and Sebenius, J. (Eds.). Harvard Business School Press, Boston, MA.

Winkler, R., Dyer, J., Saaty, T., and Harker, D. 1990. Special issue on AHP. *Management Science*, 36:247–275.

Zadeh, L. A. 1965. Fuzzy sets. *Information and Control*, 8:338–353.

Zeckhauser, R., Keeney, R. L., and Sebenius, J. (Eds.). 1996. *Wise Choices*. Harvard Business School Press. Boston, MA.

Glossary of Concepts and Terms

In a field such as decision analysis, where precision of communication is critical, it is important to use consistent terms for related but distinct concepts. Language in this field is still evolving and professional DA practice varies. I have tried to standardize on the boldface terms below, chosen primarily for their connotation to lay deciders, and only secondarily to the technical community.

Regular italics, here and in the main text, represent glossary terms introduced previously where the meaning may need refreshing. Adjectives that are in parentheses below are dropped in the text where the meaning should be clear. Alternative terms for the same concept in common use are shown in braces { ··· }. Notes after terms, if any, are *cues* to meaning, not precise definitions. Numbers in parentheses are chapters in which the term is introduced.

Action: committing resources (usually following a *choice*) (1)

Actual judgment: based on what the assessor really knows (cf. *hypothetical* judgment) (10)

(Decision) **aid:** help with deciding (1)

(Decision) **aider:** provides *DA* or other aid to *D* (1)

Anchor: 0 and 100 (or −100) points on a rating scale (5)

Approximate equivalent, substitute: close enough to be useful (4)

APU: probability-weighted *average personal utility* {subjective expected utility} (7)

(Arbitrary) **assumption:** an assignment of value or probability, without reference to its realism (e.g., for analytic convenience) (10)

Rational Choice and Judgment: Decision Analysis for the Decider, by Rex Brown
Copyright © 2005 John Wiley & Sons, Inc.

Single-**Aspect** model: only models uncertainty **or** multiple criteria (7)

Assessment updating: use of Bayes theorem to revise a probability, based on new evidence {Bayesian updating} (3)

Assessor: *judger* of a factual possibility (3)

Attribute: any property (descriptive or evaluatory) of a possibility {distinction} (5)

Average value: sum of possible values times probability, e.g., *average personal utility* (APU) (4)

Background knowledge, **&:** in addition to any specified knowledge (10)

Base: Interpretation of zero on scale (5)

Binary possibilities: two (7)

(Causal) dependence: *covariation* where direction matters {influence} (10)

Certain equivalent: single quantity, judgmentally equated to a gamble {certainty equivalent} (4)

Choice: selecting among identified options, a phase of the decision process (1)

Choice fork: branches are options {act fork} (4)

Civic decision: *D* takes a *private* position on a public issue (e.g., government policy) (1)

Clairvoyance: {perfect information} (10)

Coarse model: structurally simple (8)

Coherent: obeys logical rules of consistency (4)

Complete model: covers all relevant considerations comprehensively, implicitly or explicitly (5)

Complex model: elaborate structure (5)

(Additive) **Component:** elements of a quantity (e.g., utility *partitioned* into additive criteria) {argument} (6)

Comprehensive coherence: all of a judger's judgments are logically consistent; judger is fully rational (4)

Conditional probability: given some specified possibility (10)

Conditioned assessment: "it all depends" (3)

Conditioning possibility: affects uncertainty about another possibility (e.g., *contributor*) (10)

Consequences: Prospects due to D's action (may be defined *outcomes* or ill-defined) (5)

Constituent: interested party on whose behalf D is expected to act {stakeholder} (9)

Continuous *UQ*: can have any value on some *scale* (7)

Contributor: *attribute* of interest because it influences some *criterion* but is not itself a criterion (5)

Core model: a coarse model addressing the *target* evaluation directly (10)

Covaries with, **covariation:** probability of one possibility varies with the value of another possibility {depends on, relevant to} (10)

Criterion: An attribute D ultimately wants more or less of (e.g., wealth) {attribute, objective} (5)

Culminating prospect: possible places that an *incremental commitment* strategy may lead to (8)

Current base: *fixed base* set at present level (e.g., bank balance) (5)

Current decision: one to be made now, before learning anything new (9)

D, Decider: Person(s) responsible for making choice (i.e., committing resources) (1)

DA, (personal) decision analysis: evaluating options by quantifying *D's* judgments, based on statistical decision theory {Bayesian statistics} (1)

Decision: process of determining what action to take (including identifying a *choice*) (1)

Decision conference: facilitated group DA (9)

Decision rule: procedure, set in advance, for making a *prospective* decision, in the event of a specified development (9)

Decision tree: graphic representation of potential developments following a choice (4)

Decomposition: expressing a quantity in terms of other quantities (e.g., net benefit = gross benefit − cost), whence **decomposed** (quantity) **assessment** (10)

Definitive choice: once-and-for-all irreversible action—not *incremental* (8)

Descriptive (analysis): what is; how the world works (4)

Diagnostic judgment: how strongly a piece of evidence indicates that a possibility is true (3)

Diagnosticity of evidence of a possibility: probability of evidence conditioned on that possibility: {likelihood} (10)

Disaggregated utility/uncertainty: expressed as some function of multiple criteria scores/probabilities (6)

Discrete possibilities: take on only a limited number of values (7)

Discrete substitution: replacing *UQ* distribution by a few values and probabilities (7)

Dummy option: unrealistic but analytically convenient option (5)

Elicitor: determines someone else's judgment (e.g., of uncertainty or preference) (10)

Emulation: aid that mimics some "expert's" judgment (1)

Enhancement: judgment made more rational (1)

(Knowledge) **Enriched** assessment: improved by new knowledge (10)

Equivalent (*substitute*): *assessor* is judgmentally indifferent between them (to **equate**) (4)

Evaluation: putting a number to a judgment, not necessarily a *preference judgment* (e.g., *assessing* a probability) (1)

Evaluatory: refers to a judgment of preference (5)

Evidence: information relevant to assessing a *possibility* (3)

External/Reality check: external to model, based on observed real world {external validation} (8)

Factual judgment, assessment: evaluation, probabilistic or deterministic, of a *possibility* (3)

Feeder model: a model whose output corresponds to the input of a core model (10)

Fixed base: unrelated to options (5)

Flipping probabilities: deriving one set of discrete probabilities from another set (10)

Gamble: choice with uncertain outcomes (4)

Gamble-defined *utility*: probability in an *equivalent gamble* between arbitrary "good" and "bad" (4)

Goal: a state that D prefers to be in (e.g., increase in a positive *criterion*) (3)

(Going through the) **GOO:** Analyzing goals, options, and outcomes in a table (3)

Good/bad anchors: *hi/lo anchors* for *utility* rating scale (5)

Hatched bar: representation of range and central estimate (e.g., mode) of UQ (7)

(Hi/lo) anchors: ends of *rating scale* (e.g., 0, 100) (5)

Holistic characterization: single description of total *possibilities* (5)

Hypothetical judgment: based on a possibility that has not (or not yet) occurred (e.g., "likelihood" in statistical theory) (c.f. *actual* judgment) (10)

Ideal rationality: perfect analysis of all available knowledge (1)

Impact: difference in *value* (*criterion score* or *contributor value*), due to exercising an option (i.e., compared with *null option*) (5)

Implementing choice: narrow variant of a broader choice (8)

Implicit fixed base: "I'd give her an 8 on beauty" (5)

(Importance) weights: relative importance of criteria, trading off units {coefficient} (6)

ICE, importance-weighted criteria evaluation: utility of options = (approximately) sum of criteria scores times importance weights {linear additive multiattribute utility} (6)

Incremental commitment: at least partially reversible option (8)

Indicative (of possibility): evidence supports truth of a possibility {diagnostic} (3)

Indirect assessment: {decomposition} (10)

Influence sketch: qualitative influence diagram, shows causal linkages between choice and utility (8)

Informant: source of judgment to be assessed (10)

Input judgment: term to be supplied in a *model* or inference procedure, from which *output* is calculated

Inside organizational act: action within organization (e.g., designing a purchasing procedure) (c.f. *outside* act) {internal org act} (9)

(Institution) executive: D employed by an institution (9)

Internal check: validation internal to model (e.g., by test of technical soundness, science, or logical coherence) (8)

Interested party: interests are affected by choice (9)

Joint probability: two or more possibilities occur together (10)

Judger: makes a *judgment* (3)

Judgment: personal assessment or other *evaluation* (1)

Judgment-intensive model: main analytic effort is on assessing model inputs (not structure) (4)

Judgmental equivalent, substitute: *judger* is indifferent between them (4)

Limited coherence: some of assessor's judgments are shown logically to be consistent (4)

Logical equivalent: implied logically (4)

Measure: numerical attribute (5)

(Aiding) **method:** variant of a decision tool (4)

(Natural) **Metric:** measure of a real quantity (e.g., money) {measure} (5)

Middleman: person or group dealing with *aider* on behalf of D (9)

(Decision) **mode:** role of decider in relation to decision (e.g., *professional*) (1)

Model: mathematical function equated to, or approximating, some entity (e.g., option utility as a function of probabilities and component utilities) (1)

Monetary conversion: *partitioned* evaluation, summing money-equivalent components of criteria scores (6)

Multicriteria model: only addresses conflicting criteria considerations (5)

Multipossibility: more than two, but not many (e.g., three-possibility) (c.f. *quasi-continuous*) (7)

Multitier plural evaluation model: evaluating choice or uncertainty at different *tiers* of model (8)

Normative: logically *coherent* (4)

Null option: do nothing (may be a *dummy* option) (5)

OA, Oral assignment: to be discussed in class-(term project only) (12)

Objectivist position: relies on data-based analysis rather than on human judgment (1)

Optimal option: best, highest *utility* (4)

Optimize: decision strategy to seek *optimal* option (4)

Option: a possible *action* to be chosen by D {alternative, deal} (3)

Option base: one option (e.g., null option) is base (5)

Organizational decision analysis: where the organization is treated as the *decider* (9)

Outcomes: distinct events due to action; a special case of *consequences* (3)

Output judgment: calculated from a *model* or inference procedure, including their *inputs*

Outside organizational act: transaction between organization (as D) and outside world (e.g., to purchase equipment) (9)

Partitioned utility: *disaggregated* into additive *components* (6)

Personal decision: a *private* decision involving D's own action (e.g., whom to marry) (1)

Personalist position: models human judgment (e.g., to maximize *personal* average *utility*) {Bayesian} (1)

(Personal) Probability: judger's uncertainty, expressed as a number, 0 to 1 {frequency} (7)

Plausible range: where the bulk (e.g., 90%) of *assessor*'s experience falls (5)

Plural evaluation: using multiple *single-pass* evaluations of the same judgment {triangulation} (3)

Plus–minus tally: deriving utility of an option as the sum of pluses/minuses for each criterion, without explicitly considering the relative importance of the criteria (4)

(Factual) possibility: possible fact, event, quantity, property, proposition (3)

Possibility fork: branches are outcomes {event fork} (4)

Preference covariation: related to value judgments (6)

Preferences: D's underlying or reported value judgments, "tastes" (1)

Prescriptive: prescribes action that should be taken (4)

Present equivalent: an amount received now as a judgmental equivalent to future amount(s) (e.g., stream of money) {present value} (4)

Prior judgment: before some specified evidence is learned (3)

Private mode: decision in private life (*personal* or *civic*) (i.e., nonprofessional) (1)

Probability: metric 0–1 obeying certain formal rules (e.g., sum to 1) {frequency, chance} (7)

$P(f)$: probability of a possibility f (7)

Probability distribution: *probability* assigned to all values of a possibility {mass/density function} (7)

Probability tree: displays *unconditional* and *conditional* probabilities of *covarying* possibilities (10)

(Probability-weighted) average: sum of all possible outcomes of a *gamble* times the probability of each {expected value, e-value, expectation, mean} (4)

Professional decision: made in a professional capacity (e.g., as manager) (1)

Prospect: future *possibility* (5)

Prospective decision: one not to be made now, but possibly later (c.f. *current*) (9)

Psychological field: all that is in a person's mind (4)

Qualitative analysis: elements are words (c.f. *quantitative*) {verbal, categorical} (1)

Quantitative analysis: elements are numbers (c.f. *qualitative*) (1)

Quantity, Q: *continuous* or *quasicontinuous* numerical possibility {variable} (7)

Quasicontinuous possibilities: discrete but too many to be worth individuals; treated as continuous (7)

Range: interval between *hi/lo anchors* (5)

To rate entity: assign numerical value to an attribute on a *rating* scale (5)

Rating scale: artificially constructed (e.g., 0 to 100) for an attribute that has no natural metric (5)

Rational: advances D's *welfare* effectively, based on all D's knowledge and judgments, constrained to be *globally coherent* (1)

Rationale: explanation of reasons for an input (11)

Realistic assumption: actual (not *arbitrary*) position (10)

Redundancy: more of one criterion decreases utility of other(s) (e.g., mace and pepper spray) {double-counting} (6)

Replacement: decision tool that bypasses and substitutes for unaided judgment (1)

Representative value: single value substituted for segment of a distribution (7)

Risk averse: D dislikes possibility of bad *gamble* outcome (4)

Risk neutral: D is prepared to "play the averages" (c.f. *risk averse*) (4)

Risk penalty: amount by which *average* utility is to be reduced to account for risk, to produce a *certain equivalent* (4)

Roll back: to analyze a decision tree by progressively replacing judgments by *logically equivalent substitutes* {fold back} (4)

Satisfice: settle on the first option satisfactory to D (4)

Scale: possible values of a quantity (5)

Scenario: a *prospect* comprising a sequence of events (7)

(Criterion) score: criterion or attribute (e.g., *impact*) value; to assign a *score* (5)

Sensitivity analysis: testing the impact of alternative input judgments on analysis findings (8)

Set (of possibilities) vs. *a possibility* (e.g., color is a set of possibilities; red is a possibility within that set) (7)

Setting: a possibility that affects an option consequence but is not itself a consequence (3)

Single-pass evaluation: produces only one evaluation of a given judgment (3)

(Sole) practitioner: professional D in "private practice" (9)

Standard base: fixed base corresponding to a normal or average situation (5)

Structure-intensive model: main analytic effort is on structure (not input) (4)

Subrational: less than *ideally rational* (1)

Substitute: a hypothetical entity (model, judgment) treated as if it were another entity (4)

Sufficient model: minimum of analysis complexity that permit options to be evaluated (8)

Surrogate metric: numerical natural substitute for a nonnatural measure (5)

Synergy: more of one criterion increases utility of other(s) (e.g., number of left and right shoes) (6)

Target judgment: object of the enquiry (1)

Tier: level in hierarchy (5)

Tree sequence: single succession of possibilities on a decision or probability tree (4)

(Decision-aiding) **tool:** specific analytic procedure to aid decision {aide} (1)

Uncertainty model: elaborates only uncertainty considerations (7)

Uncertainty range: within which UQ is assessed with specified probability (e.g., 90%) (7)

Unconditional (probability) assessment: based only on what assessor actually knows (c.f. *hypothetical*) {marginal} (10)

(Scale) **unit:** 1% of rating scale range (5)

UQ, Uncertain quantity: {continuous variable} (7)

Usable decision aid, tool: useful to real D {prescriptive} (1)

(Personal) **Utility:** any quantified measure of welfare, satisfaction, happiness, etc. for D, reflecting D's preferences (1)

(Numerical) **value:** number assigned to an *attribute* (e.g., *measure, contributor*) {degree} (4)

WA: Written assignment to be submitted (term project only) (12)

Welfare: {satisfaction, happiness, good} (1)

~X: not X (10)

Index

Advocacy, decision aid as, 168
Allison, G., 56, 159
Alternatives, decision, *see* Options
"Anything else", accounting for, 190–191, 203–204
Assessment. *See also* Probability
   conditioned, **42–43**, 187–188
   decomposed, 189–190
   direct
      discrete possibilities, 181
      uncertain quantities, 182
   indirect
      discrete possibilities, 183
      uncertain quantities, 183–188
   updating, 43, **187–188**
Average personal utility (APU), **59–60**, 119

Baron, J., 12, 23
Barclay, S., 159, 228
Bayesian updating, *see* Assessment updating
Beach, L., 14, 45
Bell, D., 12
Bresnick, T., 11, 26

Brown, R.V., 11, 12, 23, 24, 25, 30, 31, 32, 44, 56, 60, 128, 143, 144, 145, 147, 148, 149, 160, 165, 166, 167, 169, 179, 180, 182, 190, 201, 228
Buede, D.M., xxii, 11, 26, 85, 139, 228
Business decisions, 23–24

Campbell, V.N., 39
Carlin, F., 142
Celona, J., 60, 228
Civic mode of decision, 7
Clemen, R.T., xxii, 11, 14, 60, 115, 228
Coherence, 127–128
Conference, decision, 164
Consequences, 80–96
Constituency, 161, **163**, **164**
Corner, J., 21, 31
Criteria, 85–86

De Bono, E., 12, 58, 144
Decision Analysis Society, 228
Decisions and Designs, Inc. (DDI), xxii

Numbers in **bold** indicate pages of special interest.

Rational Choice and Judgment: Decision Analysis for the Decider, by Rex Brown
Copyright © 2005 John Wiley & Sons, Inc.

243

Decision Science Consortium, Inc. (DSC), xxii
Decision tree, **62–64**, 68–74
Distribution, probability, 116–119

Edwards, W., xxii, 142, 146
Equivalent, certain (CE), 80, **120**, 122, 123.
    See also Substitution
Evidence, 44, **193**, **194**
Expected value, *see* Average

Festinger, L., 56, 203
Flanders, N., 66, 169
Fong, G., 14
Frequency, *see* Probability
Fuqua Business School, 228

GOO, going through the, **38**, 52
Government decisions, 25
Grayson, C.J., 30

Hammond, J., xxii, 4, 12, 132, 134, 214
Hogarth, R., xxii, 141
Holistic description, 82–83
Howard, R.A., 54, 60, 164
Human factors, **141–143**, 182–183

Ideal judgment, **54**, 128
Importance-weighted criteria evaluation (ICE), 105–108, 205–206
Influence
    diagram, 151
    sketch, 151–154
Information, 147
    value of, 193–194
Institute for Operations Research and Management Science (INFORMS), 228

Janis, I., 141

Kahnemann, D., 141, 142, 200
Keefer, D., 21, 31
Keeney, R.L., xxii, 4, 25, 28, 66, 85, 134, 157, 205, 228
Kelly, C.W., 182
Kirkwood, C., 21, 31
Klein, G., xxii, 58, 66
Knowledge, *see* Information
Krantz, J., 14
Kwit, R., 11

Larichev, 58, 169
Laskey, K., 39
Lindley, D.V., 44, 143, 144, 145

Mann, L., 141
March, J.G., 56, 165
McNamee, P., 60, 228
Merkhofer, M.E., 137
Monetary conversion, **104**, 162
Multiattribute utility analysis (MUA), linear additive, *see* Importance-weighted criteria evaluation
Multiple criteria, **83–84**, 101, 130, 202–203
Murphy, A., 180

Oliver, R.M., 151
Options
    specifying, 136–138
    incremental commitment, 127
Organizational arrangements, 165–167

Partitioning criteria, 102–104
Personal
    mode of decision, 5
    decision analysis, 59
Peterson, C.R., 14, 44, 164
Phillips, L.D., 164
Phillips, M., 164
Plural evaluation, **44–45**, 143–145, 192
Plus-minus tally, **52–54**, 102–103, 204–205
Porter, H., 167
Powell, E., 48
Pratt, S., 44, 190
Preference
    interpretation, 199–200
    elicitation, 101–112, **200–208**
Probabilistic risk assessment (PRA), 191
Probability, 178–198
    assessment, 179–193
    personal, 178–179
Professional
    mode of decision, 6, **155–168**
    practitioner, 156
Prospective decisions, 167

Qualitative aid, **37–46**, 58
Quantitative aid, **51**, 57–58

Raiffa, H., 4, 25, 44, 60, 134, 143, 205
Rationality, **8–11**, 54–58, 128
Regulation, **25**, 169–177
Resources, analytic, 228–229
Risk aversion, 121

Saaty, T., 144
Savage, L., 60

Scale
 base, 88–92
 metric, 86–88
 rating, 88–94
 units, 92–95
Schlaifer, R., 24, 44, 60, 64, 122, 129, 143, 179, 193
Sebenius, J., 228
Sen, A.K., 161
Sensitivity analysis, **146**, 179
Shachter, R., 139
Shapira, Z., 56, 165
Simon, H., 30
Single-pass evaluation, 44, **143–144**
Smith, J.Q., 151
Software, decision analysis, 158–159
Stewart, R.R., 182
Strategy, decision aiding, 132–157
 analytic, 133
 modeling, 138–141
Subjective expected utility (SEU), *see* Average personal utility
Substitution
 judgmental, 60–61
 logical, 61

Term project, 16, **210–226**
Tversky, A., 44, 56, 141, 142, 144, 228

Ulvila, J.W., 11, 24, 25, 30, 148, 160, 166, 167, 182, 201
Uncertainty, choice under, 115–124
U.S. Department of Energy, 27
Utility
 gamble-defined, **59**, 128, 130
 institutional, 159

Value judgments, *see* Preference
Von Winterfeldt, D., xxii

Waste management, 27, 28
Watson, S.R., xxii, 30, 56, 139, 147, 228
Weinstein, M., xxii, 6, 28, 228
Winkler, R.L., xxii, 180

Zadeh, L.A., 192

Printed in the United States
134672LV00003B/51/A

```
BF      Brown, Rex V.
448
.B76    Rational choice and
2005       judgment.
```

35010000531010

$94.95

DATE			

BAKER & TAYLOR